PAEDIATRIC
DEVELOPMENTAL THERAPY

PAEDIATRIC DEVELOPMENTAL THERAPY

EDITED BY

Sophie Levitt

BSc (Physiotherapy) Rand
(Formerly) Supervisor of Therapy Studies
Department of Developmental Paediatrics,
The Wolfson Centre
Institute of Child Health
University of London

FOREWORD BY

Paul H. Pearson

MD, MPH
President of the American Academy for Cerebral
Palsy and Developmental Medicine (1982–83).
McGraw Professor of Adolescent Medicine
University of Nebraska College of Medicine

BLACKWELL SCIENTIFIC PUBLICATIONS
Oxford London
Edinburgh Boston Melbourne

© 1984 by Blackwell Scientific
Publications
Editorial offices:
Osney Mead, Oxford OX2 0EL
8 John Street, London WC1N 2ES
9 Forrest Road, Edinburgh EH1 2QH
52 Beacon Street, Boston,
   Massachusetts 02108, USA
706 Cowper Street, Palo Alto
   California 94301, USA
99 Barry Street, Carlton,
   Victoria 3053, Australia

First published 1984

Set by Burns & Smith, Derby
Printed and bound at
The Alden Press Ltd., Oxford.

DISTRIBUTORS

USA
   Blackwell Mosby Book Distributors
   11830 Westline Industrial Drive,
   St. Louis, Missouri 63141

Canada
   Blackwell Mosby Book Distributors
   120 Melford Drive, Scarborough
   Ontario M1B 2X4

Australia
   Blackwell Scientific Book Distributors
   31 Advantage Road, Highett
   Victoria 3190

British Library
Cataloguing in Publication Data

Paediatric developmental therapy
   1. Child development deviations –
      Treatment
   I. Levitt, S
   618.92   RJ135

   ISBN 0-632-00968-3

CONTENTS

LIST OF CONTRIBUTORS

Hilary Baddeley BA, MCSP, CertED, DipTP, Senior Teacher, School of Physiotherapy, Addenbrooke's Hospital, Hills Road, Cambridge

Lorraine A. Burr SROT, Head Occupational Therapist (Paediatrics), Occupational Therapy Department, Northwick Park Hospital, Watford Road, Harrow, Middlesex

Jean M. Cooper PhD, FCST, Principal, The National Hospitals College of Speech Sciences, 59 Portland Place, London

Ester Cotton MCSP, Remedial Gymnast, (Formerly) Consultant Physiotherapist, The Spastics Society, 16 Fitzroy Square, London

Sylvia A. Hyde MCSP, District Physiotherapist, Hammersmith Special Health Authority, Physiotherapy Department, Hammersmith Hospital, DuCane Road, London

Patricia Kennedy SROT, Senior Occupational Therapist, Newham Paediatric Service, Elizabeth Fry School, Suffolk Road, London

Clare Latham LCST, Senior Speech Therapist, The Institute of Child Health, The Wolfson Centre, Mecklenburgh Square, London

Sophie Levitt BSc, (Physiotherapy) Rand, SRP, (Formerly) Supervisor of Therapy Studies, Department of Developmental Paediatrics, The Institute of Child Health, The Wolfson Centre, Mecklenburgh Square, London

Finuala Murphy MEd, MCSP, DipTP, Lecturer, University of Dublin, School of Physiotherapy, Trinity College, Dublin

Susan Rushfirth MCSP, Physiotherapist, Wandsworth Community Mental Handicap Teams, Gardiner Hill Unit, Burntwood Lane, London

Dorothy Seglow SRP, Senior Physiotherapist, Watford Centre for Spastic Children, Watford, London

Pauline Watter MPhysiotherapy (Qld), Senior Research Assistant, Department of Physiotherapy, University of Queensland, St. Lucia, Brisbane 4067, Australia

Alison Wisbeach SROT, Head Occupational Therapist, The Institute of Child Health, The Wolfson Centre, Mecklenburgh Square, London

FOREWORD

This is a book that is long overdue. It will find an eager audience among all disciplines working with children who have developmental disabilities. Physiotherapists and occupational therapists in particular will find it a useful introduction and a valuable reference source for the special 'developmental' aspects of working with children. Only a sound understanding of child development — cognitive, motor, language, emotional and social, and their interactional relationships — will allow the therapist firstly to assess the child's needs properly, secondly, to select the most effective therapeutic programme and, thirdly, and most important as Sophie Levitt points out in her opening chapter, objectively to evaluate the effectiveness of therapy.

This last point cannot be emphasized enough, especially at a time when therapists are being exposed to a wide variety of 'systems of therapy', e.g. Ayres, Bobath, Doman and Delacato, Kabat and Knott, Peto, Rood, Votja, etc. While each purports to have a sound theoretical base, there is little sound scientific evidence for the effectiveness of any one of them. I would particularly underline Lorraine Burr's cautionary statement in the introduction to Chapter 10 on the unproven nature of claims that sensory motor techniques can influence visual and motor perception. This in itself does not condemn any one approach *in total* since at this point in time we have little else to offer. Rather the experienced therapist, including the editor of this book, generally takes an eclectic position, choosing from each 'system' those techniques which in *their hands* and from careful observation and continuous assessment seem to work best for certain problems and for certain children. This, as much as anything, places the weight of responsibility on the therapist to maintain an objective, questioning attitude about the 'results of treatment.'[1]

I was pleased to see Hilary Baddeley's chapter 'Motor Learning'. A basic understanding of 'the mechanics underlying motor control and the variables that influence motor learning' is essential to application of therapeutic techniques and the evaluation of their effectiveness. Finuala Murphy's chapter 'The Physiotherapist in The Neonatal Unit' will introduce many therapists to a new and exciting area of involvement. Dorothy Seglow describes Professor Peto's programme of 'conductive education' in her chapter 'A Pattern of Early Intervention', while making some important points about mother–infant interaction. The chapters on speech and language development, communication, the cerebral palsies, muscle disorder, brittle bones and the child with severe visual impairment all contain important

[1] Pearson Paul H. (1982) The results of treatment: The horns of our dilemma. *Developmental Medicine and Child Neurology* **24**, 417–18.

factual information and treatment suggestions that will be of value to both the student and the experienced therapist.

A major strength of this book, in addition to its factual content, is its emphasis on the importance of the therapist maintaining an awareness of what is happening to the whole child and to the family, and on teaching parents to be competent parents (not therapists) to their child and in handling his particular disabilities. Probably no one member of the treatment team has a greater opportunity to know the child and his family than the therapist who literally has her hands on the patient and is working with the parent on a regular basis. As Sophie Levitt points out, 'The body is not separate from the mind.' The truly effective therapist must not only hone her treatment skills but develop understanding and sensitivity to the psychological aspects of management. By so doing she can be of direct help to the child and the family[2] and serve to alert the other members of the team to potentially important changes in the child or the family. At all times the therapist must assist the family to focus on the child's strengths and aim at an improvement in his self-confidence and the development of a positive self-image, to paraphrase Lorraine Burr. Quite probably this is the most important contribution any one of us can make in our care of children with developmental handicaps.

Paul H. Pearson

---

[2] Freeman Roger D. and Pearson Paul H. (1978) Counselling with Parents. In *Care of the Handicapped Child* (Ed. Apley John), Ch. 5. C.D.M. No.67, Spastics International Medical Publications, London.

The purpose of this book is threefold. *Firstly,* to present the roles and contributions of physiotherapists, occupational therapists and speech therapists to all those concerned with the care, treatment and education of the handicapped child. *Secondly,* to reflect the advances in thinking and practice of therapists in paediatrics and abnormal child development. New fields as well as new ideas in traditional fields of therapy are included in the book. *Thirdly,* to reveal the fundamental interaction between paediatric medical conditions and the child's whole development. This is presented from the viewpoint of the therapists in paediatrics, who are specialists and are often called Developmental Therapists.

This book is not only by therapists for therapists but for all disciplines. It is addressed to nurses, teachers, child-care staff, parents and social workers, with the suggestion that they consult their own therapists for any further explanation and application. Different therapy disciplines may appreciate knowledge of the advances not only in their own fields but also in those of their team workers. I have aimed to compile one book relevant to all the therapies. The links between therapy and education are referred to by a number of the authors, but encompassing all the advances of both therapy and special education is too vast a task for this volume!

Since physiotherapists, occupational therapists and speech therapists are part of diagnostic and assessment teams, this book offers information on their contributions to the different medical consultants, psychologists and others in such teams. Administrators may also find helpful information on the roles of the therapists in their organizations, centres or hospitals by referring to this book. The therapies in paediatrics are not static and like other professions have made great advances. They can no longer have the image they had many or even a few years ago.

I have invited leading experts to join me in conveying the most up-to-date image of paediatric developmental therapy. Their hard work and enthusiasm is much appreciated. Each of their viewpoints and special experience has been respected even though these do not always coincide with one anothers or with my own. This genuinely reflects current approaches in our fields. The controversies and continuing saga of the different systems of therapy in physiotherapy and occupational therapy have been given some reference but not great emphasis as so much has already been written on this in the past. The reader is referred to other publications so that a particular interest in any one system can be pursued elsewhere. Today, however, many therapists prefer to respect and draw on the ideas of many systems of treatment according to the needs of the individual child. This book helps the reader to achieve an open mind and offers many practical ideas for dealing with the various paediatric problems.

The paediatric conditions selected for this book are those more obviously related to developmental disabilities. However, all paediatric conditions, which are well described in other publications, should be viewed with the same developmental attitude expressed in this book. Some authors in the book are more profoundly developmental than others in their philosophy. It is my belief that paediatric therapy will become increasingly aware of child development and that the medical disease processes will be seen as problems of function and therefore as an integrated part of the child's whole development.

For the sake of clarity, children will be referred to throughout as male and therapists as female. In fact, considering that therapists are more often female and boys are more often handicapped than girls in many conditions, this may be acceptable. The use of 'he' and 'she' will thus be clear and consistent throughout the text.

Sophie Levitt

ACKNOWLEDGEMENTS

I would like to thank all the contributors to *Paediatric Developmental Therapy* for giving so generously of their talent and time. It has been a privilege working with such well-known clinicians and lecturers.

Although many acknowledgements are given in this book for knowledge gained from other professions as well as from our own colleagues, we have been unable to mention many others who have helped us and who are too numerous to mention by name, but our thanks are given to them all. Nevertheless a few must be mentioned in connection with specific chapters.

Chapter 1. This owes much to stimulating discussions with Elinor Goldschmied, teacher, psychiatric social worker and Consultant for Children's Day Care Centres. *Chapter 2.* My thanks to Professor K. Holt, Dr P. Sonksen and the staff of the Wolfson Centre for their encouragement and helpful discussions. *Chapter 4.* Thanks are extended particularly to Dr J. Reynell and Ms M. Moodley. *Chapter 5.* Ms C. Latham is indebted to her husband Dr P.J. Latham for his patience and valuable criticism. *Chapter 6.* Ms F. Murphy thanks the staff in the Premature Baby Unit, St James' Hospital, Dublin for all their help and co-operation. *Chapter 7.* Ms D. Seglow thanks the Watford Spastic Centre and Dr J. Luder for their encouragement and permission to use the photographs. *Chapter 8.* Ms S. Rushfirth thanks Karen Burchett MCSP, Senior Physiotherapist, Charlton Park School, for all her help with the illustrations. Parents are thanked for permission to publish photographs of their children. *Chapter 9.* Thanks are due to all the leading authorities mentioned who have all influenced my work. Also thanks to Dr J. Foley and the staff of the Cheyne Spastic Centre, Cheyne Walk, London. *Chapter 10.* Thanks are especially given to Dr P. Mesker and his staff *(the Netherlands)* and to Suzanne Naville *(Switzerland)*. Both parts of Chapter 10 were kindly read and critical comments offered by Ms Karen Christensen, Occupational Therapist *in Denmark*. Parents are thanked for photographs. *Chapter 11.* I owe special appreciation for discussions and advice given to me by Christine White *(Canada)* and Christine Howell *(London, U.K.)* and Dr Werner Schutt. I would like to thank the Ontario Crippled Childrens Centre, Rumsey Road, Toronto, Canada for their kind hospitality and permission to publish the photographs of their equipment and to reproduce the developmental chart. *Chapter 12.* Parents are thanked for permission to publish the photographs. *Chapter 13.* Ms A. Wisbeach thanks Dr C. Paterson, Professor K. Holt, Ms L. Clarke, Occupational Therapist, and Tony Blakey for reading and correcting the script and appreciates permission to use the Sillence Classification. Margaret Grant is thanked for her patience, understanding and help. *Chapter 14.* Acknowledgement is made for the inspiration and knowledge gained from Dr P. Sonksen, Ms M. Kitzinger, Psychologist, and formerly to Dr P. Zinkin, Dr J. Reynell, Psychologist, and

Social Workers Ms M. Black and A. Hagen, members of the Vision Teams, Wolfson Centre, with whom I have had the pleasure of working. The Vision Team directed by Dr J. Jan and, particularly, Ann Sykanda, Therapist, are also extended special appreciation for all they have taught me on my various visits to them at The Childrens Hospital of British Columbia, Vancouver, Canada. Parents are thanked for giving me the delightful photographs of their child. *Chapter 15.* LIC Rehab of Stockholm, Sweden are thanked for kindly sending us the photograph of the Hansa Car Seat.

I am particularly grateful to Dr R. Lovell (Physicist) who patiently read and corrected the literary aspects of so much of this book. His advice and lessons in logic have been invaluable. All those who typed and retyped the manuscripts are warmly thanked. Blackwell Scientific Publications have been most patient, helpful and encouraging and Phyllis Holbrook, Anne Brown, Griselda Campbell and Jennifer Munka have been a source of strength throughout.

Professor Pearson has done us the honour of writing the Foreword for which we are most grateful. All those parents who have helped us with permission to use photographs and posing their children for us are thanked. We appreciate the trust and kindness of all the parents and children with whom we work. Their courage is an inspiration to us and to them we dedicate this book.

CHAPTER 1
CHILD DEVELOPMENT
AND THE THERAPIST

Sophie Levitt

Paediatric therapy for a short-term illness, minor injuries, various localized muscle and joint conditions and some respiratory problems does not overtly seem to affect the child's development. Therapists, especially physiotherapists, have been able to treat the malady and send the child elsewhere for his development. However, therapists faced with the cerebral palsies and other chronic handicaps come directly into contact with these children's problems of development. The more severe the physical, sensory or mental handicap and the more multiply handicapped a child is, the more blatant are the problems of development.

In order to help the multiply handicapped child, therapists have worked in teams with many other disciplines as well as more closely with one another. This has brought contact between therapists and professionals well versed in child development. Not only have therapists gained knowledge of children for severe cases but they are increasingly aware that such knowledge is relevant to sick children and children with short-term conditions treated in hospitals.

All children have different levels of understanding and of following instructions and they communicate in particular styles according to their levels of development. Training a handicapped child to feed, dress, wash and generally take care of himself depends on what development levels the child has achieved as well as on his handicap. Clearly one would not ask a child with a fractured arm to use it in self-care, but once the fracture is mended the child could restore function of the arm in self-care activities. However, if the child is, say, only two years old, one would not suggest that he laces his shoes or eats with a knife and fork. All babies and children are at different levels of motor control and the selection of exercises or motor activities depends not only on their handicap or medical pathology but on their age. All children relate differently to people, to objects including physiotherapy equipment and toys, and to environments, according to their development as well as to their personality.

Therapy techniques of 'drilling away' at medical signs and symptoms, as frequently as possible, are no longer the whole story. Physiotherapists, for example, are increasingly asked to research their work and demonstrate progress of the physical problem. Research is expected to show improvements in tone, deformity, weakness and abnormal reflexes — although curing abnormal knee jerks has not been shelved in the physiotherapy pigeon hole!

Responsibilty for physical gains should be taken and objectively demonstrated. However, a small physical gain can often show a giant stride in the child's self-confidence. Physical progress may show greater advances in the child's exploratory activities with perceptual, cognitive and speech developmental progress. After all, the body is not separate from the mind and many interactions can be demonstrated in our work as therapists. Unfortunately constructive relationships are not always examples of such interaction. Excessive focus on physical achievement may take so much time and energy that the child and his parents may lose opportunities for family life, development of the child's interests and intellectual pursuits. Results of therapy are for the whole child and not purely for a limited part of him. Results of therapy are of importance not only for the whole child *now,* but for the adult he will become.

As we all wish to help the child no matter what our specific disciplinary background, what essentially is the child's need as a person? Perhaps it helps if we think of our own personal experiences and feelings.

Do we not each find in ourselves that which we do not consider acceptable? Has not each one of us a 'defect' such as fat hips, ugly teeth, spectacles, or we feel we are too short or too ungraceful? What have we done about our unattractive bits, our private unpleasantness? We may, like famous comedians or clowns, develop a wonderful sense of humour. We may exaggerate our defects and make others laugh. In their amusement we feel ourselves accepted and reassured. We might overcompensate and work hard within our particular area of weakness. Historically, we can recall the famous orator who was a stutterer, a great painter whose hands were arthritic, a composer who was deaf. Today we hear of an amputee who climbed a mountain or walked halfway across Canada or piloted a plane. There are many amazing examples. We might, on the other hand, hide our defects by drawing people's attention to what we find attractive in ourselves. In the same way, a child in a wheelchair can be a witty conversationalist, a good singer or an archery expert. Finally, we may become obsessed with our defect, demanding excessive attention and reassurance that we are still acceptable. The handicapped person may arouse pity and guilt in those around him, obtaining attention and apparent love and reassurance.

As therapists we cannot allow the child to laugh at himself when he is too young. We cannot agree to overcompensation, to hiding defects or 'using' defects to exploit others.

We have to confront defects because we are trained to treat them. However, whilst treating the child's deficiencies and unattractiveness we must not convey the message that he himself is unattractive or totally deficient. How have we been helped to feel worthwhile, to gain confidence and to preserve our self-esteem in the presence of our inadequacies? It is these experiences that inspire our work with the handicapped.

When one obtains self-confidence and a sense of personal worth it also becomes possible to accept more easily being different, and occasionally an outsider.

The therapist, therefore, cannot focus only on the abnormalities but must search for the potential in the child's development. It is also worthwhile to be wary of the teachings of child development experts who hold up the normal as the ideal. Neither therapists, nor parents, should see the handicapped child as a less than normal child, forever destined to fail or, at best, partially fail. Such negatives do not do much for the child's self-esteem. He is, after all, like each one of us, a unique person, a different person with assets and defects. He too must find, with our guidance, his own ways of developing into an independent, socially acceptable adult. There are more obstacles in his way, not only in his handicap, but also in many of those who surround him.

Like some teachers and psychologists we cannot just concentrate on his assets and build up his personality and education and help him to enjoy life. There are also therapists who prefer the camping, excursions, playgrounds and sports for the disabled rather than the difficult confrontation in the treatment session. We can do both without evading the handicap which may carry such difficult messages for the child. How do therapists face the pain, despair and disappointment in the child whilst having to treat the handicap?

1 The therapist can concentrate exclusively on the abnormalities with skills we are well equipped to offer. This will be done with no entry into the child's feelings and internal sufferings. We need not sink into the child's dismay that he cannot fully be the image of himself he may hope for. This would make us brisk and efficient. Although physical gains are possible in this context the child may be cheered by them. However, he often attributes them to his physiotherapist and not to his own ability to achieve. He remains isolated from his therapist and even isolated from his body which she is responsible for treating. Dependency on her does not breed self-confidence. As he is not in full communication with his therapist, co-operation will vary and seem illogical, and even move towards hostility.

2 The therapist may well recognize the child's sadness and despair and immerse herself in them. The outcome of this may be utter exhaustion and no-one can tolerate that for very long. Such therapists become frustrated and dissatisfied and can only remain in the field if they become 'hardened' and protect themselves by assuming cold and efficient roles. This they cannot tolerate and leave the field altogether. Their valuable technical skills are then lost to child and parent.

3 There are ways of delegating responsibility for the negative emotions of the child to other experts or superiors. These ways help a therapist nestle under the wing of her superiors. Respect for other experts almost raises them to the level of having a monopoly on knowledge of human emotions. We therapists may then evade the sadness but feel forever inferior to others in dealing with the whole child. It would be preferable to retain our rapport and friendships with our patients by receiving advice on emotional problems from those particularly specialized in such aspects. Only when we reach our limitations, and this varies from person to person and from child to child, should we refer our emotional and social problems of our work elsewhere.

4 Finally, there are day-to-day routines which can be created for therapists

to avoid becoming brisk and efficient or drowning in the tears of their patients: Teamwork helps, where the team not only share their technical expertise but share their personal experiences of the child's interests, personality, what motivates him and how his despair manifests itself. How each team member deals with all these aspects is shared so that the whole child can be helped. Where there is no team and the therapist is isolated in a rural area, or as a conductor to a group, or as a visiting community therapist, day-to-day methods of supporting such a therapist must be found.

It is worth having support groups or interaction groups for therapists. Someone skillful and experienced in leading such groups is needed. Sensitivity and knowledge of group work with child care personnel is essential. Through such discussions and team discussions better methods of organization and discovery of new ways of working will emerge.

The sharing of the total burden of the child's rehabilitation is not only between professionals but between the therapist and parents of the child. We need to communicate to the parents but also be open to communications from parents. Sharing the total care and development with parents involves listening to what they desire from therapists. This may not be the therapist's priority but it is wisest to start from what parents need for their child. We must listen to their anxieties. Do not immediately reassure parents, for it is attentive listening and empathy which will serve them best.

PARENT PARTICIPATION

From the initial assessment by therapists the parent should be expected to participate. A questionnaire should be given personally by each therapist to discover what parents find their child can do and under what circumstances he does well in his daily life. Headings of feeding, dressing, washing, toiletting, play activities and communication should be the framework of such a questionnaire. Movements and postures and methods of locomotion in relation to these daily life activities compose the questions to parents. For example, the posture of head and trunk in sitting, movements of the arm and hand, action of the face and tongue muscles and getting to and from the dinner table would be relevant to feeding. In addition, discover how much the parents understand of what feeding movements and utensils and their relationships should be understood by the child. Social situations of feeding and emotional problems with feeding will add to the integrated picture of the feeding assessment and the plan for therapy.

The examination of the child for therapy need not only be a therapist's activity. Some specialized assessments are only possible by the therapist. However, many, if not all, parents can be asked to undertake some of the assessment methods with their child. Not only could this reveal functions which the parent knows how to motivate, but it reveals the parent's ability to handle, communicate with and relate to the child. If parents are observed working with their child, they may also show how much they focus on the child's defects and how much they emphasize the child's abilities.

The assessment of the child involves also assessment of the parents. If one of the parents is not the only 'key worker' for a time, the therapy assessments and therapy programme will have to be carried out with either the health visitor, playgroup worker, nursery-nurse, nurse or other child-care person who must relate to the child.

Participation in assessment as well as in therapy by the key-worker helps to tilt the priorities towards the experience and knowledge of the therapist. Nevertheless compromises must be made as therapists may study many children, but parents may know their own child best in some respects. Promotion of parents' participation recognises their value as parents. They will co-operate better if they are given confidence in their own parenting and will bring many valuable ideas and suggestions to share with therapists. Appropriate therapy methods will also be selected for parents. Some parents will be assessed as those who can do more for their child whilst others may only be able to manage one or two therapy methods. Time changes parents as time changes the child, so there must be regular reassessments until the baby grows and develops to an adult. Therapists rarely have the experience of such a long follow-up and this fact makes it essential that parents are given the information, the confidence and the courage to continue in what must be their personal follow-up of their child.

THE COMPREHENSIVE ASSESSMENT

Therapists and parents have to see the child as a whole. They must know the child's development in:

1 speech and language and other communication techniques;
2 self-care;
3 posture, locomotion and voluntary movements;
4 sensations, i.e. vision, hearing, touch, proprioception, vestibular, also development levels of perception;
5 cognitive abilities;
6 emotional and social development.

Many developmental workers have created developmental checklists which parents can use with the assistance of therapists to avoid dogmatic adherence to any age 'norms' and sequences.

The presence or absence of handicaps in the above development areas should be known. Is hearing present and how much? What medical diagnoses are there of vision, of sensation, perception and motor planning? Although a defect may be present in one area of development, does it affect other avenues of development in the child? These events do occur and the chapters in this book discuss them according to the particular condition of the child. Very few therapists on the forefront of developmental paediatric therapy today see the problem in only one area of the child's development.

Naturally therapists prefer assessing within a team. However, if isolated, each therapist must ask for observations from other colleagues in therapy and school. Contact with them must be maintained. Visits and study of other specialist viewpoints is important to obtain the areas of overlap and an integrated picture and programme for each child.

INTEGRATED THERAPY PROGRAMMES

The mother, nurse, teacher and other child-care workers have certain common requirements from the therapists. These deal with:

1   what methods of communication they should use and develop;

2   what techniques to use for feeding, dressing, washing, toiletting and playing with the child, and what methods to use to encourage his own efforts and abilities;

3   how to stimulate motor development and hand functions, and what methods are best to discourage undesirable movements;

4   what aids or equipment are required to help the child function and to correct any abnormalities — hearing aids and spectacles as well as splints and furniture have to be correctly cared for and of relevance to each child's handicap;

5   how to carry the child correctly if he should be carried at all;

6   how to motivate the child through the above developmental levels and use of equipment. What toys and play activities to use to obtain the above aspects. How to enjoy the child and take pleasure in his successes as he develops from stage to stage.

The child-care worker integrates all these many aspects and should not be bombarded with too heavy a development programme. The therapists will have to carry out some of the programme and decide within the team exactly what is indicated. Medical and psychological consultants will guide therapists, and social workers will give the family background so that the programme is more relevant and acceptable to each family.

THE THERAPIST'S ASSESSMENT

A developmental assessment by the physiotherapist, occupational therapist or speech therapist is supportive for the child-care worker as it is based on the following approach.

1   *What levels of development has the child achieved?* These abilities must be reinforced so the child consolidates what he has achieved.

2   *Which levels of development are just emerging?* Therapists have their own methods of revealing the 'flicker' of what is to come. This is encouraging to parents and child, and methods to build up these emerging abilities will be used.

3   *Which levels are not yet reached in the child's specific areas of development?* This is better than giving the child's abnormalities as static. They may be in some conditions and must be accepted if this is the case. One must then avoid the

hold-up of other areas of the child's development. This should be demonstrated in all cases. Today many conditions, such as mental handicap, cerebral palsy or other neurological conditions, are no longer 'static'. Obtaining the developmental picture includes the child's abilities and disabilities and presents him in a dynamic process of change. Medical signs and symptoms in a developmental context are more palatable and more accurate.

Individuals with the same signs and symptoms in babyhood, childhood or even older childhood may or may not remain the same. The child will certainly be different due to his individual personality, drive and particular functional development. Therapists view the functional development more than ever before. The function may change the degree of pathology as well as the degree of developmental delay. This has been shown in many medical conditions. The chapters in this book discuss how this is possible even though the condition remains incurable.

The therapist's specific assessment and reassessment vary according to their speciality and within each speciality. Different approaches are discussed in the chapters that follow. There is, today, an overlap between the assessments in treatment and the assessments in teaching or training handicapped children.

TREATING OR TEACHING

Once the assessments are made a programme is planned, carried out and then re-evaluated. The child does not progress from one developmental stage to the next as an automatic process, he must learn how to do this. Teachers have various strategies of helping the child develop. Their knowledge is of immense value to therapists. There are many different educational views on learning and a few appear in this book. Behaviourism is discussed in Chapter 8 but many of its methods are already used by therapists. Other motivation methods are mentioned by others in the book.

The main points to remember are:

1   the child's developmental stages must be small enough so that he experiences success;

2   the child should participate as actively as possible;

3   the tasks for training or treatment must have meaning for the child; he should also enjoy doing them and appreciate their use for him and for his independence, if he is able to understand this;

4   his attention should be focused on what he can manage and he may need help to concentrate appropriately;

5   the task must be well analysed for each child — all aspects of a task must be considered so that failure is not inevitable, and this requires teamwork so that analyses are well done;

6   opportunities to practise any task must be available to each child — repetition should be facilitated in real-life situations;

7   rate of progress should be at the child's own pace;

8   praise and pleasure in the child's efforts as well as in his achievements, no matter how small, should be clearly shown to him.

CONCLUSION

These approaches in assessment, programme plans and day-to-day work with children help to build their self-esteem, their confidence and their sense of being worthwhile people in our world. It is their world too.

Table 1.1 Brief outline of development progress (average ages given). Based on the work of Sheridan (1975) and others (see note on p.12).

Age	Gross motor (includes touch, kinaesthesia, body image)	Vision and fine motor (includes various perceptions)	Hearing and speech (communication)	Social, emotional, self-care
1–3 months	Supine/prone. Head to one side. Head lag on pull-to-sit. Prone head raise and rising on forearms. General flexion beginning to decrease. Jerky kick in supine. Prone creeping movements; pelvis flattens, legs start to externally rotate and extend	Watches mother's face. Turns to light. Grasp reflex. Thumb in palm, fingers flexed. Reflex hand flaring open. Begins eye focus and follow horizontally at 6″–10″ (15–25 cm) side to midline	Startles to loud sounds. Stills to familiar, gentle sounds. Eyes 'corner' to nearby sound. Cries when hungry or if uncomfortable. Guttural sounds	Sleeps often. Sucks well. Smile becomes social by 8 weeks. Alert expression. Feeding reflexes decreasing. Dressing is passively accepted
3–6 months	Head in midline, turns side to side. Decreasing head lag. Vertical head control. Prone head control, on fore-arms and later on hand support. Hands opening on weight bearing. Hands to midline, arm waving. Reciprocal kick smoother. Rolling over from prone. Sits trunk support, lean on hands or with grasp. Fully extended hips and trunk in prone lying	Visualy alert, gazes around. Vertical eye follow, oblique, half circle 6″–12″ (15–30 cm). Visual fixation and convergence. Visual-tactile link. Visually directed reach. 'Hand regard'. Held object placed in hand later regards it, mouths it, uses palmar grasp. Hands open. Reach and grasp starts. Visual recognition of everyday objects	Differentiates cry pattern. Coos, gurgles and vocalizes in response to overtures. Achieving babbling by 6 months. Eyes dilate to sound. Turns to sounds horizontally then in two stage to localize down and later arc-like movement to see sound below or later above him. Associates sounds with everyday situations. Communicates with movements, e.g. begins arm lift to indicate wish to be picked up	Responds to friendly handling. Recognizes people, situations, showing pleasure, excitement. Eating semi-solids. Uses active lip, tongue, swallow actions. Watches mother dress, wash and care for him. Hands may be placed on bottle

Table 1.1 *continued*

Age	Gross motor (includes touch, kinaesthesia, body image)	Vision and fine motor (includes various perceptions)	Hearing and speech (communication)	Social, emotional, self-care
6–9 months	Rolling, back to stomach, and vice versa. Vertical head, trunk control to sit alone. Squirming, creeping and pivotting, abdomen on surface. Reach — grasp to play with feet, body parts. Pats mirror image. Takes weight and steps if held upright. Holds all fours position, on hands, on one hand and reach. Full extension of arms, legs, body	Mouthing objects, watches dropped objects but forgets them when out of his visual field. No squint, mature visual convergence. Objects held simultaneously in one hand or in each hand. Pass object from hand to hand, explore, turn over with lively interest. Palmar grasp matures to radial grasps. Object drops	Chuckles. Imitates intonation sound rhythms. Practises vocalizations. Laughs, squeals and screams. Turns quickly to mother's voice. Localizes sound in arc and then sharp oblique look to source below, above, then behind him. Listens attentively.	Recognizes tone of voice. Modifying responsiveness to strangers. Holds bottle, cup and drinks. Holds and bites, chews rusk. Begins to put out arm for dressing in supported sitting.
9–12 months	Roll to change positions lying, sitting. Crawl and standing supported. Sit alone 10 minutes and increasing time. Tilt and saving are completely achieved. Sit and turn, lean and re-adjust. Crawls, bottom shuffles, pivots in sitting. Pulls up to stand. Stands holding on or alone at 12 months. Cruises holding on. Walks two hands, one hand and alone in some at 12 months	Takes object out of container only. Reaches out for offered toy and does this but cannot release. Quick visual appraisals and selection of object for attention. Watches moving object/person at 10 feet (3 m), with recognition 10–20 feet (3–6 m). Finger isolation and used for exploration. Pokes, prods and later points with index finger. Thumb and finger grasps 'scissors' becoming pincer grasp. Release by pressing against surface or throws. Looks for object out of sight	Babbles using purposeful sounds. Vocal imitation. Begins to understand words, gestures. Recognizes name, 'no' and may articulate some understandable words. Understands more than says. Waves 'bye-bye'. Mature localization of sounds established. Reach for sound without sight now possible.	Reacts to encouragement, discouragement, shows many emotions such as affection, annoyance, joy and fears. Plays pat-a-cake, peek-a-boo and searching for hidden toy. Offers toy to familiar person. Suspicious of strangers. Holds spoon, may take to mouth but overturns it. Messy feeder. Finger feeds, pushing into mouth. Drinks alone if guided. Chews. Participates in dressing. Imitates

Table 1.1 *continued*

Age	Gross motor (includes touch, kinaesthesia, body image)	Vision and fine motor (includes various perceptions)	Hearing and speech (communication)	Social, emotional, self-care
12–18 months	'Bearwalk' (12 months in some). Walking alone after walk one hand held. Wide base, arms held at sides at shoulder level 'on guard'. Pronated feet. Stopped by fall, adult or furniture. Begins quicker walking becoming stiff run. Pull up from lying to standing holding on in last phase. Kneeling upright unaided. Squats at play. Stand and stoop to pick up toy without falling. Crawls upstairs, comes down on buttocks, begins walk up. Points but cannot name though knows body parts; tactile localization improving (18 months)	Picks up small crumbs, objects with finer pincer grasp. Fine release develops. Build tower of 2–3 cubes after demonstration. Scribbles; crude grasp, or pincer. No dynamic tripod yet. Points to pictures and enjoys looking at book. Turns 2–3 pages at once. Visual fixation with each eye or both at 10 feet (3 m), recognizing some miniature toys, rolling balls 2-⅛'' (53 mm). Visual perception: form constancy. Mouthing objects decreased by 15–18 months	Attends to words spoken to him. Uses about 6–20 words. Echoes some words. Obeys simple instructions. Points to body parts. Jargons in conversational cadences. Jabbers loudly. Enjoys nursery jingles. Names of people and things understood. Sound localization matures including other voices	Picks up cup/spoon, takes to mouth. Puts out arms and legs for dressing with sitting balance. Takes off shoes, socks, hat. Restlessness to indicate toilet need. Bowel control being attained. Plays alone but near others. Imitates. Uses lids, containers and objects in and out of them
18 months–2 years	Runs less stiffly, changes direction and can stop himself. Walks upstairs holding on, two feet per step, walks down, holding. Begins to know self in relation to space, size, objects. Throws ball with direction. Walks into ball to kick. Squats and rises to stand without support. Walks backwards pulling toy by string. Discriminates hot/cold touch	Removes paper wrapping from small sweet. Circular scribble and dots. Imitates vertical line. Enjoys picture book and finer details. Turns single pages; book placed right way up. Hand preference beginning. Finer control of building with cubes, tower of 3–6	Uses about 50 words. Understands more. Refers to self by name. Defines objects and toys by use. Puts 2 or more words together. Joins in nursery rhymes	Indicates toilet needs. Better able to undress. Unzips. Drinks without spilling. Replaces cup to table. Completely independent with spoonfeeds; no longer turns over spoon uncontrolled. Make-believe play. Very actively curious. Does not realize dangers. Emotionally labile.

Table 1.1 *continued*

Age	Gross motor (includes touch, kinaesthesia, body image)	Vision and fine motor (includes various perceptions)	Hearing and speech (communication)	Social, emotional, self-care
2–2½ years	Climbs stairs but needs rail downstairs. Alternature feet only ascent. Runs. Climbs easy apparatus. Push and pulls large toys but not able to manoeuvre them around obstacles. Jumps two feet together. Stands on tiptoe. Kicks large ball. Tricycling beginning or 'walks' feet along ground. Gait pattern mature	Builds tower of 6–8 cubes and lines the blocks 'in train'. Quick recognition of detail in picture books, his own photo. Imitates horizontal, circle and V. Paints, dots, strokes. Recognizes miniature toys, 2–⅛'' (53 mm) rolling ball at 10 feet (3 m). Recognizes simple formboard and uses it by 3 years. Holds crayon in cylindrical grasp then first two fingers with thumb stiffly held	Knows full name. Talks to himself at play. 200 or more words but also infantilisms. Questions, pronouns. Stuttering if eager. Enjoys simple stories and says some rhymes. Names some body parts and follows directions e.g. up, down, sideways	Eats skilfully with spoon. May use fork. Puts on hat, shoes. Pulls down pants for toilet but not replaced. Dry through night if lifted. Active, restless and rebellious; tantrums. Make-believe play and may join in with others. Cannot understand sharing the adult or toys yet
2½–3 years	Stairs up with alternate feet. Later steps down alternate feet. Agile climbing. Avoids obstacles, turning, going backwards. Tricycles. Momentarily stands on preferred foot, balances. Runs or walks on tiptoes. Walks on a narrow plank with help	Each eye used separately sees tiny objects. Builds trains, pyramid and imitates bridge of three. Imitates finger plays, thumb wiggle. Copies cross, man with head and one other part or features drawn. Matches red and yellow mainly. Cuts with scissors. Paints at easel. Tripod grasp improves	Listens to a story attentively. Modulates speech. Large vocabulary intelligible. Descriptions. Unconventional grammar. Repeatedly asks for favourite stories. Counts without knowing meaning of quantity. Increase follow direction words	Eats with fork and spoon. Washes hands, needs help drying. Toilet trained 3–5 years. Take off and put on all clothes except buttons. Attempts to be tidy. Likes to help adult and siblings, plays with peers. Understands sharing. Some confusion with left and right in dressing
3–4 years	Climbs ladders and trees. Stands on one leg 5 seconds. Hops on same leg. Throw and catch ball mature; use of bat	Copies diagonal line. Visual: part-whole relationships. Use of pencil with dynamic adult tripod begun. Draw-a-man head, trunk, legs, arms, fingers. Matches about 4 colours. Threads small beads. Grips strongly either hand increased	Speech grammar correct. Connected descriptions of recent events. Jokes and long stories and fantasizes. Counts to 20	Spoon and fork skilled, wash and dry. Brushes teeth. Dressing with buttoning not laces. Out of doors play with large materials, takes turns. Appreciates past, present and future. Protective to you

Table 1.1 *continued*

Age	Gross motor (includes touch, kinaesthesia, body image)	Vision and fine motor (includes various perceptions)	Hearing and speech (communication)	Social, emotional, self-care
4–5 years	Runs lightly on toes. Dances, skips, hops 2–3 yards on either foot. Walks on a narrow line	Dynamic tripod improved and used. Copies square, letters. Writes a few letters. Draws a man, house with detail. Counts fingers. Colour matches and names	Fluent speech. Acts out stories. Enjoys jokes	Knife and fork. Undresses and dresses. Relates to friends.

NOTE: The table helps to review the therapist's knowledge of normal child development, showing simultaneous activities in different areas of development. It is *not* a developmental test, a test of intelligence nor a predictive set of observations. Interpretation of delay or unusual functions should only be made after discussion with doctors and psychologists.

The normal development areas overlap and interact. This is why each discipline should have some idea of the function of each channel of development, although having more expertise in one or two.

The table is useful as a screening assessment.

Use the table as a general guideline for the next stages in therapy for motor, communication and self-care as well as for associated visual, auditory and sensory-motor development. Individual modifications will have to be made for each child. The activities are selected in broad stages of development to allow for such individual variations. Set ages are avoided.

The activites are chosen in each stage according to experience of the therapist's special concerns in training.

Referral to this table may be made in relation to many of the chapters in this book, so that modifications are appreciated and the reader is given a basic developmental background.

REFERENCE

Sheridan M. D. (1975) *The Developmental Progress of Infants and Young Children* 3e. HMSO, London.

MOTOR DEVELOPMENT

Sophie Levitt

Motor development is, unfortunately, often presented as a chart of motor milestones. The child is, for example, expected to hold up his head, then to roll over, then sit, then crawl, pull up to standing and walk. Checklists may have many more items of motor functions and have no reference to developmental ages. Others recognize the vast amount of study on developmental 'norms' by physicians and psychologists such as Gesell (1971), Illingworth (1979), Sheridan (1975), Griffiths (1967) and McGraw (1966). The list of developmental motor functions is labelled in 'ages' and developmental sequences of these motor ages are given for children.

Many experienced developmental physiotherapists find such lists unacceptable and have made many of their own adaptations of these checklists according to the child and his particular paediatric condition. However, such developmental charts are perhaps useful in conveying the important message that there is a sequence in the development of motor capacity. Health and education workers and those treating an occasional child in a general practice must appreciate this. In training motor-handicapped children to walk it would be clearly illogical to do so before the child can sit or carry out other earlier motor acts than walking. Should a baby of, say, 6 months have poliomyelitis, spina bifida or a rare muscle disease affecting his legs, the use of walking exercises would be absurd as part of the physiotherapy programme.

Using checklists with numerous motor skills is also helpful for detection of handicap. However, there must be a specialist examination by developmental physicians and physiotherapists to confirm that there is in fact a handicap and not a variation of normal child development.
The reasons that physiotherapists and occupational therapists are not using checklists, or the developmental sequences of normal milestones, are that many variations occur and milestones are not analysed.

Variations of normal motor development occur in all children, normal or abnormal, because of genetic and environmental influences. Unusual movement sequences are found in individuals who are normal children. There are different routes to the same developmental motor achievement. Robson has collected a number of normal children with 'preferred head turning' and bottom shufflers who had never crawled but walked normally. (Robson 1970; Robson & MacKeith 1971.)

Variations of sequence due to handicap Developmental sequences have to be modified because of the particular handicap as described in various chapters in this book.

Variations due to cultures and environments Many studies in child development show how position affects development. If the practice of nursing the baby in prone is greater, then the stages of prone development to crawling are more advanced than sitting. Children spending much time in supine advance more quickly to sitting instead of crawling. In blind children, prone is not spontaneously used and crawling may not occur at all. Treatment with therapy approaches emphasizing prone creeping patterns often achieve crawling earlier than sitting balance. African mothers carrying their babies on their backs lead to earlier head control than in babies elsewhere. Yucatan Mexicans, who rarely put their babies on the rough ground of their homes, have babies who show different motor developmental sequences (Solomons & Solomons 1975), and many other instances can be found.

Other examples of motor development variations are:

1 Body size and body proportions will affect the selection and pattern of motor milestones and sequence.
2 Children with respiratory problems dislike prone as well as those children mentioned above.
3 Malnutrition delays the rate of development, and the child's body size occasionally affects the sequences used.

THE TOTAL MOTOR ABILITY AND MILESTONE ANALYSES

The motor abilities must be analysed for adequate therapy. The positions of the head, trunk, pelvis, hips, knees and feet, the shoulder girdle, shoulders, elbows and hands vary in the different postures and movements which comprise the particular motor ability. Detection of abnormality can thus be made by the physiotherapist who has studied what the normal positions or patterns should look like. Treatments may improve the parts of the motor pattern and show how the child is progressing. Yet assessment of the total motor ability of 'rolling' or 'reach and grasp' or 'walking alone' is too general and may seem to show the same results for a long time.

The observation of the motor patterns needs an expert eye and today there are increasingly objective bio-engineering methods, films, sequence cameras, light points on joints, and other methods to help the human eye become more expert. The notation systems of Benesh and Laban help improve careful observation.

The detection of greater detail does not necessarily lead to treatment to obtain 'normal patterns of movement' as this may not be possible if the

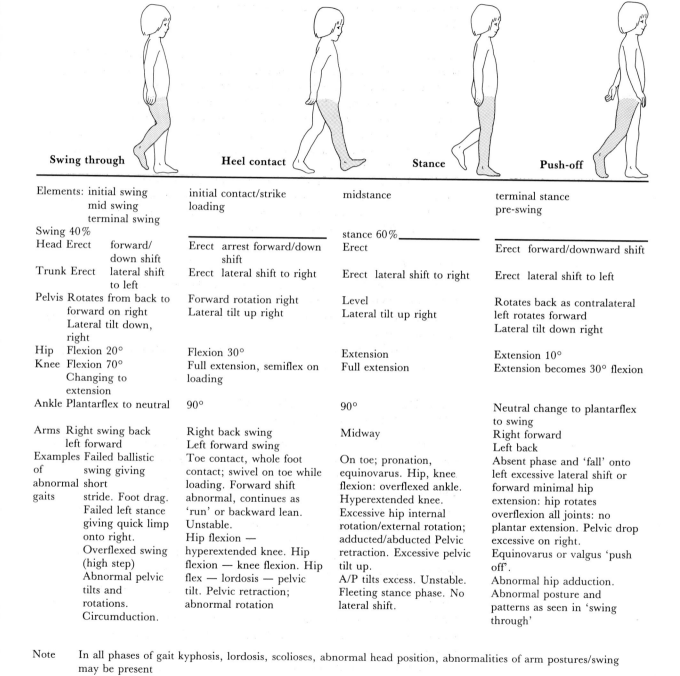

Swing through	**Heel contact**	**Stance**	**Push-off**
Elements: initial swing mid swing terminal swing	initial contact/strike loading	midstance	terminal stance pre-swing
Swing 40%		stance 60%	
Head Erect forward/down shift	Erect arrest forward/down shift	Erect	Erect forward/downward shift
Trunk Erect lateral shift to left	Erect lateral shift to right	Erect lateral shift to right	Erect lateral shift to left
Pelvis Rotates from back to forward on right Lateral tilt down, right	Forward rotation right Lateral tilt up right	Level Lateral tilt up right	Rotates back as contralateral left rotates forward Lateral tilt down right
Hip Flexion 20°	Flexion 30°	Extension	Extension 10°
Knee Flexion 70° Changing to extension	Full extension, semiflex on loading	Full extension	Extension becomes 30° flexion
Ankle Plantarflex to neutral	90°	90°	Neutral change to plantarflex to swing
Arms Right swing back left forward	Right back swing Left forward swing	Midway	Right forward Left back
Examples of abnormal gaits Failed ballistic swing giving short stride. Foot drag. Failed left stance giving quick limp onto right. Overflexed swing (high step) Abnormal pelvic tilts and rotations. Circumduction.	Toe contact, whole foot contact; swivel on toe while loading. Forward shift abnormal, continues as 'run' or backward lean. Unstable. Hip flexion — hyperextended knee. Hip flexion — knee flexion. Hip flex — lordosis — pelvic tilt. Pelvic retraction; abnormal rotation	On toe; pronation, equinovarus. Hip, knee flexion: overflexed ankle. Hyperextended knee. Excessive hip internal rotation/external rotation; adducted/abducted Pelvic retraction. Excessive pelvic tilt up. A/P tilts excess. Unstable. Fleeting stance phase. No lateral shift.	Absent phase and 'fall' onto left excessive lateral shift or forward minimal hip extension: hip rotates overflexion all joints: no plantar extension. Pelvic drop excessive on right. Equinovarus or valgus 'push off'. Abnormal hip adduction. Abnormal posture and patterns as seen in 'swing through'

Note   In all phases of gait kyphosis, lordosis, scolioses, abnormal head position, abnormalities of arm postures/swing may be present

Fig.2.1   Right leg gait analysis (child over 2 years of age). Note also: speed, base, rhythm and step sizes, endurance (distance), EMG. (Compiled by Sophie Levitt.)

nervous system is severely damaged or muscles permanently paralysed. It does help, however, to pinpoint where abnormalities exist and what might be the appropriate aim of treatment. Figure 2.1 gives gait analysis as an example.

PATTERNS OF MOTOR ABILITIES

These may be:

Immature in a child as if he is functioning like a younger child or a baby. He may be mentally retarded without any other physical damage. There may be intelligence with brain damage or dysfunction, as in the cerebral palsies or clumsy children. He may lack motor experiences for various reasons, primarily because of visual handicap, mental retardation or social deprivation.

Pathological motor patterns   These may be due to particular paralyses or extreme weakness of certain muscles, as in spina bifida, polyneuropathies or poliomyelitis. Muscular defects and specific bony deformities create abnormal patterns of motor skills. The cerebral palsies are notorious for the presence of a variety of pathological patterns frequently interacting with primitive patterns.

Compensatory patterns   These occur in all motor-delayed and motor-disordered children. There are many postures and patterns of locomotion in rolling, creeping, crawling and walking. Normal muscles or the stronger muscles may be overused, balance reactions exaggerated and hand actions abnormally used to create a series of abnormal patterns so that the child can adjust to gravity or mechanical forces within and without his body. Abnormal compensatory patterns are used if children are pushed beyond their motor developmental levels and they compensate in the best ways they can in such circumstances. Pathological patterns may be reinforced unnecessarily or other unusual patterns are used.

ANALYSES OF MOTOR PATTERNS

These analyses must be done to achieve greater precision in treatment. Not only does detection of specific abnormal patterns, leading to deformities and inefficiency, take place but the cosmetic appearance of the child can be improved. Function with complete independence may sometimes only be possible with abnormal patterns. Experienced therapists must judge the situation in each child. All therapists, teachers and parents should then follow the agreed approach.

Teachers can help analyse motor patterns into components for learning once teamwork exists with therapists. Rewarding achievement of each component and other teaching strategies are discussed elsewhere (see Chapters 3 and 8).

Analyses of motor patterns must also include their speed, rhythm, strength and how long the child can maintain the motor pattern or his endurance. Unfortunately none of the analyses discussed above appear in the developmental checklists.

GRADING OF MOTOR ACHIEVEMENT

Grading of motor pattern and degree of independence needs recording. This is often difficult. At least the degree of independence can be given as: absent; partial, unreliable, just emerging; and final reliability.

Variability of sequences due to schools of thought

There may be great differences of opinion about motor sequences. Observation of the normal child is influenced by the treatment system; for example, Temple Fay (1955) and Vojta (1974) place emphasis on the prone developmental sequences. Vojta builds up the aspects of stabilization, rising and other postural mechanisms through various prone creeping techniques. These mechanisms are expected to transfer to all other motor capacities. Reflex rolling and roll-and-rising methods are also used. No work is done with the child in the sitting or standing sequences. Bobath (1967), on the other hand, emphasizes extensor activity in prone showing this as basic to upright sitting and standing. She and also Rood (1962) consider the stimulation of the extensor pattern of the Landau reaction crucial for standing. Bobath frequently refuses to train crawling in cerebral palsied children and delays walking if adequate motor ability is not present in the earlier extensor lying patterns, rotation and balance reactions called the Equilibrium reactions. Other aspects of the normal are stressed as fundamental only in relation to what the abnormal cerebral palsied require in various systems of therapy. This does not mean that observations of what is normal must be taken to apply to all normally and abnormally developing children.

Cotton (1974), also working with cerebral palsied children, has pointed out sequences and patterns of motor development which are different from the other schools of thought. Within many of the programmes of motor training in the Peto approach, Cotton has used predominantly sitting and standing sequences. In another publication and in Chapter 9 I have tried to incorporate many different viewpoints in the normal developmental guidelines I have found useful (Levitt 1982).

Motor developmental sequences have been viewed differently in different disciplines. Many educational colleagues have seemed to use the cognitive, perceptual aspects and the exploratory motor actions resulting from these aspects as the framework for developmental stages of motor control. All therapists and teachers nevertheless agree that it is sensory-motor experiences which train motor abilities. However, the emphasis on obtaining a good reliable motor apparatus is given by physiotherapists working with children who have physical handicap. Those without physical handicap but with other handicaps called 'non-motor' may still not have a ready-made motor apparatus. Physiotherapists are well equipped to provide methods for increasing strength, balance, co-ordination and flexibility in the neuromotor system. All disciplines interact to understand that motor development is neither a problem of neuro-motor activity nor just secondary to psychomotor and sensory defects. Nor is it only because of environmental deprivations such as parent rejection, institutions or poverty which may cause lack of general developmental stimulation.

This chapter will now discuss motor development which concerns all disciplines who may be 'caretakers' of disabled children. This chapter will consider using a similar approach to Chapter 4: the nature of movement, factors affecting development, and procedures to facilitate movement and posture. Specific conditions requiring more detailed information have been discussed elsewhere in the book.

THE NATURE OF MOVEMENT

Although the word 'movement' is used, it is a shorthand term. Unless a person can maintain him or herself against gravity, adjust to move and continue to balance, very litle movement would be possible. Even in lying, minor adjustments of the body occur to allow a leg or an arm to be moved; for example, a person in water who moves a limb has to activate his trunk muscles or he will roll over out of control. Therefore when using the word 'movement' we must be talking of both movement and posture.

If one studies the view of many different disciplines concerned with children's movement, the following main reasons for encouraging children to move emerge:

1   movement for fun and fantasy;
2   movement for physiotherapy;
3   movement for function;
4   movement for fitness;
5   movement for finding out about the world.

The motor handicapped child needs all these movement experiences. Far too often these movement experiences seem to be divided and separated among different disciplines. There do not seem to be enough hours in the day to adequately deal with all the above needs. How do we contain the many hours going to and from swimming, horse-riding, playgrounds and sports for the disabled and also have adequate physiotherapy treatment sessions for severe deformities and physical handicaps?

Solutions vary with each child and with the team's view of the child. Unfortunately, if one discipline has control of any one team, the viewpoint, rather than the child, may decide what is best. As physiotherapists cannot evade the physical handicap and are aware how this can limit the child's total development, this viewpoint should be considered. It is possible for the physiotherapy aims of prevention and correction of many deformities and of encouraging desirable patterns of motor abilities to be incorporated in many viewpoints. Fun and fantasy are present in play activities, music and drama and art therapy. Correction of abnormal postures and stimulation of corrective motor patterns need not be isolated from all this. In fact the child's motivation by these activities is used to provoke his desirable motor actions. Action songs can involve stretching out bent arms, balancing, corrective leg actions, and head and back muscle activity. Therapists and teachers can combine their aims this way.

Horse-riding, swimming and adventure playgrounds present many opportunities for corrective motor patterns. The therapist can subtly check the corrections in many cases so as not to distract from the child's enjoyment and creative abilities. In sports and play activities the correction may also make the activity possible. Sitting upright and equally on each buttock on a horse is excellent treatment for hemiplegia, or poor balance in many other conditions, as well as making horsemanship itself better. The physiotherapist should be invited to observe in all the child's activities to advise and supervise so that as much as possible is incorporated into each activity of the day. Additional motor activity throughout the day is important to keep the child fit so he develops endurance and speed in his motor control.

When children are taken on excursions to the zoo, circus and into shops, physiotherapists can again suggest using whatever motor capacity the child has and also motivate the motor control that is just beginning or emerging.

Movements for function are those movements and postures required for self-care. The physiotherapists should be analysing what these are with the occupational therapists. Which postures and movements are needed for feeding, dressing, washing and toiletting must be studied in normal children as guidelines. The developmental levels from normal children are only guidelines as once again they have to be modified in terms of the child's handicap and in terms of his other non-motor handicaps. Achieving aspects of daily functions on his own is often highly motivating to a child. They are further reinforced if the child is ready intellectually to use them in imitation and pretend games.

Movement for finding out about the world of people and objects is also greatly dependent on the child's intellectual development. The physiotherapist will have to work closely or, if isolated, learn from teachers and psychologists about the intellectual levels of the child. Speech therapists interested in the child developing understanding 'smooth', 'sharp', 'big', 'small', 'deep' and 'shallow', and many other meanings, guide the other therapists. The child will use his hand movements and large body movements to learn these and other meanings of objects in his world. Applying his movements and postures to experience his world he simultaneously experiences who he is and what he can do to his world. Physiotherapy not only gives the child movements and postures he can use but also must check that the child does use them in the world outside the physiotherapy department. If the therapist makes such observations outside her clinic, she will also detect many of the child's interests in his world which could act as motivations for the emerging motor abilities as well (Levitt 1974).

FACTORS AFFECTING MOVEMENT

The physiotherapist must assess the child to find out what physical factors affect his motor development. She will also assess how delayed the child is in his motor development with regard to the delay in his neurological development. Neurological and other physical factors will distort as well as delay motor development. It is a complex situation and requires paediatric development knowledge. Most undergraduate courses in physiotherapy and occupational therapy do not have the time or the specialist to train therapists for such work. Post-graduate or post-registration courses and experience are usually essential for assessments of children with delay and disordered development. See Table 2.2 at the end of the chapter.

PHYSICAL HANDICAPS

These handicaps will be further discussed under the relevant chapter headings in this book, as well as within this chapter.

NEUROLOGICAL BACKGROUND (Fig.2.2)

There is a normal sequence of development of reflex reactions. The infantile or primitive reflex reactions at birth become integrated and disappear as the nervous system matures. More mature reactions begin to appear, becoming more obvious at various ages in babyhood and early childhood.

A delay of development may be due to lack of stimulation of the more mature reactions due to deprivation of use. If a child is relatively immobile for any reason there will be lack of use of the mature reactions. These reactions are called the *postural reactions* and they form the gross motor abilities. If there is no curiosity in the child to explore or if he is fearful of exploring due to mental, visual and perceptual delays, then these postural reactions within gross motor abilities are not activated. They will present as abnormal signs and symptoms of motor inadequacy. There need not be any pathology in the nervous system from the physical point of view.

However, if there is damage to the nervous system, especially in the brain, then the development of the more mature neurological reactions will also be delayed. In addition, the pattern of their development both in sequence and in the pattern of each reaction may be disordered.

The postural reactions appear at different ages in the normally developing nervous system and have been studied by authorities such as Bobath and Bobath (1964), Paine and Oppé (1966), Milani-Comparetti and Gidoni (1967), Vojta (1974) and many other paediatric neurologists.

Terminology varies and the following phrases, based on the terminology of Martin (1967), have been found helpful.

1 Postural fixation This involves stabilizing the body against gravity. Stabilization of parts of the body as well as of the total body is required. This

Fig. 2.2 Neurological reactions in development.

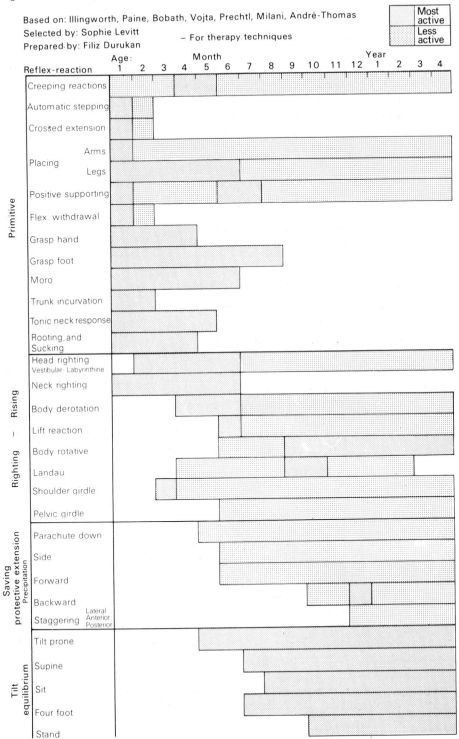

Based on: Illingworth, Paine, Bobath, Vojta, Prechtl, Milani, André-Thomas
Selected by: Sophie Levitt — For therapy techniques
Prepared by: Filiz Durukan

develops gradually as the child develops and the normal sequence may be used as guidelines.

2   Counterpoising   This is maintenance of posture or of the stability of the body against gravity whilst a part of the body moves. In order to allow movement without falling over, the other parts adjust to preserve the equilibrium. For some movement, postural adjustment, *especially* of the trunk, may be subtle and merely a slight body sway. For other movements, more in range, in vigour or in strength the postural adjustment will have to be greater and will be more clearly observed.

3   Tilt reaction   If the whole body and not just a part of the body is tilted out of alignment, there will be a tilt reaction. The trunk will adjust in the opposite direction to which it is being tilted.

4   Saving reactions   If the tilt reaction cannot preserve the child's balance against gravity he will fling out his arms or legs in saving reactions. These reactions are also called protective reactions, parachute reactions and staggering or hopping reactions.

5   Rising reactions   If the child has to assume a position against gravity and also change his position he will use righting or rising reactions.

Being able to rise from lying to standing or from sitting to standing does not mean he can maintain or posturally fixate once he has got there. Furthermore, once there, any movement of an arm, say to feed himself, to reach for a plaything, or to lift his leg to step or climb, involves posture with counterpoising. Should the child wish to be able to sit, stand or maintain any other posture on a tilting surface such as a bumpy cart, a boat or a see-saw, he will activate his tilt reactions to prevent falling. If he does topple over, he will save himself with a saving reaction in his limb or limbs. This saving reaction usually throws out the limb so as to widen the child's base for balance. If the fall is too vigorous, this will lead to injury of limbs but if it is a less heavy fall, the limbs will prop and maintain the wider base to save him.

All these reactions occur at different times in the motor stages of the child. Normal sequences of neurological reactions of posture-balance exist to guide the therapist (Fig.2.2). The physiotherapist can plan what needs activating and which methods can be used by those caring for the child. Specialized physiotherapy methods may also have to be used in special treatment sessions.

SENSATION AND MOVEMENT

The reactions above, as well as voluntary movement, depend on sensory input. All sensory pathways have to be checked and records made of any loss. Where tactile sensation and proprioception are intact, these pathways of afferent input may still be disused from lack of motor experiences. There may even be 'symptoms' of sensory or perceptual problems which are really reflecting a delay due to lack of sensory motor practice. This delays understanding of sensations although sensory awareness may be present.

The motor training needed for the motor delay in blind, mentally retarded and intelligent children who are deprived of such experiences also improves sensory aspects. Increased stimulation of the sensory systems often increases motor actions. However, when there is brain damage or dysfunction the sensory input may not get through the complex connections and integrations in the brain and normal motor actions are not guaranteed.

Not all children like being handled. They may react with voluntary tension or increase pathological spasms, involuntary movements already present, in protest. Gradual acceptance takes place with sensory stimulation under the child's own control, using his own hands and the hands of his mother or 'special adult'. Some handicapped children will continue to refuse handling and so other approaches through play, use of music and speech, in group work and other ideas may help them to move.

Motor development with associated sensory development cannot only be a neurophysiological process. Just observing a child's fascination with tactile, temperature, proprioceptive and vestibular input during play with his hands and large body movements and balance reveals this. The child is seen as explorer, scientist or student of what is happening to him and what he learns as he experiments with his hands, body and mind as he develops from one motor stage to the next. He is learning the meanings of his sensations and of his sensory-motor and motor actions.

It is no longer enough to describe motor developmental patterns of each milestone without asking what process is needed to achieve them. Motor learning must be studied and physiotherapists will gain much from contemporary research in psychology and human movement studies (see Chapter 3; Cratty 1967).

PROCEDURES FOR TRAINING POSTURE, MOVEMENT AND HAND FUNCTION

Procedures will vary according to the child and his condition. There are many techniques which cannot be discussed in one chapter, or detailed without relating them to particular problems and demonstrating their application. Courses and personal demonstration are best.

There are techniques used by physiotherapists and those selected by physiotherapists for others responsible for the handicapped child. (Brinkworth & Collins 1969; Pearson & Williams 1978.)

The main objectives of motor development methods which include treatment techniques are:

1 to prevent and correct deformities;
2 to activate and strengthen paralysed, disused or weak muscles;
3 to reduce muscle tightness in association with hypertonus, or with habitual positions without hypertonus;

4   to counteract any abnormal reflex reactions, involuntary movements or spasms which disrupt or prevent function.

Some of the aspects above overlap and some may not exist in every child. The general approach consists of the following practical points.

The child's positions must be varied throughout the day and night.

The parts of the child's body, particularly the most involved parts, must move or be placed in a variety of positions other than the habitual ones.

Procedures will include the following.
1.   Stimulation of mobility and postures in developmental sequences for the child.
2   Specific active movements practiced to counteract abnormal patterns. This is structured in play activities and daily living activities as well as in specific neuromuscular techniques.
3   Passive stretching and passive movements.
4   Passive corrections by splinting, plasters, calipers and equipment.
5   Positions of the child in boots, calipers and equipment must be supervised. If there is sensory loss or sensory unawareness or disinterest, abnormal positions may be assumed and the correction by the special aids may be lost and even abnormal positions created. The positions used by the child in lying, prone, sitting, kneeling or standing may be held in abnormal ways so that deformities and pathological movement pattern are made worse.
6   Positions which have been found to decrease hypertonicity, involuntary movements and floppiness are advised.
7   Positions in which action is facilitated with the help of gravity, or because the abnormal hypertonus has relaxed, are selected for children, in developmental contexts.
8   Specific emphasis is placed on motor abilities in developmental sequences according to the child's handicap not only according to the child's individuality. Children with spina bifida, paraplegia or severely handicapped lower limbs, require more practice with press-ups on hands, for arm and shoulder strengthening. Others with potential activity in their legs need extra practice with appropriate motor abilities using their legs. Children who have excess action of their flexors require more of the motor abilities in the sequence which involve the extensor muscle groups. There are many other examples.
9   Compensatory, pathological and immature motor patterns have to be corrected and discouraged, and techniques both passive and active applied. When these abnormal patterns are the only ones possible for a child to use for independence in a special skill, then other activities in his day should use patterns to counter them. Careful assessment and planning must be made in these cases.

10   Surgery may have to be used in selected children. Pre- and post-operative regimes will be necessary. Developmental motor actions may change post-operatively; pain and swelling may need more treatment with gradual acceptance of the different motor levels promoted in the child. Hospitalization may also be difficult for the child so that his motivation to move will need special consideration. Splintage and calipers may change and these too will have to be sensitively introduced to the child and their advantages demonstrated to him.

THE DEVELOPMENT FRAMEWORK
FOR MOTOR DEVELOPMENT (See Figs 2.1 and 2.3)

Figure 2.1 on page 15 provides guidelines. However, it is best to follow the sequences of positions: prone, supine, sitting and standing during the same period. Figure 2.3 shows some of the main developmental motor abilities which most if not all children should learn. Not all sequences will be at the same developmental age in different cases, but in general one attempts to keep to approximately the same trimesters in prone, supine, sitting and standing positions. Some ideas worth using in many motor retarded children will be given, but many other publications and the child's own therapist will provide the methods.

Prone development

Over wedges, or mother's lap or on floors of various textures encourages head raise and turn, coming up on forearms and sway from side to side on forearms. Help the child get up on to his knees, maintain his weight, sway, whilst he lies across mother's lap or cushions. Progress in time to coming up on hands, helping him open them out. Help him flatten his hips on the surface in order to get up on forearms and on hands. Also help the child reach well forwards along the floor to hold a toy. His arms above his head will increase his back extension.

   In prone development, the child is now being helped to activate weak neck and back extensor muscles, stretch out bent arms and hips, and strengthen shoulder and pelvic girdle muscles as he takes his own weight on his limbs. If there are any asymmetrical postures, they are easily corrected when the child takes weight equally on both arms or knees. Also stretch the spine to counteract any lateral curves as he lies prone.

   Hand function commences by having the child's hands meet when he is on forearms or reach out for a toy in front, to the side and up behind him according to his level of capacity. As he reaches back he may roll over on to his side or further. Help him rolling from on his stomach to his back as this is easier than vice versa. Also, practice sidelying and half rolling.

   Encourage the sensory experiences of touch, hearing and vision in prone. However, remember that Down's babies, blind and other multiply handicapped children need time to accept prone as an unusual proprioceptive

Function	0–3 months	3–6 months
PRONE		
SUPINE		
SITTING		
STANDING WALKING		

Fig. 2.3 Developmental levels

6–9 *months*   9–12 *months*

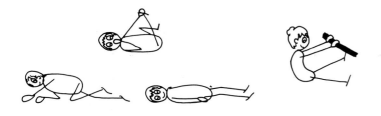

Fig. 2.3   Developmental levels *continued*

experience. Only when they are happier in prone would they concentrate on other sensory input. Also consider that the child may be genetically predisposed to supine and bottom shuffling so that prone development may not be relevant to him. Some of these children can still be taught crawling, as can blind children who dislike prone. But in these cases not too much pressure should be put on the child to carry out prone activities.

The next stages in prone include the hands and knees position, body sway laterally, forwards and backwards and then other activities leading to crawling. Creeping along the ground may be trained before crawling or it may be omitted. However, such additional patterns of locomotion plus the added body image experiences are valuable for all children particularly if they are blind, mentally handicapped or both. The child can explore the continuity of the ground and other aspects of space but cannot use his hands unless he sits back on his heels. Crawling is not trained or encouraged if hip and knee flexion is excessive, plantar flexion is present or leg deformities in all these positions are present. Locomotion on proneboards on castors is used and efforts made to get the child straight up in standing and stepping with full-trunk-support-positions. Proneboards inclined on to tables so the child can play and other positions with hip–knee extended and feet held at 90° will be given more emphasis than crawling on hands and knees. 'Bearwalk' pushing low trolleys is also preferable if this is the level of development of the child.

From prone getting up to sitting, standing and to other positions must also be trained, especially in children immobile due to lack of curiosity, fear, or lack of experience. Weak and spastic muscles will benefit from the changes of position. Rotation of the body in order to change position is of special benefit to children with spasticity.

Supine development

Many handicapped children spend too much time in supine. They must be taught how to turn their heads and then reach over to a toy or mother's face to promote rolling over. Help children come up to sitting and lifting their heads, propping on a forearm or hand according to their level of rising.

Lying supine often aggravates many abnormal reflex reactions in cerebral palsied children, so that sidelying, prone or well-supported sitting is better for sensory training and use of their hands. Involuntary movements may be worse in supine and decrease in other positions.

If supine is used, train the child to keep his head centred, correct any curves of the body to one side and help the child keep legs apart and turned out but with *straight* knees. This position counteracts many abnormal positions of 'frogging' or spastic adducted legs. Motivate hand-to-hand actions and let the child see his hands at play with rings, bells, paper and toys held in both his hands. Let him clasp hands or the toy and bring it over sideways looking at his hands and so lead into the rolling action of his body.

Once rolling methods are selected progress to roll and get up on to arms or knees, or into hands-and-knees postures. From there rise to supported standing, or change to sitting with hands propped or sitting alone.

Sitting development

Having taught the child to come up to sitting there is no reason to believe he can maintain sitting. Begin training sitting by head control in the vertical position long before you expect sitting. Do this by carrying the child upright, sitting him on your lap and talking to him face to face, holding his shoulders and generally use the upright head position in feedng, dressing and bathing if possible. Prop the child up on cushions with his head and body in midline, bring his shoulders forward using the semicircle of a chair back or firm pillows. This helps him bring hands together in midline and play. All the development of hand use should be motivated in the sitting position where the hands will be used most often. Sitting balance needs continued training as this will make it possible to combine sitting and hand function, each function reinforcing the development of the other. It is most unwise to wait until sitting is obtained independently before hand function is developed to the same developmental level as the sitting. Work on hand activities in well-supported sitting if there is not any balance present, but assessments must continue to confirm how much balance emerges and when it does so. Then hand activities should be used with as much balance as the child can achieve without disrupting his concentration.

Sitting on laps, swings, soft sponge, or inflatables and tilting sideways, forwards and backwards without balance loss are important activities at the correct stages. Also seat the child on the floor and tip him over to touch the floor to discover it. Train him to save himself and prop with each arm, in all directions. Forwards to the side and later backwards propping is the developmental sequence for many retarded children but other handicaps may change the rate and pattern of achievement slightly.

In order to gain stability in sitting, have the child grasp with both hands. Spastic, athetoid and floppy children should hold their elbows straight and activate their shoulder muscles keeping their bodies straight or forward from their hips. Make sure all children sit evenly on their two buttocks and take weight equally through their feet or legs depending on the sitting position being used. Various floor seats, chairs and wheelchairs are selected for different children and carefully checked for size and specific adaptations (see Chapter 15).

Play in sitting and changing from sitting to other positions are important and the developmental guidelines should be consulted for each child. If the child has a round back and sits backwards off his buttocks then concentrate on reaching for dangling toys overhead, put arms up for dressing or throw balls from overhead and try other such ideas to motivate arm elevation. Reaching backwards with body rotation also helps to correct round shoulders and backs. All these activities may depend on the child's development of his postural reactions and are selected according to these levels.

Development of standing and walking

At first the child has to be trained to take weight on both feet. The feet should be plantigrade and procedures to obtain this will be chosen according to the cause of deformities of the feet. Meanwhile head and trunk control in the vertical position is developed in sitting positions. The development of head and trunk control when the child is prone or supine contributes little to standing balance as it takes place with different visual and proprioceptive input. Supine and prone development train the child to get up to standing but do not train standing as such. Strengthening the back in prone and the shoulder and pelvic girdles and abdominal muscles plays a part but strength does not automatically lead to its application in other activities. Therefore early weight bearing in standing is recommended for handicapped children who are a long way from standing alone. If this is done with care taken to correct the hips, knees and feet of the child and *full* support of his trunk, then standing is worthwhile. Special equipment, splints or calipers may be required. Modifications to training of standing without support must be made with assessment of each child by physiotherapists.

Stepping with a reasonably wide base, on plantigrade feet, is facilitated when standing is fairly well practised. Standing, with weight swayed from foot to foot in all directions and with postural reactions of the trunk and head achieved fairly well, must precede the training of stepping. If not, compensations in the form of abnormal gaits are created. Some children will themselves begin to walk before all their postural reactions are developed and it is difficult to prevent this. The therapy programme then concentrates on the earlier motor abilities with building up of postural reactions needed for better patterns of walking. Other older children may also need direct gait training.

Deformities of the legs will need correction to make upright standing and walking possible or in a better pattern. Until standing and walking are attained, mobility in sitting and other postures is essential. Wheelchairs, chariots, playthings, proneboards on wheels, tricycles and other aids have to be found. Walking aids will also be selected for each child and at each stage of development. Wheelwalkers, crutches, quadripods, tripods and ordinary sticks or a stick will be chosen.

Development of hand function

The development levels are followed for the use of hands in play activities, feeding, dressing, washing and bathing. Many children with visual, mental and physical handicaps need to have pleasurable activities to make them aware of their hands, accept touch and seek out touch and grasp. Encourage this by having the child accept his or mother's hand on his hand (see Chapter 14). Place his hand in bowls of lentils, marbles, wooden balls, cellophane and other rustling paper and encourage play. A treasure basket of articles from the kitchen, bathroom and other objects as well as natural objects, such as cones, leaves, shells, pebbles and stones, holds endless fascination for children and provides further development of hand use and hand–eye co-ordination (Goldschmied 1980).

Development of hand actions includes hand-to-mouth movements, hand to hand, hand-to-body and hand-to-foot. Position the child so that he can achieve these. Hand actions such as opening, palmar grasp, fingers and thumb grasps, fingering and thumb use can be trained with a selection of toys which demand this for rewarding play. Exercises to obtain these movements are also indicated for those handicapped children who cannot respond physically to such toys. Rhymes and action songs with hands are greatly enjoyed by handicapped children who have a variety of problems.

Grasps must be developed in all positions of the child's arm as well as in prone, supine, sitting and standing. The handicapped child will need to use his hands for grasp and support far more than the normal child. If he is relatively immobile, hand use is also more important as so much is learnt through manual exploration and dexterity. In prone, sitting, kneeling or standing positions, the child should be placed next to a table. He can then pat, stroke, scratch, bang and explore the table surface. Toys can be used on the table instead of being precariously held in the air. Suction bases or Dycem non-slip mats secure the toys or may themselves serve as tactile experiences for the child. Long cords and table edges are some of the devices used to save the toys from falling too far away from the child. Securing the toys to the table by a long cord is useful in cases where the child throws his toys. He may do this as a developmental stage around ten months, to discover how well he can use his arm, how far it is to the floor, what might happen to the toy when it hits the floor and what happens in the behaviour of adults when he throws toys. Handicapped children will tend to prolong this throwing stage rather longer than normal children for the needs mentioned. However, if it continues for an excessively long time to the annoyance of all, then behavioural methods should be used and disapproval naturally shown. If constructive play is also being fostered, then this will help to decrease throwing by a child. Training release into large boxes, buckets and progressing to release into smaller containers should be part of this development.

Motor-training

Although motor development ideas have been given, the details of training have not been discussed in only a short chapter. Motor training involves training the child's attention and clarifying for him what aspect of the motor action he should concentrate on. He cannot attend to every component of a motor pattern, but may need to keep his attention on the goal of this pattern. The therapist should decide what he can manage. He must achieve his action not only in the special treatment session but practice it in everyday life. When motor components are taught, feedback for his success should be clearly conveyed. Touching, looking at visual cues and general handling guide the child in what he is expected to do. Learning methods should be used and are discussed in Chapter 3.

It has already been stressed that it is essential to train motor abilities in the functions of daily life and not only in a physiotherapy department. As the application of motor abilities to the skills of daily living depends on all areas of child development, a team of consultants (medical, educational and psychological), therapists, teachers and parents is of immense value for motor development and treatment.

CONCLUSION

A review of the many factors affecting motor development has been given. Relationships of treatment and teaching have been mentioned which are further elaborated in other chapters. Details of technique cannot be given here although a general approach and some practical suggestions have been made.

The motor development suggestions are applicable to most children with motor retardation as in mental handicap such as Downs Symdrome; in intelligent blind children; in neurologically or orthopaedically handicapped children or in children who are deprived or disadvantaged for social reasons.

Specific treatment or training programmes will depend on each child's individuality, condition and age as well as levels of development. In the chapters that follow more specific discussions about selected conditions will be made. However, it is the child's own therapist who must be consulted for her assessments, plan of therapy and selected techniques and equipment.

Table 2.1   Assessment for therapy of motor problems. Main areas which may require assessment after checking medical diagnoses, history, drugs being used, past therapy programmes, surgery.

Gross motor levels in prone, supine, sitting, standing and stepping
   Analyse each motor ability — components, patterns
                                               — time, speed, rhythm
                                               — relevant reflex reactions
Fine motor development in prone, supine, sitting, standing
   Analyse each motor ability — components, patterns
                                               — time, speed, rhythm
                                               — relevant reflex reactions
Eye—hand coordination and visual development and visual assessment
Hearing assessment and hearing use in developmental stages
Sensory assessment and sensory integration. Auditory-visual-tactile:
   Vestibular-proprioceptive-tactile: visual-motor and other sensory-expressive
   integrations
   Description of sensory performance in different body positions
Oral function. Feeding reflexes. Abnormal patterns. Hypersensitive
   oro-facial musculature and muscle hypotonus/hypertonus
Development of feeding, dressing, washing, toiletting
Play activities. Motor and perceptual, cognitive and social
Communication related to therapy and personal relations
   to therapist
Problem behaviour. Mannerisms. 'Blindisms' hyperactivity
   affecting training procedures
Attention span and stages of attention development
Deformities. Threatening: present but unfixed. Fixed contractures
   Measurement of deformities. Leg lengths. Limb girths

Muscle status. Paralyses, weakness, strength. Fixator or phasic action.
Ranges of action. Synergies
Joint ranges. Head. Trunk. Limbs
Aids and appliances. Relevance and fit. Effectiveness
Rewards specifically appropriate for child

REFERENCES

BOBATH B. (1967) The very early treatment of cerebral palsy. *Developmental Medicine and Child Neurology* **9,4.**

BOBATH K. & BOBATH B. (1964) The facilitation of normal postural reactions and movements in the treatment of cerebral palsy. *Physiotherapy* **50,** 8, 246.

BRINKWORTH R. & COLLINS J.E. (1969) *Improving Mongol Babies.* National Society for Mentally Handicapped Children, London.

COTTON E. (1974) *The Basic Motor Pattern.* The Spastics Society, London.

CRATTY B.J. (1967) *Developmental Sequences of Perceptual Motor Tasks.* Educational Activities Inc., New York.

ELLIS E. (1967) *The Physical Management of Developmental Disorders.* William Heinemann Medical Books, London.

FAY T. (1955) The origin of human movement. *American Journal of Psychiatry* **111,** 644–52.

GESELL A. (1971) *The First Five Years of Life.* Harper and Row, New York.

GOLDSCHMIED E. (1980) *Il Bambino Nell'Asilo Nido — Guida per le Educatvici El Genitori.* Fabbri Editori, Milan.

GRIFFITHS R. (1967) *The Abilities of Babies,* 4e. University of London Press, London.

HOLLE B. (1977) *Motor Development in Children: Normal and Retarded.* Blackwell Scientific Publications, Oxford.

HORTON M. & McGUINNESS J. (1975) Movement notations and the recording of normal and abnormal movements, p. 124–31. In *Movement and Child Development* p. 124–31. (ed. Holt K.). Spastics International Medical Publications, Heinemann, London.

ILLINGWORTH R.S. (1979) *The Normal Child,* 7e. Churchill Livingstone, Edinburgh.

LEVITT S. (1975) A study of gross motor skills of cerebral palsied children in an adventure playground. *Child: care, health and development* **1,** 29.

LEVITT S. (1982) *Treatment of Cerebral Palsy and Motor Delay,* 2e. Blackwell Scientific Publications, Oxford.

McGRAW M.B. (1966) *The Neuromuscular Maturation of the Human Infant.* Hafner, New York.

MARTIN J.P. (1967) *The Basal Ganglia and Posture.* Pitman, London.

MILANI-COMPARETTI A. & GIDONI E.A. (1967) Routine developmental examination in normal and retarded children. *Developmental Medicine and Child Neurology* **9,** 631.

PAINE R.S. & OPPÉ T.E. (1966) *Neurological Examination of Children.* Clinics in Developmental Medicine 20/21. Heinemann, London.

PEARSON H.P. & WILLIAMS C.E. (Eds) (1978) *Physical Therapy Services in the Developmental Disabilities.* Charles C. Thomas, Springfield, Illinios.

ROBSON P. (1970) Shuffling, hitching, scooting or sliding: some observations in 30 otherwise normal children. *Developmental Medicine and Child Neurology* **12,** 608.

ROBSON R. & MACKEITH R.C. (1971) Shufflers with spastic diplegic cerebral palsy; a confusing clinical picture. *Developmental Medicine and Child Neurology* **13,** 651.

ROOD M. (1962) The use of sensory receptors to activate, facilitate and inhibit motor responses, automatic and somatic in developmental sequence. In *Approaches to Treatment of Patients with Neuromuscular Dysfunction* (Ed. Sattely G.C.). William C. Brown, Dubuque Iowa.

SHERIDAN M. (1975) *Children's Developmental Progress from Birth to Five Years. The Stycar Sequences,* 2e. NFER Publishing, Windsor.

SOLOMONS G. & SOLOMONS H.C. (1975) Motor development in Yucatan infants. *Developmental Medicine and Child Neurology* **17,** 41–6.

VOJTA V. (1974) *Die cèrebralen Bewegungstörungen in Säuglingsalter.* Ferdinand Enke Verlag, Stuttgart.

CHAPTER 3
MOTOR LEARNING

Hilary Baddeley

The subject of motor learning has attracted the interest of psychologists for at least a century. Many techniques for studying motor behaviour have been developed, and I believe that they can be of value and relevance to physiotherapists. Psychologists are primarily concerned with understanding the mechanisms underlying motor control and the variables that influence motor learning. Such research findings can throw light on clinical problems for the practitioner and suggest fruitful strategies for training or retraining motor skills.

Research concerned with the practical application of principles derived from laboratory studies is, however, still at an early stage, and consequently this chapter will not offer a prescriptive account of how children should be treated.

The omission of any reference to the strategies employed to attempt remediation of learning disorders in young children is recognized. The work of Professor Ayres (1980) represents a leading example of an approach where improvement of sensory integration is sought by providing appropriate augmented sensory input. Although there are encouraging reports that both cognitive and perceptuomotor function appear to be enhanced by such methods, as yet little scientific evaluation as to the effectiveness of this, and similar methods, has been carried out.

Instead, the aim of this chapter is to provide an introduction to the subject of motor learning under five headings. First, the problem of separating maturational from learning factors to account for changes which occur during motor development in childhood will be discussed. Second, the development of learning theory by psychologists will be outlined. Associative learning, as studied by behaviourists, notably the American psychologist, B.F. Skinner, will be briefly explained, giving examples and applications relevant to physiotherapy. The approach of cognitive psychologists will also be included, showing how studying people in terms of the way they process information helps to identify the variables that are important in aiding learning. Leading on from this, the third part will be concerned with the topic of feedback, showing how specific and automatic control mechanisms are common to many species, and some of the consequences of defective feedback that patients with neurological damage sometimes incur. The fourth section will attempt to show how the novice may change his use of feedback as he becomes skilled at some motor task. The role of attention in motor learning, and the implications for training both normal and brain-damaged subjects are included here. Lastly, variables which have been shown to influence skill acquisition are described, with particular reference to those which are open to manipulation by the therapist.

MATURATION AND LEARNING

An understanding of normal motor development is crucial for anyone concerned with identifying deviations from this pattern and for those attempting to remedy motor delay or abnormality. The basic abilities of locomotion and manipulation are acquired during childhood and it is against this background that more complex skills can be learned in later life.

The problem of separating the effects of maturation from changes in motor behaviour attributable to experience is not simple. In the developing organism environmental stimuli may be necessary for growth and differentiation of anatomical structures. Structure and function are inextricably linked, so that not only does structure determine function, but function modifies structure. For example, exercising muscles has an influence on bone shape. This, in turn, enables muscles to operate more effectively. The changes in structure of the bones of the hand reflect the changes in grasping ability that occur between six and twelve months in the developing child. Initially the flat hand is used to grasp objects, by a year the thumb and index finger can be used in a pinch grip. The bones and joints change their configuration and accomodate this change in motor ability.

The issue of genetic versus environmental determinants of motor behaviour is a most important one, with far-reaching implications for child care and preschool education in the normal child.

It may appear that babies *learn* to walk, and that parents carry out activities aimed at fostering the mastery of this motor ability. However, when evidence from cultures with different child rearing practices is considered, this may seem to be primarily not a learning but a maturational consequence. In a classic study by Dennis (1940), two groups of Hopi Indians were compared. One group followed traditional rearing patterns binding their babies to cradle boards for the early months, only occasionally loosening them for changing. The other group influenced by European practices, allowed their infants to move freely from the outset. It was found that despite the extreme difference of opportunity to learn, both groups walked independently at about the same time, fifteen months. The role of learning in the young human being must, nevertheless, be considered alongside the process of maturation. Development is not only of the neuromuscular system, but as has already been mentioned, also in the size and shape of the skeleton.

As the nervous and other systems mature, so the potential for learning increases. Environmental stimuli may well be crucial in eliciting each new behaviour. The difficulty lies in identifying precisely what these events might be. Deprivation studies using primates and other non-human subjects such as cats, have attempted to increase the information available concerning the importance of sensory input at various developmental stages. It is important to bear in mind that perceptual learning is not a purely passive process, and an animal's own active movements crucially influence what it learns from what it sees and hears. Laboratory experiments that tamper with this feedback loop show that it is a key to developing and maintaining spatial orientation in advanced mammals (Held 1965).

Important though this area of research is to the student of perception and perceptual motor development, most of the discussion of motor learning in this chapter will be related to studies of the mature, intact human subject.

LEARNING

One of the basic forms of learning is classical conditioning. For example, reading recipe books can make one salivate, or hearing a creaking door in a reputedly haunted house can make your heart pound with fear. It is not that the words in the recipe book or the sound in the haunted house in themselves elicit the reflexes of salivation or tachycardia, but they have become associated with the smell of food or a fear-evoking situation. These relatively automatic forms of learning can be distinguished from instrumental or operant conditioning which involves action in advance on the part of the subject in order to gain some effect or reward. For example, one turns the handle of a door because you have learned that this is what you need to do before the door will open.

B.F. Skinner's work with animals, particularly pigeons, has shown that giving a reward when the animal performs an action, or something approximating to the action, conditions that desired response. Animals can be trained to perform not only the one act, but quite complicated sequences can be systematically built up. If an animal trainer at the circus is observed closely, it can be seen that he frequently offers a titbit of food to the animal. This not only demonstrates to the audience that he is kind to animals, but it rewards the animal motivating him to repeat the trick, and giving the animal feedback or information concerning the aptness of its behaviour.

Skinnerian instrumental conditioning has been usefully applied in many clinical contexts. Phobic patients have, for instance, been taught to master their fears using techniques based on learning theory, and this general approach known as behaviour modification, has been sucessfully applied to a wide range of problems. These range from the improvement of social skills in adolescents to the control of violent behaviour in head-injured patients.

In physiotherapy, the principles can be used to aid patient compliance. This is particularly helpful if the patient has to cope with short-term pain or unpleasantness in order to achieve long-term benefit.

A patient known to the author will serve as an example of the manner in which therapists without specialized training in psychotherapy were able to cope with a patient and achieve cooperation where previously there had been stubborn refusal to make any effort on his part. A homeless alcoholic vagrant was knocked down while staggering across the road and sustained multiple injuries. This necessitated a lengthy period of hospital treatment, during which time he consistently resisted attempts to aid his recovery, and frequent reports of abusive and hostile behaviour were made. On transfer to rehabilitation, things did not improve, and so it was decided to adopt a strategy of rewarding, or reinforcing, any behaviour which we judged demonstrated even a very small effort at cooperation. Having received so much chastisement whilst in hospital due to his difficult behaviour, he was very surprised to receive praise for even small acts such as standing up in the parallel bars. We deliberately ignored the swearing and verbal abuse, and after a short while he began to do new activities spontaneously, seemingly trying to please us, thereby getting 'rewarded' again. Although his muscles were weak and he was not at all fit, gradually he performed lengthier series of movements before getting praised. His behaviour continued to improve and he became progressively more reasonable and cooperative. By initially rewarding him for very slight improvements we had succeeded in breaking the vicious circle of bad behaviour which had led to negative responses from the therapist, which in turn had led to more bad behaviour. The crucial feature here is not of course that we were kind to the patient, but that we behaved systematically and consistently in a way that would induce him to change his behaviour.

Work with animals and people has shown that the way reinforcement schedules are designed can influence the amount of learning that takes place. It is also important to identify the reward that is most effective. Initially the rewards are most likely to be extrinsic and immediate, like sweets for children or recording scores on a displayed chart. Ultimately rewards become internalized in many subjects, so that they are prepared to carry out activities to achieve goals that they want themselves.

Negative reinforcement or punishment, although effective at discouraging an activity, is not nearly so powerful as reward in training to perform some positive act.

FEEDBACK

The term feedback is derived from control engineering and refers to the process whereby a system monitors its environment and reacts accordingly. A simple example would be in a central heating system containing a thermostat. Heat is supplied until the room exceeds the preset temperature, whereupon the system switches off the heat, switching it on again when the temperature drops below the critical level. The relationship between the furnace and the thermostat forms what is termed a closed-loop system of control. Each component influences the other. Psychologists use this term to describe motor actions which are monitored continuously by feedback. The term 'open-loop' control refers to those sequences of movements, or motor programmes, which can be selected from a store of programmes held in motor memory and run off in response to some environmental demand. Unlike the closed-loop control model, such programmes, or engrams as they are sometimes called, are not linked continuously to feedback. Instead the movement is compared with a stored copy or efferent copy held in motor memory store as a trace produced by the previous execution of the movement.

Automatic adjustments to the vicissitudes of the ground when walking are mainly under closed-loop control. Studies of insect locomotion have identified three elementary units of motor control whereby environmental variability can be automatically adjusted for. Wilson (1980) describes the way a cockroach progresses using these three automatic adjusting mechanisms. One comprises a series of oscillators which rhythmically drive each leg. A second involves an inhibitory reflex which prevents the initiation of a leg swing until the appropriate phase of the walking sequence. A third consists of a servomechanism which adjusts the strength of the signals sent to the muscles of support and propulsion so as to compensate for the variation of the loads to be supported and moved. All the insect's small brain has to cope with is the speed of progression, sending out command signals of either faster or slower.

These three units of action operate automatically in the control systems of all species, including man. Yet, of course, intact man possesses far greater ranges of degrees of freedom than the cockroach. His central control mechanisms can send a far greater number of command signals than just fast or slow.

Although caution must be exercised in generalizing the evidence derived from work with the animals such as insects or birds, some interesting experiments have produced results which suggest that motor output can occur in the absence of feedback. Studies on the development of birdsong provide one example. The vocal system of birds can be affected by severing the hypoglossal nerve which innervates the vocal system bilaterally. When Nottebohm (1970) severed the nerve on one side or the other, paralysing certain muscles, parts of the song dropped out. The remaining elements of the song, however, occurred in the proper sequence. The missing auditory or proprioceptive feedback was not necessary for triggering the remaining elements.

We constantly use feedback in interacting with our environment. The relationship between action and feedback is one that has been extensively studied in people as well as animals. The role of vision, for example, is very important in maintaining balance, and probably has a more important function than either proprioceptive or vestibular feedback. This is particularly so in childhood. Lee (1980) carried out experiments using a 'moving' room' apparatus. The subject stands on a stationary floor, but the walls of the room are suspended in such a manner that they can be moved backwards and forwards as a unit without disturbing the floor. The way subjects' posture is affected by moving the walls can be observed. When small children stood in the room the effect of only moving the walls a few centimetres caused them to fall down. When the walls were moved away from the children, they lurched forward in a surprised way. In adults the effects were less dramatic, but definite increases in sway could be observed. It appears that the visual stimulation is more powerful as a source of feedback than either proprioception or vestibular stimulation. It is interesting that this is particularly true in children who have not had so much experience in integrating various sources of feedback.

The discussion so far has outlined some of the features that characterize either peripheral, closed-loop control, or central, open-loop motor control systems. What are the changes that take place to account for the way the clumsy efforts, requiring a great deal of attention, that can be seen when the learning of a new movement skill is begun, become rapid, accurate and requiring minimal attention when the skill has been mastered? This is a subject of much present-day research, and is largely beyond the scope of this chapter. That certain permanent changes do take place is evident when it is considered what can be observed in the learner's behaviour.

The general pattern of any given skill becomes under automatic control, requiring minimal and only intermittent attention, freeing the subjects attentional capacity to concentrate on fine-tuning and adjustments. Learning to drive a car will be a familiar experience to most. Initially one has to concentrate on each element of the complex pattern of coordinated movements involved in controlling the car's direction, and speed, let alone take appropriate action in regard to the traffic conditions. Gradually with experience each component becomes more automatically executed, so that the driver's attention can be focused on where he wishes to go, not on how to make the car move there.

In therapy the retraining of motor skills, or, in some instances, the teaching of movement skills for the first time, has to be approached against a background of impoverished or altered feedback. The disadvantage this is likely to present may be appreciated by considering the crucial role that feedback plays during the early stages of skill acquisition. The exercising of closed-loop control will be disrupted in instances where the perhipheral mechanisms are disordered. Here an analogy could be drawn from a mechanical and moving system such as an industrial crane. If any part of the mechanism is broken then it will fail to operate correctly whatever the crane operator does in terms of pushing knobs and levers in the control box. Physiotherapists assess the moving parts of their patients so as to identify disorders such as loss of joint range or muscle weakness. They check for other potentially hampering abnormalities such as visual field defects. Some of these disorders may be open to remediation, and an important aspect of a physiotherapist's job is directed to this end. If the central control is out of order, as in brain damaged patients or an untrained crane operator trying to manipulate the parts of the crane, then the problem will not be solved by paying attention to peripheral disorders.

Patients with brain damage may have many problems in processing afferent information. Visual agnosia, cortical sensory loss or sensory inattention are neurological deficits suffered by stroke patients. In these circumstances therapeutic strategies are more likely to meet with success if the therapist can identify the source of the problem and then provide augmented or alternative feedback. The neuroanatomist, Brodal gives an account of his experiences during recovery from a stroke. He reports that when the therapist moved his arm passively, it enabled him to extend his arm in a manner hitherto impossible. This is not to suggest that the feedback from passive movement is the same as when the arm is moved actively. However, in the absence of active movement ability, the feedback from the passive movement could be utilized to organize a movement pattern in some way approximating to a normal movement (Brodal 1970).

Further information concerning the role of feedback in the performance of manual tasks has recently been provided in a single case study of a patient with severe peripheral sensory pathology (Rothwell *et al.* 1982). His performance on a number of laboratory tasks was surprisingly successful. For example, he was able to move his thumb accurately through 3 different distances at different speeds. Yet despite demonstrating these and other abilities in contrived circumstances, he found his hands quite useless to him in everyday life. He could not grasp a pen and write, do buttons or hold a cup of tea. Part of his difficulty lay in the absence of any automatic reflex correction in his voluntary movements, and also in an inability to sustain constant levels of muscle contraction without visual feedback over periods of more than one or two seconds. He was also unable to maintain long sequences of simple motor programmes without vision.

SKILL ACQUISITION

Understanding the processes of motor learning has progressed to a point where a number of important factors which can influence learning have been identified. In designing training schedules it is important for the teacher or therapist to have knowledge about the characteristics of the learner, the nature of the task to be learned and the programme which will best convey the skill to the learner (Holding 1965).

Careful assessment is important, particularly when neurological deficits are present. Patients with brain damage may have a number of disabilities which make motor learning more difficult. This may be because they cannot comprehend what is being asked of them. Alternatively, they may be unable to make use of feedback, or indeed they may have sensory loss of a cortical type. Some may have sensation preserved, yet be unable to attend to the information from one side of their body. The hemiplegic patients who demonstrate unilateral neglect are familiar to many therapists, and the evaluation of the patient's limitations and potential in respect of this and other relevant factors is the only way that appropriate treatment can be planned. Augmented or alternative feedback techniques may help the patient gain closed-loop control over the initial stages of relearning movements that have been lost through disease or injury. Recent work by Aitken and Bower (1982) has been concerned with the possibility of providing alternative feedback for congenitally blind children by means of augmented auditory input. The children wear a helmet containing a device for detecting echoes which bounce off solid objects in the child's auditory field. This technique has shown promising results with young children, although they appear less able to make use of the information when they begin to acquire language. Results with adults, however, have so far been disappointing.

Another very important source of feedback for the patient is provided by giving him knowledge of the consequences of his attempts. Knowledge of results, or KR as it is often abbreviated, is only effective if it is as accurate as the therapist can provide. Offering praise, as has already been discussed, has value, but if it is given indiscriminately, may only serve to confuse the patient. More accurate feedback of KR can be given using mirrors or videotape played back. Much interest is being shown in the possibility of biofeedback systems. The patient is provided with either visual or auditory feedback in response to his efforts by means of circuitry linked in series with the active muscles. He is given instant and accurate information regarding the correctness of his attempts either by watching the trace on an oscilloscope screen or hearing blips or sounds. On each practice he attempts to match the effect of his action to the effect of a correct movement, which he has been shown beforehand. A simple example of biofeedback relating to the relative weight distribution that a patient takes through each foot when he is standing can be achieved using two sets of bathroom scales. The readings on the dials provide instant visual estimates of the proportion of the body weight taken through each leg.

As has already been described, the demands on the learner's attentional capacity are heavy when a novel skill is first attempted. The therapist can aid the patient, ensuring that he is not overloaded by breaking the task down into smaller elements which are manageable, and then gradually building these up until the composite movement is mastered.

IMAGING

Laboratory experiments have shown that subjects remember how to execute a linear positioning task more accurately if they imagine performing the task before carrying it out (Johnson 1982).

Patients may well be helped to perform movements correctly if they are instructed to imagine the movement before attempting it.

DISTRIBUTING PRACTICE

Learning a motor skill requires practice. The amount of practice depends on the person's abilities and the complexity of the skill in question. With some tasks learning is more efficient when practice sessions are kept short with intervening periods of either rest or alternative activity. Long periods of continuous practice may be counterproductive, with fatigue and discouragement to the learner. A study of learning to type, carried out on Croydon postmen, showed that distributed practice sessions, that is 'little and often', were superior to fewer longer sessions in producing skilled typists (Baddeley and Longman 1978).

The motor abilities that normal people use in everyday life need to be generalized to many and varied situations. No skill is learned in isolation, it is grafted on to existing skills, some of which may help and some hinder learning. When one skill helps another, there is said to be positive transfer of training. Learning the piano would, for example, transfer positively to learning the organ. Negative transfer is said to occur when two skills tend to interfere, as with playing squash and playing tennis. The stimulus is similar, a rapidly moving ball, yet two different types of stroke are demanded.

The aim in teaching a skill is to ensure that it transfers positively from the learning environment to the much more complex and varied situations occurring in the outside world. In the case of the therapist, it is important to bear in mind that once a skill is mastered, it should generalize to all the circumstances needed in daily life. The initial stages are probably guided best under consistent conditions, but when this has been achieved, variability should be gradually introduced. Walking training, initially over smooth, unobstructed ground, should progress to walking over carpet, round corners, over rough ground, and so on. Unfortunately, hospitals and rehabilitation units are often very different from patient's homes. A patient may be able to push open a door and sit on a raised toilet seat as well as managing his clothes whilst in the hospital. On discharge, he finds he cannot turn the door knob, manage the low toilet seat or, in fact cope with many of the activities he had been able to perform in the hospital environment. Given a willing relative, he may simply cease to try to cope with such tasks and relapse into quite unnecessary dependency.

CONCLUSION

The rapidly expanding field of psychological study of motor control and learning is already contributing valuable information with relevance for therapists trying to train or retrain skills. Therapists, on the other hand, are particularly well placed to observe the motor disabilities consequent upon disease and injury. It is hoped that the communication and collaboration between these and allied professions will continue to develop and flourish.

REFERENCES

AITKEN S. & BOWER T.G.R. (1982 Intersensory substitution in the blind. *Journal of Experimental Child Psychology* **33**, 309–23.

AYRES A. J. (1980) *Sensory Integration and Learning Disorders.* Western Psychological Services, Los Angeles.

BADDELEY A.D. & LONGMAN D. (1978) The influence of length and frequency of training session on the rate of learning to type. *Ergonomics* **21** (8) 627–35.

BRODAL A. (1970) Self observations and neuroanatomical considerations after a stroke *Brain* **96**, 675–94.

DENNIS W. (1940) The effect of cradling practices upon the onset of walking in Hopi children. *Journal of Genetic Psychology* **56**, 77–86.

HELD R. (1965) Plasticity in sensory-motor systems. *Scientific American* **213**.

HOLDING D.H. (1965) *Principles of Training.* Pergamon Press, New York.

JOHNSON P. (1982) The functional equivalence of imagery and movement. *Quarterly Journal of Experimental Psychology* **34** A, 349–65.

LEE D. N. (1980) Visuo-motor coordination in space-time. In *Tutorials in Motor Behaviour* (Eds. STELMACH G. E. & REQUIN J.). North Holland, Amsterdam.

LEE D.N. & ARONSON E. (1974) Visual and proprioceptive control of standing in human infants. *Perception and Psychophysics* **15**, 527–32.

NOTTEBOHM F. (1970) Ontogeny of birdsong. *Science* **167**, 950–6.

ROTHWELL J. C., TRAUB M.M., DAY B.L., OBESO J.A., THOMAS P.K AND MARSDEN C.D. (1982) Manual motor performance in the deafferented man. *Brain* **105**, 515–42.

WILSON D.M. (1980) Insect walking. In *The Organisation of Action* (Ed. GALLISTEL C.R.). Lawrence Erlbaum Assoc., London. (Reprinted from *Annual Review of Entymology* **11** (1966).

CHAPTER 4

SPEECH AND LANGUAGE DEVELOPMENT

Jean M. Cooper

The development of communication, taken as one aspect of total child development, is the concern of all professionals who deal with the developmentally disabled child. During the first few years of life, the child is engaged in the process of developing communication skills which he will use throughout his life. These early, formative years are of considerable concern for those who are professionally trained to work in the area of communication problems, i.e. speech therapists.

Since communication abilities and disabilities have a profound effect on all areas of development some knowledge of the processes involved in acquiring such disabilities during these early years is also important for other professionals whose expertise is essential in identifying and managing handicapped children.

The purpose of this chapter is to focus on the communication process as an integral part of overall child development. By describing briefly the nature of language, its development and the factors affecting its development, and by citing a few of the procedures that will facilitate this development, a better understanding of the role of verbal communication in the child's intellectual, social and emotional growth may be achieved.

THE NATURE OF LANGUAGE

Before discussing the development of speech and language (verbal communication) in particular, we should perhaps consider the whole range of human communication. Communication can take place using any of the five senses, i.e. auditory, visual, tactile, olfactory and gustatory and much study and research takes place about all these aspects. This academic study is known as Semiotics.

Whilst verbal communication is the main means of human communication, it is important to see it in relation to the other modes particularly when we are concerned with the handicapped child. Combined auditory and visual disability poses special problems in relation to communication and severe physical and/or mental handicap may, in addition, affect the tactile modes. In such circumstances the development of any communication system is extremely slow.

Verbal communication is made up of three interrelated components, language, speech and hearing. The normal development of speech and language is dependent on hearing.

The terms speech and language are frequently interchanged. Language is the broader, more encompassing term of which speech is one part.

Speech is one of the means through which language is manifested. The three main elements of this aspect of language behaviour are vocalization, articulation and prosody.

Language may be defined as the ability to understand and use a system of symbols (and for purposes of this chapter particularly verbal symbols) in thinking and as a form of communication. A symbol is something that can stand for, or represent, something else, e.g. a cup can be represented by a toy cup, a picture or a word. The use of the symbol can convey the concept without the actual object being there. However, there must be understanding or knowledge of the object itself, i.e. a concept of the object. At first the object itself is only recognized in a familiar setting and conceptual understanding only develops when the child understands that an object continues to exist even when it is not present.

Thus language comprises both a receptive and an expressive aspect and, what is less observable, an integrative aspect — all of which are dependent not only upon audition and motor function but also upon cognitive processes, and may be modified by other functions such as perception and motivation. As our language ability develops we can engage in more abstract and complex behaviour and we can communicate not only about the 'here and now' but we can recall past events and make predictions about future ones.

THE DEVELOPMENT OF LANGUAGE

Underlying the development of verbal communication is the progressive maturation of the brain with its increasingly refined interconnections and co-ordination of electrical impulses. This maturation process proceeds at varying rates but with remarkable consistency of sequences. Likewise the progressive development of communication skills is based upon the fact that each subsequent stage of development is dependent on the prior establishment of a prerequisite stage. Because of the wide variation in the rate of language acquisition one of the most important points to remember is to consider it always in relation to the child's total pattern of development.

The sequence of stages in development of the receptive and expressive aspects of language is fairly consistent as it is determined by the stages in cognitive development upon which it is dependent. It is the intellectual basis which very largely determines the rate at which language develops, e.g. we have already seen how concept formation must precede symbolic understanding.

Figure 4.1 illustrates some of the processes that are involved in the development of verbal communication and which are now briefly described.

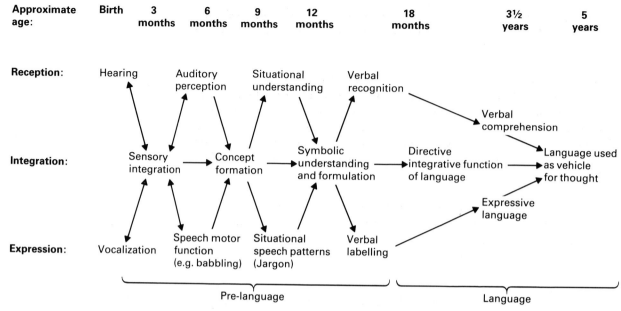

Figure 4.1 The integration of some processes involved in the development of verbal communication (after Cooper *et al.* 1978).

Hearing and auditory perception   The infant receives a wide range of auditory stimuli and in order to make use of this he has to learn to detect, select, discriminate and integrate the signals received. One of the basic requirements for learning is the ability to attend, and there appear to be certain developmental stages through which the child passes in acquiring this ability.

First stage (normally 1st year of life): the child's attention is held only momentarily by whatever is the dominant stimulus in the environment and he is easily distracted by any new stimulus.

Second stage (normally 2nd year of life): the child can now concentrate on a concrete task of his own choice but in order to sustain this concentration his attention is rigid and inflexible. He finds it difficult to tolerate intervention or any attempts to modify the task by an adult.

Third stage (normally 3rd year of life): the child is now more flexible but his attention is single channelled, e.g. either auditory or visual. The control of this has still to be focused by the adult.

Fourth stage (normally 4th year of life): the child is now beginning spontaneously to control his own attention but it is still single channelled.

Fifth stage (normally 5th year of life): the child can now assimilate verbal directions related to the activity in which he is engaged without having to stop and set the focus of his attention.

Sixth stage: integrated attention is now well established and sustained.

Situational understanding   Before the child's understanding of symbols emerges, and subsequent verbal recognition and comprehension, he will demonstrate an understanding of familiar phrases. These phrases are part of a regularly occurring sequence of events such as the child's response to 'pat-a-cake'. The individual words do not have meaning but the child responds to the familiar interaction pattern in the right context.

Verbal recognition and comprehension   As symbolic understanding develops from the recognition of objects, and the situational clues are reduced, the child can begin to select objects in response to naming. At first he can only assimilate one concept at a time but by about two years he can begin to relate two concepts in a phrase such as 'put the *dolly* on the *chair*.' Between $2\frac{1}{2}$ and 4 years of age there is a rapid advance to verbal comprehension and he is able to follow directions including three or more concepts.

Vocalization   It could be said that language acquisition begins with the birth cry. Certainly it develops out of the reflexive activities of the early months and the emotional interaction between mother and child in the early weeks is considered by many authorities to be crucial.

Babbling   Crying is gradually replaced more frequently by sounds of pleasure such as cooing and gurgling which the infant makes when in a supine position. Then, as the infant sits up, his repertoire of sounds becomes much more extensive and more interaction begins to take place between infant and mother (or "caretaker"). Sounds are repeated back to him and he in turn responds by repeating these sounds.

Jargon and situational speech patterns   By about ten months of age the infant begins to imitate not only a wide range of sounds but also inflection and rhythmic patterns and this sounds as if he is almost producing real sentences and trying to tell us something. These utterances normally have an environmental referent such as a person, object or action.

When asked what were the first words used by the child the answer is often 'all gone' or 'bye-bye' or 'more'. As with situational understanding the phrases are linked to a specific situation and, as such, cannot be considered as real symbolic language.

This stage of development usually precedes the first meaningful word. Older retarded children often remain at this stage for a long time acquiring phrases often used in the right situation but which are not representational. It is an important stage of development, and parents and all those handling the child should be encouraged to develop the child's repertoire by introducing such phrases into daily activities.

Verbal labelling and expressive language   The first real words that emerge normally between 12 and 15 months, are usually concerned with familiar objects in everyday use. At first these are dependent upon back-up clues but later, when consolidated, will be used without a concrete referent.

By two years of age the child can relate two concepts in a phrase. From then on there is a rapid advance in language development. Part of the growth in vocabulary is due to the fact that he is now questioning a great deal and using his own language to direct his activities. In fact the child begins to depend more and more upon language as a vehicle for his thinking and with this dependency the need to be understood becomes a vital part of his social and emotional growth.

This directive, integrative function of language develops in the following way.

First stage: in the early stage of the child's development the adult's attempt to introduce language into a child's activities is of little value; indeed it may even be disruptive to the child's behaviour.

Second stage: adult verbalization may then be helpful in guiding the child's activity, e.g. 'put one on top' may help the child to build a bridge with his bricks which he might not have been able to do without this verbal direction.

Third stage: the child then takes over the role of verbal guidance for himself, by talking aloud first of all as an accompaniment to his play and then later to help plan and direct his activity. Even children with a very limited amount of expressive language will be heard giving themselves simple directions, e.g. 'put car there', etc.

Fourth stage: after a time it is not necessary for the child to externalize this verbal guidance and verbal thinking becomes internalized except when dealing with a new or difficult task. Even as adults we sometimes revert to externalized or sub-vocal language when working out a particularly difficult activity.

As a child approaches about four years of age he sometimes finds his language inadequate and hesitations may occur in his speech patterns from time to time. Parents sometimes get anxious about this phenomenon of 'normal non-fluency' and need to be reassured. It is also important for them to remember that no child develops constantly and consistently in all areas of performance. There will be periods where development appears to level off while the child consolidates the skills he is busy acquiring. This should be expected and explained to parents.

FACTORS AFFECTING THE DEVELOPMENT OF LANGUAGE

The normal development of speech and language is the result of a fortunate combination of factors. Normal physical structure and physiological function, integration of the central nervous system, adequate intellectual ability, emotional stability and environmental stimulation are all needed. Hence the development can be delayed permanently, or impeded temporarily, by problems arising in relation to any of those factors. The various disorders that may result can occur either separately or in combination, e.g. central nervous system impairment and mental retardation in the cerebral palsied child.

However, it is not the purpose of this chapter to deal exhaustively with all the deficient forms of language handicap and their possible causes. That is the concern of the professional trained to deal with the evaluation and management of speech and language disorders. Nevertheless it may be helpful to consider, in a general way, the problems likely to be encountered in relation to the stages of development as seen in Fig. 4.1 and as described earlier in this chapter. It is intended only to aid the recognition of what is normal and what may need further help. There is always the danger, when attempting to use any classificatory system, of thinking of language problems as consisting of discrete entities. To some extent any separation, or grouping, of problems is artificial and there is often great overlap and interaction between any of the processes. However, Table 4.1 may be a useful guide in considering some of the problems related to developmental language handicap.

Table 4.1   Groupings of problems related to language handicap

Central		Peripheral	
Non-verbal	Verbal	Endogenous	Exogenous
Problems of attention	Problems of verbal comprehension	Anatomical or structural abnormality	Environmental deprivation or inadequacy
Problems of concept formation	Problems of verbal expression	Physiological dysfunction	
Problems in symbolic understanding			

Some specific handicaps may produce certain general trends in the pattern of language development and these will be discussed very briefly.

Deafness   For this group of handicapped children there is a tendency for verbal expression to develop a little in advance of verbal comprehension. Their vocabulary may also develop in advance of sentence construction. They often develop other forms of 'symbolic language' such as gesture to substitute for their somewhat limited verbal language and this is necessary to help them in their intellectual development.

Blindness   For this group there is a particular difficulty in developing object labels as often they have less opportunity of associating the object with a concrete referent. They need a lot of experience in handling objects when they are being named for instance.

Cerebral palsy   This group of children are at risk with both central and peripheral aspects of language, and it is particularly important for a comprehensive assessment to be carried out to identify the predominant difficulties and to facilitate the development of some sort of communication.

Mental retardation Whilst there is nothing specific about early language development in this group as with most other groups, the need to build a solid foundation of conceptual and symbolic understanding is most important. With some of the handicapped children there may well be the need to develop alternative means of communication and this subject will be considered in Chapter 5.

HELPING LANGUAGE DEVELOPMENT

Most language responses are learned, and one must consider the principles of learning when trying to explain the differences between children. The stronger the motivation to use language, the more effective reward it brings and so the more developed language behaviour becomes. There is some evidence that the less verbal child is likely to be spoken to less often than the highly verbal child.

It has been shown that the most rapid development of language is between $1\frac{1}{2}$ and $4\frac{1}{2}$ years of age. It seems appropriate, therefore, to provide help at this stage before deviant patterns become established and any further learning difficulties are encountered.

Let us now consider some of the ways we may help in the development of some of the aspects referred to.

Attention The beginning of this skill is dependent on motivation and reinforcement. The child must want to attend to that particular stimulus and his response needs to be rewarded so that it is likely to occur again. The best reward is one inherent in the situation but sometimes it needs to be a simple reward like a hug or a kiss or even being given a sweet. Whilst at a basic level the response to the sound of a human voice as a stimulus is to pause and listen, at a later stage the child needs to make finer discriminations of speech. Such discriminations will involve even more subtle attention skills and certainly must be rewarded.

Symbolic understanding It is necessary to stress the importance of helping the child towards more imaginative play in order to lay the foundations for language development. The young child needs opportunities for play with domestic objects and simple toys. He needs the opportunity of imitating someone using objects to comprehend the function of play. Later he can be helped in the recognition and use of smaller (miniature), more representational toys. At a later stage pictures, i.e. two-dimensional representation of objects, can be recognized.

Through play, sequencing activities can be developed and again this helps to lay a good foundation for language. Syntax requires the ability to sequence or organize information in the form of sentences, words and sound within a word.

Verbal comprehension Each communication to the child needs to be as meaningful as possible and related to daily living situations. Also in the early stages of development it is important that the language that is used has a concrete referent. References to time and space require a more advanced stage of language as a thinking process.

Rewarding success in verbal comprehension need to be stressed. It is easy to reward the child for naming something correctly but it is just as necessary to reward him for understanding verbal information. Children imitate a great deal of what they hear and therefore the language addressed to the child is a major input for their learning.

Verbal expression At first it is important to focus on the content of the child's verbal output rather than the finer points of production such as the articulatory, syntactic and prosodic features. Correction of these should be deferred until language use has met the practical communication needs of daily life.

The request for verbal information should be genuine and not a demand of linguistic performance, e.g. rather than 'Tell me what that is called' or 'Say car' it is better to ask 'What is that?', etc.

Environmental stimulation Opportunities for utilizing language and for the child to benefit from a rich language environment are very important. But as with any diet neither the ingredients nor the quantity should be indigestible. It is important to help structure this opportunity for the child and therefore helping the child with learning strategies is far more important than bombarding him with more and more material that he is not necessarily ready to assimilate.

Finally, it cannot be sufficiently stressed that normal language development must be integrated into the child's total daily living environment. It cannot be confined to certain activities, or time of the day or days of the week.

CONCLUSION

In this chapter an attempt has been made to provide an introduction or overview of the development of speech and language, emphasizing the relationship between developing language skills and cognitive skills. The intention has been to increase interest and develop some understanding in the area of communication among professionals involved in the day-to-day contact with the handicapped child. A multidisciplinary approach to language facilitation should be encouraged to ensure that such children derive the maximum benefit from any intervention programme.

REFERENCES AND FURTHER READING

COOPER J., MOODLEY M. & REYNELL J. (1978) *Helping Language Development*. Edward
    Arnold, London.

COOPER J. (1976) Working with parents on early language development. In *Early
Management of Handicapping Disorders* (eds. Oppé T.E. & Woodford F.P.). Elsevier
Scientific, Amsterdam.

CRYSTAL D. (1980) *Introduction to Language Pathology*. Edward Arnold, London.

Department of Education and Science (1972) *Report of the Committee of Enquiry into the
Speech Therapy Services*. Chairman: Prof. Randolph Quirk. Her Majesty's Stationery
Office, London.

HOLT K.S. (1977) *Developmental Paediatrics*. Butterworths, London.

JOHNSTON R.B. & MAGRAB P.R. (1976) Introduction to developmental disorders & the
interdisciplinary process. In *Developmental Disorders* (eds. Johnston R.B. & Magrab
P.R.) University Park Press, Baltimore.

KNOBELOCH C. (1976) Speech & language. In *Developmental Disorders* (eds. Johnston
R.B. & Magrab P.R.). University Park Press, Baltimore.

MARGE M. (1972) The general problems of language disabilities in children. In
        Principles of Childhood Language Disabilities (eds Irwin J.V. & Marge M.).
        Appleton-Century-Crofts, New York.

PIAGET J. (1954) *The Construction of Reality in the Child*. Basic Books, New York.

SKINNER B.F. (1957) *Verbal Behaviour*. Appleton-Century-Crofts, New York.

WOOD N.E. (1964) *Delayed Speech & Language Development*. Prentice Hall, New York.

CHAPTER 5

COMMUNICATING WITH CHILDREN

Clare Latham

Communication can be defined as the act of conveying one's meaning to others. It is an adaptive process involving two or more participants who modify their behaviour to facilitate the sharing of ideas, feelings and interests. Communication is not a term interchangeable with 'speech and language', for whilst the verbal channel is important, effective communication can only be established by the combination of verbal and non-verbal abilities. It has been suggested that only one-third of what is communicated is done so through words and the remaining two-thirds is conveyed by non-verbal means (Mehrabian 1972). Adults are generally unaware of the depth and subtlety of their communication skills. Information is automatically given or sought on a wide variety of subjects in a way that is distinctive and mutually acceptable (Argyle 1981). It is worth examining the communication process a little more closely.

The giving of information requires four areas of skill:
1   being able to state ideas in words that will be understood by the listener;
2   monitoring that those words are being understood;
3   being sensitive to the listener's need to seek clarification, confirmation or additional information on any points;
4   being able to change roles and become the listener at the appropriate moment.

The role of listener should not be thought of as passive. First, interest must be shown mainly by use of eye contact and encouraging facial expression. Second, the listener has to comprehend not only the meaning of the words but also the meaning of the facial expressions and gestures of the speaker. Third, the listener must use his own facial expression to indicate when confusion has arisen or clarification is needed. He also must know how to change roles and, in turn, become the speaker.

These subtle communication skills of both giving and receiving information are not present at birth but, like speech, take many years to develop and continue developing and changing throughout life.

Communicating with children is less easy than with adults because of the inequality in the level of communication skills. As the more able partner in communication, it is up to the adult to adapt to the situation but, unless one is familiar with children, these adaptations may at first feel strange. In this section, I shall highlight some of the adaptations imposed on adults and some of the responses they can expect children to give.

Whatever information we, as adults, feel that a child should know or act upon, it has to be presented in a way that the child can begin to understand and accept. It is first of all important to show a desire for equality and thus eye-to-eye contact must be established. This means bending down, sitting or kneeling down to the child's level or, in appropriate circumstances, picking the child up. The words chosen and the length and complexity of sentences should be appropriate for the child's developmental level. It is difficult to monitor how well a child is receiving information, as the ability to interject and to seek clarification when points are not understood may not be fully developed. When a child does not understand what is being said to him, he tends, in the main, to terminate the interaction in ways that often appear rejecting to the adult. Typical strategies that children use in this situation include turning, walking or running away, diverting attention to a new subject or creating a new situation such as a request for the toilet.

When the adult adopts the role of listener, adaptations are also required. It is important to realize that children may take longer to respond to a request than do adults and it is essential to give them adequate time. In the case of very young children, their initial verbal attempts are often not understood by strangers and it can be difficult to decide whether to pretend to have understood what the child said rather than to intimidate the child by constant requests for clarification. A useful clue is that the child's facial expression will often indicate the importance to the child of his statement or request and thus when it is necessary for the adult to try and understand. In this situation, it is best to ask the child to show you what he wants or to say it another way. If this approach works, then it is a good plan to let the child know how his attempt should have sounded by stating the adult version 'Oh, you wanted a biscuit'. Thus the child learns not only how his attempt should have sounded but also he begins to learn vital strategies for dealing with temporary breakdowns in communication.

The presence of specific handicapping conditions can cause great difficulty in the child's acquisition of communication skills and it is important to be aware of how and why this may occur.

THE BLIND CHILD

The eye-to-eye contact, which is one of the most important early communications between mother and baby, is denied in cases of severe visual handicap. This means that voice becomes a more important link. The visually handicapped child does not turn to sound as early as the normally sighted child but this does not mean that attention is not being paid. To supplement the voice, it is most important to use touch and to keep tactile input at a high level. Many mothers spontaneously do this and it is essential to reinforce this natural behaviour. The lack of eye-to-eye contact makes the initiation of verbal exchanges rather more difficult and blind children heighten their responses to tone of voice and eventually become able to initiate communication vocally. Facial expressions to indicate pleasure or displeasure are obviously present but the subtleties of eye expression are absent and this lack becomes more obvious as a child grows older. Without the subtle cues of eye-to-eye contact to initiate, and eye avoidance to terminate, a conversation the blind child is more heavily dependent on tone and pitch of voice to gain such information. The inability of the blind child as the listener to sustain eye contact is sometimes read by sighted people to indicate a lack of interest but if one looks more closely, the tense face and concentrated stilling will reveal that the child is listening attentively. Whilst the hands are the 'eyes' of the blind, social custom does not allow them to feel the vital facial expressions used during a conversation (see also Chapter 14).

THE CHILD WITH CEREBRAL PALSY

Apart from the most severely affected individuals, the child with cerebral palsy has some control and use of his eyes. The potential for eye-to-eye contact is therefore present. Unfortunately, the delay in acquisition of head control means that such contact is by no means as easily established as in the normal child, and therefore care must be taken to provide the child with an appropriate means of stabilizing his head to allow him to make the most of his eyes. The motor patterns which are the essence of severe cerebral palsy do tend to work to inhibit communication. In mother–baby interaction it becomes obvious that it is movements involving flexion which bring mother and baby together and facilitate communication. In cerebral palsy the dominant movement is generally extensor and does of course tend to move mother and baby apart. Again it is important to be aware of this and pay special attention to appropriate positioning of the child in any situations where communication may take place. As the child grows older, the presence of a pseudo-bulbar palsy and the difficulty in maintaining control over expiration may impose severe limitations on the quality of vocalization that the child can achieve. General motor difficulties may prevent the child from visually exploring his environment and making the most of the 'look and see' learning by which children build up their vocabulary. Later concepts in language development, including those of size, speed and physical relationship may be impaired in cerebral palsy.

Even when speech has developed, further difficulties can be encountered. Problems of motor control affect not only the organs of articulation but also the facial muscles and thus facial expression. This often results in a totally inappropriate expression for the word used and total lack of subtlety in facial movement.

Whilst some degree of intellectual deficit is common in cerebral palsy, frequently children are to some extent 'locked in' with an intellect in advance of motor function. This group of children has been greatly helped by recent advances in non-verbal communication whether by gestures, graphic systems or communication aids. The provision of an appropriate communication system can allow a child to express himself at a level more appropriate to his innate intellectual ability. It must be remembered that often a great deal of hard work is necessary before a child can actually use a system to communicate. The 'locked in' child has had no opportunity at all to practise even the most basic communication skills of initiating or terminating interaction and this lack of experience becomes very obvious when a communication system is provided and the child seems at a complete loss as to how to use it. It is important that he is taught and then gains experience in these very basic processes. Most methods of alternative communication are slower than speech and sometimes the speed can be so slow that the thread of conversation gets lost and the child will also need help in preventing this happening. When communication is provided by a machine, the child has the added difficulty of having to look down at a keyboard or display, thus losing the vital eye-to-eye contact he requires to monitor the success of his interaction. In addition, he will have limitations imposed by silence and the inability to interject or ask for clarification verbally. These difficulties may so discourage the user that he is inclined to give up and it is, therefore, most important to give adequate help and support to allow the different problems to be overcome and the art of communication to be mastered.

THE CHILD WITH MENTAL HANDICAP

A child with mental handicap is slow to develop through all the stages described in Chapter 4 and some form of speech or language therapy is usually indicated. For some children, the handicap will be so profound that they will never become verbal and some form of very basic alternative communication will have to be used. For other children, acquisition of spoken language can be facilitated by using a sign or symbol as an intermediary which will eventually be replaced by speech. The majority of mentally handicapped children are able to acquire speech and this, of course, should be a primary goal of therapy. It is very important, however, to realize that speech is of very little value without the communication skills to back it up. Therapy techniques used in the past have been aimed at eliciting speech in imitation of the adult but this approach often results in a child who remains unable to produce anything other than a monologue or constant stream of questions whose answers are never awaited. In other words, the ability to participate in a dialogue is never mastered. Teaching the function of language in communication is a much harder task than producing speech but it is a particular vital one (see Chapter 4).

ASSESSING CHILDREN'S COMMUNICATION SKILLS

Assessing communication is a difficult task. The adaptive nature of the process demands that the communication will vary according to the person, the situation and the topic of discussion. It follows that testing a child's communication in a given situation with one person will assess only one small part of his skills. It is necessary to observe the child in different settings and with those who feature most in his life. Practicalities often make such a venture impossible so that questioning may be the only way to gain such information. To this end, many practitioners have developed their own checklist (Macdonald 1980). Figure 5.1 is a checklist I found useful as part of my assessment.

ASSESSMENT GUIDELINE	Test Results to Date		
Name	Intellectual —	Symbolic Understanding	—
Age	Language Understanding —	Hearing	—
Diagnosis	Expression —	Vision	—

People/Agencies involved in Patient's Communication Difficulty

PRESENT METHOD OF COMMUNICATION	
1. *Use of Speech* If patient has some speech, describe [i.e. number of words, length of sentence, clarity]. If no speech, state if/how yes/no are indicated.	d) Can attempt to join in a conversation. e) Tries to include others in conversation. Comment if necessary.
2. *Use of Facial Expression* Describe these and what they mean.	6. *Communicating Behaviour* a) Seems to make little attempt to communicate. b) Tries to communicate but gives up easily. c) Persists at communicating and in a variety of ways.
3. *Use of Hand, Body and Eye Gestures* Describe the use of these and in particular if any are used for direct communication, i.e. pointing or eye pointing to desired item.	d) Checks to see if his communication has been received, i.e. monitors well. e) When communication attempts are not clear, how do child/parents/teacher/siblings react.
4. *Use of Vocalizations other than Speech* State what they mean, e.g. vocalizes to gain attention, in anger, in response to others, etc.	7. *Speed of Communication* a) Frustratingly slow. b) Laborious. c) Moderate. d) Quick and easy.
5. *Response to Other's Communication* a) Sustains eye contact when being spoken to. b) Follows other people and to where they are looking with interest. c) Reciprocates friendly facial expression.	8. *Use of Current Communication* a) Patient can indicate physical needs. b) Can express his feelings. c) Can communicate socially with strangers. d) Can relate events that have happened in the past. e) Can be independent of family in his interaction with others.

Figure 5.1

Such a checklist is only a guide to one's observation. As our knowledge improves, observations will be more specific. However, a checklist can be helpful, particularly to parents who may feel that communication with their child is adequate. This will probably be correct, but the child needs to communicate with others if he is ever to become independent. As the parent tries to answer some of these questions, it often becomes apparent to them exactly what their child can or cannot do with his method of communication.

COMMUNICATION SYSTEMS

To meet the communication needs of those children whose speech and language is impaired, alternative or augmentative systems have been developed. These systems are used in one of three ways:

1   as a permanent method of communication for children who have little or no chance of developing intelligible speech because of the severity of their handicap;

2   as a temporary measure to encourage the development of communication skills and to alleviate frustration in a child who will eventually become verbal but in whom the acquisition of speech will be delayed;

3   as part of specialized teaching strategy for children with developmental speech disorders.

For this chapter, I have selected the six most commonly used systems in the United Kingdom. They are all standardized and taught by qualified instructors. In addition, I have described how to use pictures and the written word. The systems can be divided into two groups: those needing only some form of strategy to use a chart or display (Graphic Systems), and those requiring sufficient dexterity to produce hand signs (Signing Systems).

GRAPHIC SYSTEMS

PICTURES

The simplest of the graphic systems is the use of clear pictures stuck on to a chart to which the child can point in some way. To use such a system, the child must understand that a picture can represent an object or an action in real life and must also possess a reliable yes/no strategy. It may be necessary to prepare a child for a graphic system by working on his symbolic understanding through the use of real objects and toys and helping him to discover a suitable yes/no response. I recommend that clear colour photographs are taken of the child's personal belongings and family. Later, those photographs can include activities of daily living, such as bathtime, mealtime, dressing drinking, etc. The size and complexity of the photographs and the way in which they are displayed on the chart should take into account any defect of vision and the limitations of the child's pointing system.

To enable children to use such charts successfully, most families require advice in two main areas. They need to know how to make the most of a limited vocabulary and also how to alter their own communication with the child. Most parents of a non-speaking child adopt the 'closed question' technique, e.g. 'Do you want a biscuit?' which requires a yes/no response. This should be changed to include as many 'open questions' as possible, for example, 'What would you like to eat?' enabling a child to make a choice and to use his chart. As the child becomes more skillful with a picture chart, the pictures can become smaller and more numerous and line drawings can replace photographs. It may be possible to go on to more abstract concepts in the form of symbols.

SYMBOLS

There are a number of symbol systems in use in the United Kingdom but the majority of children use Bliss Symbols. This system requires a well-developed symbolic understanding, i.e. more than understanding photographs and line drawings but not as advanced as understanding the written word. A degree of discrimination between symbols is necessary. The child's ability to make such discrimination can be gauged by using the Pre-Bliss Assessment published by the Resource Centre (see Address (1) at end of this chapter).

Blissymbolics is a language in its own right, with its own internal structure and, as such, it is an effective method of communication. It is possible to follow most spoken English rules but syntactical subtleties cannot be indicated. A wide variety of sophisticated equipment is available for use with the Bliss system and this makes it particularly suitable for physically handicapped children and its application is expanding. The written word accompanies the symbol and thus the child can communicate with those unfamiliar with the system. Further information is available from Address (1).

THE WRITTEN WORD

Children who have good reading skills can use the written word for communication. Like pictures and symbols, words can be placed on a chart to which the child can point. The most sophisticated of modern communication aids function through the written word. These take the form of word processors, some with the ability for artificial speech. To use these, a relatively advanced degree of reading and spelling ability is essential. Many children will develop their abilities from using three-dimensional objects, through pictures and symbols to using written words and it is important for involved professionals to be aware of when a child has reached his limits or when a more advanced system is indicated.

SIGN SYSTEMS

The use of hand gestures to aid communication is well known. Whilst being natural and spontaneous, they are as transient as the written word and in most cases can only be used with others familiar with the signs.

AMERIND

AmerInd is based on the ancient 'hand talk' of the American Indians and has been developed into a simplified gestural code by Skelly (1979). It is not a language with grammatical rules but a code or signal system. Signals are not based on words of a particular language but on ideas or concepts. There are two important features of this system. First, most of the signals are concrete and require limited symbolic understanding and, secondly, Skelly has shown that most signals can be understood by the uninstructed. Its current use is with the severely mentally handicapped. Information is co-ordinated in Great Britain by Address (2).

SIGN LANGUAGE

Sign languages have been developed by deaf people throughout the world as an effective means of communication. In the United Kingdom, British Sign is used. It is a language in its own right, with its own grammatical structure that does not follow the rules of spoken English. Recently, it has been considered important to approximate British Sign to spoken English. To do this, the same signs are used but firstly they are changed to follow spoken word order and secondly spoken English syntax is incorporated. This is done in one of two ways. In Sign-Supporting English it is achieved by finger spelling where necessary and in Signed English there are individual signs for grammatical structure. Further information is available from Address (3).

THE MAKATON VOCABULARY

The family of communication systems derived from British Sign is completed by the Makaton Vocabulary (Walker 1978). This is a specialized vocabulary of British Signs based on a developmental language programme. Like Sign-Supporting English and Signed English, it also follows spoken word order but there are no signs for detailed grammatical function and use of finger spelling is limited. Some syntactical structures can be used but effective communication is possible without their use. Children require some dexterity but most signs are either one-handed or if two hands are required, both hands are used in the same position. The vocabulary is widely used amongst the mentally handicapped as the simpler signs require minimal symbolic understanding. Its application is expanding. For further information see Address (4).

THE PAGET-GORMAN SIGN SYSTEM

The approximation of British Sign to spoken English is a recent development. During the first half of this century, it was felt that the lack of approximation was preventing deaf people from learning to read and write. The need for a sign system which followed exactly the rules of spoken English caused the Paget-Gorman Sign System to be designed. Word order and syntax are exactly as in spoken English.

It may be argued that with the further evolution of British Sign, two systems are not necessary. By virtue of the fact that it is a contrived system, the very structured rules of Paget have proved useful in teaching children with aphasia and allied language disorders. There is no doubt that Paget requires more dexterity than any of the other systems and this may be important in considering its application. Further information is available from Address (5).

CUED SPEECH

Unlike the other systems mentioned, Cued Speech can only be used in conjunction with actual speech. It is designed to clarify the ambiguities in lip reading by the use of eight hand signals or cues made in four different positions close to the mouth. In clarifying the ambiguities in lip reading. Cued Speech enables a deaf child to gain a fuller understanding of language and assist them towards clearer pronunciation. Further information is available from Address (6).

CONCLUSION

In conclusion, we should remember that communication is an adaptive behaviour which allows a sharing of ideas, feelings and interests. By definition it involves two or more people and the responsibility for effective communication is shared by those involved. The normal process entails a complex, changing repertoire of verbal and non-verbal clues which children take many years to learn.

Children who fail to achieve intelligible speech are severely handicapped, not only in their communication but also emotionally and educationally. The cause of their difficulties varies and their needs are different. Every effort should be made to help speech develop wherever this is possible. Sometimes, however, the use of one or more of a range of augmentative communication systems will be required. The use of such systems may be temporary or permanent but, whatever the reason for their use, they are like speech, a medium for interaction. They can be taught but will only be of value if they are seen to be useful in communication. This is a difficult task requiring changes by all those concerned with the child if satisfying and meaningful communication is to be achieved.

ADDRESSES

(1) Mrs E. Davis
     The Blissymbolics Resource
         Centre
     The South Glamorgan Institute
         of Higher Education
     Western Avenue
     Llandaff
     Cardiff
     S. Wales

(2) Mrs S. Leavesley
     7 Chester Close
     Lichfield
     Staffs

(3) The Royal National Institute
         for the Deaf
     105 Gower Street
     London, WC1E 6AH

(4) Mrs M. Walker
     31 Firwood Drive
     Camberley
     Surrey

(5) Mr B. Newey
3 Gipsey Lane
Headington
Oxford, OX3 7TT

(6) Mrs J. Dixon
The Principal
The National Centre for
Cued Speech
London House
68 Upper Richmond Road
Putney
London, SW15

REFERENCES AND FURTHER READING

ARGYLE M. (1981) *The Psychology of Interpersonal Behaviour*. Penguin Books Limited,

CARRIER J.K. *Jr.* (1976). Application of non speech language system with severely language handicapped. In *Communications Assessment and Intervention Strategies*, p. 523–48 (ed. LLOYD L.L.). University Park Press, Baltimore.

McDONALD E. (1980) *Teaching and Using Blissymbols*. Blissymbolics Communication Institute, Toronto.

MEHRABIAN A. (1972) *Non-Verbal Communication*. Aldine Publications, New Jersey.

SKELLY M. (1979) *Amer-Ind Gestural Code based on the Universal American Indian Hand Talk*. Elsevier Press, New York.

WALKER M. (1978) The Makaton vocabulary. In *Ways and Means* (ed. TEBBS I.). Globe Education, London.

CHAPTER 6

THE PHYSIOTHERAPIST IN THE NEONATAL UNIT

Finuala Murphy

There is considerable variability within the wide range of normality in development. Diagnosis in infancy can be very difficult and it may be many months before a positive diagnosis can be ascertained. What looks like pathology may not necessarily be so, but may rather be part of the normal developmental process. It is not the initial severity of neurological signs that might be important in prognosis, but their persistence or time of disappearance that determines the long-term outcome. Infants have a tremendous power of recovery (Held 1965). From the studies of Dubowitz (1981), it would appear that persistent asymmetry of posture and hypertonus, with diminished mobility in the legs in the neonatal period, consistently correlates with later abnormality.

THE ROLE OF THE PHYSIOTHERAPIST

The role of the physiotherapist in the neonatal team is one of observation, recording development, stimulating normal reactions, preventing abnormal postures and deformities and advising on posture, positioning and the handling of infants in need or 'at risk'. Physiotherapists are also actively involved in the care of the infant's chest. In addition, by being in regular contact with the infant and his parents we may aid him in establishing positive relationships.

BONDING

By handling and cuddling an infant the physiotherapist has the opportunity of helping the newborn infant to establish bonding (attachment) and to encourage responses to tender love and care which introduce him to his first and foremost experience with the world of human stimuli (Stern 1979).

Parents play a very important role in the development of their baby and must be allowed to participate in its care from the very beginning. The importance of bonding cannot be stressed too strongly as the findings of Klaus *et al.* (1972), Schaffer & Crook (1978) and many others suggest that there is a sensitive period for attachment, shortly after birth. The release of maternal feelings seems to depend heavily on the infant's capacity to exhibit behaviours that characterize adult communication, creating interaction between mother and child. This interaction initiates caretaking behaviour in the parents. The intricate visual, tactile and auditory stimulation between mother and baby serves to unite them. Bonding is essential for the infant's emotional and intellectual development.

Hospital organization which leads to very early separation of the baby from his mother has been found to contribute to 'abnormal maternal child relationships, including rejection, neglect and finally battering', (Korner & Thoman (1970). Every effort should be made to facilitate mother-child interaction and even ill infants in incubators can be visited regularly. The mother should be encouraged to touch through the portholes and stroke and talk to her baby. Breast feedings should be established whenever possible, even in the intensive care unit.

Some mothers, and fathers too, are shocked and lack confidence in their caring abilities when confronted by a small infant, surrounded by medical equipment and intensive care. Mothers, no matter how inexperienced or clumsy they appear to be, must never be made to feel inadequate when handling their babies.

INFANTS REFERRED FOR PHYSIOTHERAPY

Not every premature or low-birth-weight infant needs intensive stimulation from the physiotherapist. Only infants, with a known birth history indicating abnormal factors, pre- or post-natally, that are likely to cause handicap, require close observation with intervention plus continuous assessment. Follow-up observation of development may be required for some months or even years.

Infants showing signs of abnormality of tone, posture or movement require treatment and continual assessment at regular intervals, often twice daily in the first few weeks of life. Close observation without actually handling can alert one to the need to intervene or to advise on positioning or sucking.

Many preterm and low-birth-weight infants are much better given minimal handling in an optimal environment (incubator) to maintain their body temperature and oxygen intake, with intensive nursing and feeding. Physiotherapy treatment is only envisaged when the infant's medical condition is stable and he is gaining weight, except in respiratory conditions when urgent treatment of the chest may be required. There are few conditions in the neonatal period that require vigorous treatment from the physiotherapist, for example, club feet, atelectasis and marked hypotonia. Small infants tire easily, hence any physiotherapy treatment must always be precise, skilful and of short duration.

STIMULATION OF THE INFANT

Physiotherapists in the neonatal unit use developmental knowledge (Sheridan 1977) and work from the neurological basis of movement described by Barry

Wyke. 'The more active a fetus is in the later stages of pregnancy, and the more handling and mechanical stimulation it gets after birth, the more rapidly will its tissue mechanoreceptors mature and the more efficient will its mechanoreceptor reflexes become' (Wyke 1975).

The learning of movement is entirely dependent on sensory experience and sensory input not only initiates but also guides motor output (Bobath 1967). The physiotherapist observes the infant's reactions adjusting her and mother's methods of handling to assist or resist these responses. Such handling therefore stimulates the infant to move and react to postural change, including positioning of his head in space.

Sensorimotor stimulation aims at activating the infant and awakening his interest in his environment, so he can interact with it. Infants spend much of their time scanning the environment and seeking stimulation. Infants placed in the semi-upright or upright position become more alert (Korner & Thoman 1970). The practice of sensorimotor stimulation is based on the premise that the sequence of development is of vital importance (Woodward 1970).

There must be repetition of the feedback from the feel of normal movement in order that the baby can learn. Much of human interaction is characterized by reciprocal reinforcement. The infant's behaviour is reinforced by food and by the mother's attention. The mother's behaviour is reinforced by the child's smiles and coos. The physiotherapist gives reinforcement to the neonate by eye contact, smiling, talking, singing, touching and cuddling. Conditioning can be developed in the first weeks of life.

Habituation occurs when the infant sees an object repeatedly or hears the same sound, he turns away to look for new stimuli and will not respond unless a different pattern or sound is offered. The speed of habituation increases with age and infants become more selective in responding to certain stimuli. Habituation represents an early adaptive learning response to the environment. It has been shown (Dennis 1960) that early experience can affect structural development, intersensory co-ordination and behavioural maturation.

Stimulation must never exhaust or distress the infant. Babies' responses to the environment differ depending on their state of arousal or mood.

BEHAVIOURAL STATES

'States are distinct conditions, each having its specific properties and reflecting a particular mode of nervous system functioning' (Prechtl 1974).

State I   Eyes closed, regular respiration, no movement.

State II   Eyes closed, regular respiration, small movements; gross body movements may occur.

State III   Eyes open; quiet; no gross movements.

(a) Normal

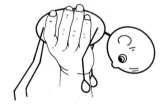

(b) Preterm

(c) Hypotonic (floppy)

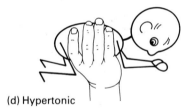

(d) Hypertonic

Fig. 6.1 Ventral suspension position.

State IV   Eyes open; gross movements; no crying.

State V   Crying.

The optimum states for assessment and treatment are States III and IV. A baby is most alert shortly before a feed but if excessively hungry he will not co-operate. Record of the state of arousal should be made so that future assessment can be done under constant conditions. Crying, hunger or sleepiness inhibit some activities and reflex reactions.

TONE, POSTURE AND MOVEMENT

Tone is estimated by the amount of resistance given by a muscle contracting when a joint is moved passively by the therapist. Tone is also indicated by the pattern in which spontaneous active movements occur and by the ability to hold postures and move against the force of gravity. The position of the head in space determines the distribution of tone throughout the body. From a study of the newborn, Casaer (1979) has demonstrated that the newborn infant has a small but definite degree of postural tone. When picked up he is neither too floppy or rigid and is easy to carry. In the upright position he makes vigorous attempts to right his head and make early visual contact. By contrast, the abnormal baby with increased tone feels stiff; he may hyperextend his neck, fist his hands or extend his legs stiffly and is difficult to cuddle. The floppy or hypotonic infant on the other hand is difficult to hold as he does not adjust his postural tone or react to movement and can easily slip through the caretaker's hands. He resembles a jelly fish or the 'rag doll' as described by Dubowitz (1969) (Fig. 6.1(c)).

The ill or very premature infant lacks tone. The mentally handicapped and the Down's syndrome baby and some cerebral palsy babies show varying degrees of hypotonia from birth.

MOVEMENTS

The level of activity is highly variable in quantity and quality in infancy. Movements in the newborn infant occur spontaneously or can be elicited by external stimuli. They are usually bilateral mass movements — the upper limbs moving more than the legs. Frequently, some infants show more activity on one side though this may not be consistent. It is most important to watch for symmetry and asymmetry of posture and movement.

Tremors, twitching and rapid, jerky movements should not be considered normal and may be due to cerebral irritation, convulsions, hypoglycaemia, hypocalcaemia or hypernatraemia. Spasmodic, momentary, jerky movements of the limbs of the newborn on awakening from sleep are common in normal neonates. Agitated tremulous movements (jitteriness) can be seen when an infant is hungry or hyperalert. Jitteriness should be distinguished from neonatal seizures. In tonic convulsions the infant goes stiff and exhibits tonic extension of the trunk and limbs. It is often associated with apnoea and cyanosis, and handling may precipitate an attack.

Movement and tone are inseparable and in infancy the supine (Fig. 6.2), prone, ventral suspension (Fig. 6.1) and vertical suspension positions are used in assessment and treatment. By using passive extension and release or traction on the limb, the speed of recoil and return to the flexed posture indicates the tone. The amount of flexion depends on the tone and the maturity of the infant, (see Fig. 6.2). Very immature and hypotonic infants remain supported on the mattress in full extension. The development of tone can be assessed by measuring the angle of the elbow and the knee (i.e. the popliteal angle). Pull to sitting from supine combined with arm traction tests the head lag and is commonly used by paediatricians (see Fig. 6.3). In the preterm baby the head needs to be supported initially. Some infants with good limb tone may show marked head lag and others have surprisingly good head control from birth. The preterm reaching forty weeks post menstrual age may show good head control with fully extended limbs in supine and they are very active in prone.

If an infant shows remarkably good head control in ventral suspension or prone (i.e. well above the horizontal) in comparison to marked head lag when pulled to sitting, it would alert one to check whether there is hypertonicity in the extensors of the neck (see Fig. 6.1 (d)).

If an infant is supported by two hands under his axillae and around his chest and placed on a firm surface on his feet, he will exhibit positive supporting reaction in his legs and if tilted slightly forward the automatic walking reflex will occur, simulating walking. The preterm baby of less than thirty-five weeks is unable to extend his trunk. The normal-term baby places the whole foot on the surface and moves in a heel–toe progression. The abnormal or hypertonic infant goes stiff and walks on tiptoe. Preterm infants have a different pattern of development and walk in a toe–heel progression or on their toes.

Normal infants sometimes catch one leg behind the other. This is not a scissors gait and must not be confused with adductor spasm (Infant postures are copiously illustrated in Dubowitz and Dubowitz (1981)).

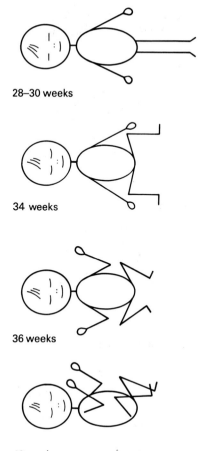

28–30 weeks

34 weeks

36 weeks

40 weeks

Fig. 6.2 Supine infants at different gestation ages.

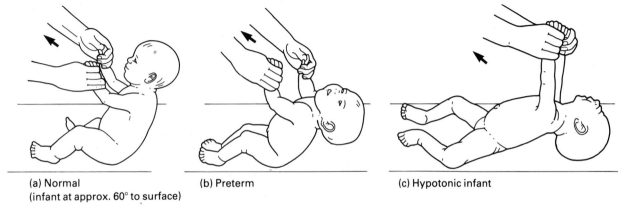

(a) Normal
(infant at approx. 60° to surface)

(b) Preterm

(c) Hypotonic infant

Fig· 6.3 Pull to sitting from supine.

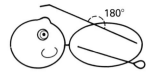

(a) Knee extension in preterm infant
    (28 weeks)

(b) Knee extension in term
    infant

Fig. 6.4   Diagram of the popliteal
angle.

RANGE OF MOVEMENT

The normal-term infant has a good range of rotation of his head to both sides. He may have a preference to turn his head to one side. He lies flexed but has a good range of extension of his spine, shoulders, wrists and fingers. The range of extension in elbows and knees is limited in the first weeks of life, but he gains extension actively within four or five months. The one exception is the infant who is born by breech delivery who may have fully extended legs at birth.

Maturity of the preterm infant can be estimated by measuring the popliteal angle. The thigh is flexed up to the abdomen by holding the knee between the thumb and index and the leg is then extended with the other hand behind the ankle. The resistance to one's pressure is felt and the angle of the knee is assessed. The more immature the infant the more extended the knee will be (see Fig. 6.4).

The normal newborn baby's hips abduct to 90° when the knees are flexed so that the thighs lie alongside the abdomen. This position is used for testing for congenital dislocation of the hip.

In the preterm infant the hip and knee extension are more complete than in the term infant, but the wrist flexion and foot dorsiflexion are incomplete.

The term infant's feet may be compressed in utero and may take a few days to unfold. It is possible to dorsiflex the ankle so that the dorsum touches the lateral border of the leg. Plantar flexion is limited in the newborn period. Infants' feet tend to be inverted but can be passively everted fully unless there is an underlying deformity. It is important to note the range for differential diagnosis between congenital talipes equinovarus and the postural type of inverted foot, commonly seen in the neonatal period.

The preterm infant differs from the term infant in that he has a greater range of neck rotation and shoulder flexion (scarf sign) depending on his maturity. The amount of flexion in the limbs at forty weeks is not quite as great.

In cases of hypotonia there is hyperextensibility of joints whereas the hypertonic infant has marked resistance to passive movement.

PREVENTION OF DEFORMITIES

The nursing positions are vital to the development of the baby. Constant changes of position are important because they prevent abnormal moulding of bones and deformities in joints. Malformation can occur in utero from temporary malposition and moulding occurs as a result of local pressure. After birth, immobile postures result in changes in the visco-elastic properties of muscles and tendons which can lead to contractures. Constant lying on one side can cause asymmetrical moulding of the skull, (plagiocephaly) or flattening of the rib cage.

Imbalance in muscle tone leads to deformity. In hypotonia deformities occur particularly in the lower limbs from immobility and the pressure of gravity or weight of the bedclothes (see Fig. 6.2).

Contractures and deformities can be prevented in neonates by careful positioning and handling. In addition, full passive range movements and very gentle passive stretchings will maintain joint mobility and overcome tight structures. Splints are occasionally required and must be applied with great care (see also Chapters 11 and 12).

REFLEX ACTIVITY

The normal infantile (primitive) reflexes are useful in the neonatal period, not only for assessment but for stimulating an infant to move. Care must be taken never to overuse reflexes or reinforce any reactions that could lead to abnormal postures or abnormal changes in tone, e.g. asymmetrical tonic neck reaction (ATNR) (Fig. 6.5; see also Chapter 2, Table 2.1).

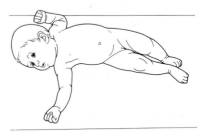

Fig. 6.5 Asymmetric tonic neck reaction posture.

For a description of reflexes see Prechtl (1977) and Illingworth (1980), noting timing of appearance and disappearance, symmetry or uneven strength in infants.

The following points and table of reflex development in the *preterm* infant are used in physiotherapy treatment (Table 6.1).

Table 6.1. Preterm development of reflex activity. Approximate time of appearance.

Gestation (in weeks)	Reflex (present but weak)
20–24	Galant
24–28	Rooting
28–34	Sucking
28–30	Grasp (palmer)
28–32	Moro — incomplete
32–36	Reacts to light
32–36	Automatic walking — erratic
32–36	Crossed extension — incomplete
34–36	Neck righting
34–36	ATNR — seen intermittently (adopts posture for sleeping).
37–39	Placing
37–39	Traction response

Reflex activity in the preterm infant is not reliable, strong or fully developed. Many responses are difficult to elicit in the first weeks of life. The tonic neck reflexes are very difficult to ascertain in term babies with normal tone and almost impossible to produce clearly in infants with low tone.

There is a great variability in the time at which some reflexes appear or disappear (McGraw 1966; Illingworth 1980). In the severely damaged infant, the responses are stereotyped and consistent, often abnormally obligatory, or they may be absent altogether. Variability of the elicited response is a typical characteristic of the healthy infant (Touwen 1978).

Reflexes are absent or weak in hypotonia and in very immature or ill infants. The Moro, the grasp reflex and traction response are asymmetrical in cases of hemiplegia, Erb's Palsy and in fractures of the clavicle or humerus. The Galant and crossed extension are absent in lesions of the spinal cord below the level of the lesion.

ORAL REFLEXES AND FEEDING

The sucking and swallowing reflexes are normally present at birth in all but the very small preterm or very ill infants. The sucking reflex may be present but the effort of sucking may exhaust the infant so tube feeding may be necessary. Sucking is initially evoked by tactile stimulation of the roof of the mouth and infants not sucking normally should be stimulated by the introduction of a teat into the mouth before feeds.

Oral reflexes are absent or weak in infants depressed by barbiturates. Satiated infants turn away from the stimulus for rooting.

GENERAL APPEARANCE

FULL TERM INFANT

Several hours after birth the newborn infant's skin flushes red all over and fades within 24 hours (erythema neonatorum) and peripheral cyanosis or blueness around the circumoral area are considered normal at this time. The heart rate is 120–140 and the respiration rate is about 40 per minute. The pattern of breathing is shallow and mostly diaphragmatic, using nasal breathing.

At birth the normal infant can see, hear, smell, swallow, suck and sneeze. He gazes intently at his mother's face as she speaks to him and within a few weeks he responds by smiling.

Physiological jaundice occurs commonly in term babies in the first week of life and particularly in light-for-dates infants. No treatment is required unless hyperbilirubinaemia develops. Septicaemia, haemolytic disease or an obstruction can also cause jaundice.

Engorgement of the breasts is common in full term infants, male and female, and resolves without treatment. The female genitalia remain large in the first month of life.

A high-pitched cry or 'cri du chat' indicates an abnormal baby.

THE PRETERM INFANT

The premature (preterm) infant weighs less than 2500 g (5½ lb) and is born before thirty-seven weeks gestation. The low-birth-weight or small-for-dates baby has suffered growth retardation in utero, and weighs less than 2500 g irrespective of the duration of pregnancy.

At birth the preterm infant is tiny with shiny, transparent, wrinkled skin. He may also have oedema. He lacks subcutaneous fat and muscle bulk, hence he is very prone to hypothermia. Lanugo (fine downlike hair) is often profuse all over the body. Infants of less than thirty-five weeks gestation lack creases on the soles of the feet, nipples are barely visible and the cartilage of the ears is not well formed.

The head appears relatively large and is without moulding, and the limbs appear short in relation to the crown–rump length. The fontanelles are small but soon gape as the brain grows faster than the skull. The abdomen is often prominent and may remain so for months. Regurgitation occurs frequently and the baby is at risk of aspiration of milk and subsequent pneumonia.

The infant is flaccid and the head is to one side, he is unable to turn it himself. Owing to weakness of the intercostal muscles and and the very mobile rib cage, recession of the sternum and costal margins is commonly seen. These infants are liable to cyanotic and apnoeic attacks.

Respiratory distress syndrome (hyaline membrane disease) occurs in immature infants who lack surfactant in their lungs. Sucking and swallowing are poorly developed. The breathing pattern is erratic in depth and rhythm and a rate of over 65 per minute indicates respiratory distress.

The posture of the preterm infant depends on his maturity (see Fig 6.2). The tone at forty weeks is less than in a term infant but he is more active and the movements are wilder and faster. His sleeping posture in prone resembles a six-week-old term infant (i.e. the pelvis is flat).

The preterm infant is at high risk for infection and intraventricular haemorrhage, hypoglycaemia, hypocalcaemia and atelectasis.

THE LOW-BIRTH-WEIGHT INFANT

These small-for-dates infants differ from the preterm in that they are more mature at birth, i.e. flexed posture, eyes and mouth closed. They are remarkably skinny with no subcutaneous fat and have dry, wrinkled skin. There is often meconium staining of the finger nails and cord. They are alert, wide eyed and resemble little old men. The tone is lower and the movements are weaker when compared to the normal term infant.

The maturity of the infant is more important for survival than the weight. Any birth injury, infection or haemorrhage increases the risk of permanent damage and the smallest and most immature infants are at the greatest risk. The Apgar scoring system (Illingworth 1972) is of prognostic value for later morbidity in these infants.

THE POST-MATURE INFANT

The post-mature infant is long and skinny and born after forty-two weeks gestation. After term (forty weeks) the effectiveness of the placenta decreases and the volume of the liquor diminishes and the infant continues his linear growth. This puts him at risk of fetal distress, anoxia or starvation and damage to his central nervous system. The causes of post-maturity are obscure.

RESPIRATORY DISTRESS IN THE NEONATE

The newborn baby is particularly liable to develop infection. The lungs at birth are not fully developed and are unable to cope with unusual respiratory disturbance. Tachypnoea is the most frequent and easily detectable sign of respiratory trouble and grunting respirations indicate distress. Coughing is a rare sound.

In the neonatal unit, chest physiotherapy techniques are used in conjunction with nursing procedures. Emphasis is placed on positioning and changing the infant's posture, at least every hour. Percussion is used over the affected area by finger tapping and vibrations in conjunction with postural drainage. It has been shown (Finer *et al.* 1978) that appropriately performed postural drainage and chest percussion to neonates with various forms of respiratory distress give a significant increase in the arterial Po_2.

In the presence of dyspnoea or cyanosis an infant is nursed in the humidified incubator and given monitored oxygen. The base of the incubator can be tilted for postural drainage and physiotherapy treatment given through the portholes (see Fig. 6.6). Infants not requiring oxygen can be treated very effectively on the physiotherapist's lap using various standard tilting positions (Gaskell and Webber 1980).

Treatment must be given with caution and of short duration. Very weak preterm infants with severe atelectasis are not placed on the unaffected side for any length of time as this position makes it more difficult for them to breath with the good lung and can easily lead to exhaustion. The prone position helps to fixate the very mobile rib cage in the preterm infant. No treatment should be given for at least one hour after a feed, and treatment is discontinued if handling causes an increase in apnoeic attacks. Infants on mechanical ventilation may require more intensive chest therapy including suctioning.

CONCLUSION

If a child is either hypotonic or hypertonic all his motor responses will tend to be abnormal and the normal basic patterns of movement may not become established. The physiotherapist aims at stimulating normal movement and normal responses. Treatment is planned on a full assessment of the individual infant's needs according to his maturity.

The handicapped infant matures more slowly and needs to be given earlier and more specific stimuli than the normal baby (Drillen & Drummond 1977). He is often passive and unable to react spontaneously to his environment, he needs help, more provoking situations and more repetitive movements to reinforce his learning. Thus the physiotherapist in the neonatal unit aims at providing a wide variety of experiences for the infant within the confines of his incubator, cot or in his mother's arms.

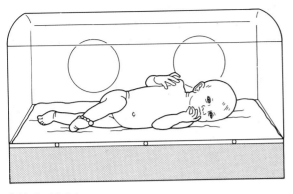

(a) Left side lying

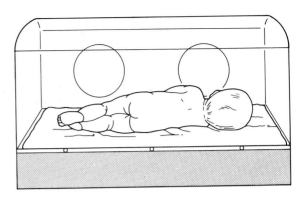

(b) Right side lying

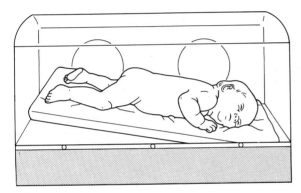

(c) Prone head down

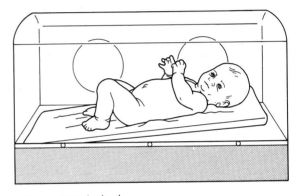

(d) Supine head raised

Fig. 6.6 Postural drainage positions in the incubator.

There is not yet statistical proof that our intervention is more or less effective than doing nothing. There seems no doubt that movement can be activated and deformities prevented and that parents benefit from the advice and support of physiotherapists. The change of parents' attitudes can be seen as they become more relaxed and confident in handling their baby.

It is difficult to prove the value of early treatment as many infants showing serious neurological disturbances in the neonatal period recover fully, and often apparently mildly affected infants may become progressively worse. It is more important to give every baby 'at risk' the initial opportunity to develop normally so that the potential for improvement is not lost.

Experience in paediatrics, knowledge of normal development, caution and common sense are essential ingredients in the assessment and management of the neonate.

REFERENCES

BOBATH BERTHA (1967). The Very Early Treatment of Cerebral Palsy. *Developmental Medicine and Child Neurology* **9**, 370–90.

CASAER PAUL (1979) *Postural Behaviour in Newborn Infants.* Clinics in Developmental Medicine, No. 72. SIMP and Heinemann Medical Books, London.

DENNIS W. (1960) Causes of retardation among institutional children: Iran. *Journal of Genetic Psychology* **96**, 47–9.

DRILLEN C.M. & DRUMMOND M.B. (1977) *Neurodevelopmental Problems in Early Childhood.* Blackwell Scientific Publications, Oxford.

DUBOWITZ VICTOR (1969) The *Floppy Infant.* Clinics in Developmental Medicine, No. 31. SIMP and Heinemann Medical Books, London.

DUBOWITZ LILY & DUBOWITZ VICTOR (1981) *The Neurological Assessment of the Preterm and Full Term Newborn Infant.* Clinics in Developmental Medicine No. 79. SIMP and Heinemann Medical Books, London.

FINER N.N. BOYD J. & GRACE M.G. (1978) Chest physiotherapy on neonates: a controlled study. *Physiotherapy Canada* **30**, 12–14.

GASKELL D.V. & WEBBER B. (1980) *The Brompton Hospital Guide to Chest Physiotherapy* 4e. Blackwell Scientific Publications, Oxford.

HELD R. (1965) Plasticity in sensorimotor systems. *Scientific American* **213**, 84.

ILLINGWORTH R.S. (1972) The Apgar Score. In *Development of the Infant and Young Child,* 5e. Churchill Livingstone, Edinburgh.

ILLINGWORTH R.S. (1980) *The Development of the Infant and Young Child, Abnormal and Normal,* 7e. Churchill Livingstone, Edinburgh.

KLAUS M.H., JERAULD R., KREGER, NANCY, McALPINE W. STEFFA M. & KENNELL J.H. (1972) Maternal attachment: importance of the first postpartum days. *New England Journal of Medicine* **286**, 460–3.

KORNER A.T. & THOMAN E.B. (1970) Visual alertness in infants evoked by maternal care. *Journal of Experimental Child Psychology* **10**, 67–78.

McGRAW M. (1966) *The Neuromuscular Maturation of the Human Infant.* Hofner, New York.

PRECHTL H.F.R. (1974) The behavioural states of the newborn infant: A review. *Brain Research* **76**, 185–212.

PRECHTL H.F.R. (1977) *The Neurological Examination of the Full Term Newborn Infant.* Clinics in Developmental Medicine, No. 63. SIMP and Heinemann Medical Books, London.

SCHAFFER R.G. & CROOK C.K. (1978) The Role of the Mother in Early Social Development. In *Issues in Childhood Social Development* (ed. McGurk H.), pp. 55–8. Methuen, London.

SHERIDAN MARY D. (1977) *Spontaneous Play in Early Childhood - From Birth to Six Years.* NFER: Nelson Publishing Co., Windsor, Berks.

STERN DANIEL (1979) *The First Relationship: Infant and Mother.* Fontana Open Books, London.

TOUWEN B.C.L. (1978) Variability and stereotyping in normal and deviant development. *Clinics in Developmental Medicine* No. 67. SIMP and Heinemann Medical Books, London.

WOODWARD W.M. (1970) Cognitive processes, Piaget' approach. In *The Psychological and Physical Handicap* (ed. Mittler P.), Methuen, London.

WYKE BARRY (1975) The relevance of mechanoreceptor maturation. In *Movement and Child Development* (ed. Holt K.S.), pp. 24–5. Clinics in Developmental Medicine No. 55. SIMP and Heinemann Medical Books, London.

FURTHER READING

BOBATH BERTHA (1971) Motor development, its effect on general development and application in the treatment of cerebral palsy. *Physiotherapy* Nov. 1971, 526–32.

BRAZELTON T. (1973) *Neonatal Behavioural Scale.* Clinics in Developmental Medicine, No. 50. SIMP and Heinemann Medical Books, London.

FORFAR J.O. & ARNEIL G.C. (1978) *Textbook of Paediatrics,* 2e. Churchill Livingstone, Edinburgh.

GORDON N. (1976) *Paediatric Neurology for the Clinician.* Clinics in Developmental Medicine, No. 59/60. SIMP and Heinemann Medical Books, London.

HOLT K. S. (ed.) (1975) *Movement and Child Development.* Clinics in Developmental Medicine No. 55. SIMP and Heinemann Medical Books, London.

ILLINGWORTH R.S. (1982) *Basic Developmental Screening: 0-4 years,* 3e. Blackwell Scientific Publications, Oxford.

KEAY A.J. & MORGAN D.M. (1978) *Craig's Care of the Newly Born Infant,* 6e. Churchill Livingstone, Edinburgh.

MUSSEN P. (1979) *The Psychological Development of the Child,* 3e. Prentice Hall, New York.

O'DOHERTY N. (1979) *Atlas of the Newborn.* M.T.P. Press.

SCHAFFER A.J. & AVERY M.A. (1978) *Diseases of the Newborn,* Section 2 — Disorders of the Respiratory System, p. 89–218, 4e. W.B. Saunders Co., Philadelphia.

SHEPPERD R. (1974) *Physiotherapy in Paediatrics.* Heinemann Medical Books, London.

VULLIAMY D.G. (1977) *The Newborn Child,* 4e. Churchill Livingstone, Edinburgh.

CHAPTER 7

A PATTERN OF
EARLY INTERVENTION

Dorothy Seglow

It has always been recognized that early diagnosis and assessment of the cerebral palsied child is essential. Early treatment of the baby is important as it will greatly influence his development. Early intervention normalizes patterns of posture and movement and can prevent increase in spasticity, which comes about through continuous use of the reflex activity that frequently results in deformities.

I worked for many years with cerebral palsied babies and their mothers in a one-to-one relationship. This today is still the most usual therapy situation, in which the child is treated and the mother is taught how to 'treat' her child — not how to live with him. We fail to realize that the parent is as much a casualty as the child and we have to help both of them.

It is normal treatment procedure to handle the baby, explain to the mother what we are aiming at, and instruct her to repeat it at home.

Most babies become distressed when handled by a stranger, but the mother has no alternative but to look on while suppressing her need to comfort her baby. After instruction the mother is asked to take over and repeat what has just been done. She then becomes the focus of attention and is anxious to do as instructed.

The mother appears to understand how she should handle her child but so often she returns to the next session and tells us that she has forgotten how we did this or that. 'It looked so easy with you but it was so different at home on my own.' Watching the mother's nervous smile, aware of her suppressed pain, I know we had not created a learning situation; she was listening but in her anxiety she could not take it in.

By making the mother dependent on the therapist, we increase her anxiety and undermine her confidence. The mother is the gateway to the child, so in that isolated one-to-one situation do we fail both of them?

During 1965 I visited the Institute for the Motor Disabled in Budapest, where Professor Andras Peto has developed a system of teaching cerebral palsied children which is called Conductive Education, and where there is a School for Mothers based on the concept that the mother is the best teacher of the young child.

My most striking experience was that here mothers were brought out of their isolation and worked together with their children in a group; a social learning situation instead of a treatment session. The group was led by one person whom they call the Conductor. An apt name, as like the conductor of an orchestra, she leads the whole group while keeping contact with each mother and child.

When I returned to my therapy in England, the relationship between mother and child was constantly in my mind, and I thought about how it develops in the normal baby. Months of expecting, dreaming and longing precede the birth of a child, a human being totally dependent on his parents. The mother reacts to her baby's needs and demands, and strives to satisfy them. The newborn 'knows' his mother; her voice, her smell, the way she holds him are recognized, and she is able to comfort where others fail. The child's dependency and the mother's love form the first strong bond between them.

From total dependency at birth, the baby develops and matures week by week and month by month, until at about 2 years of age he can stand and take his first steps away from his mother, manipulate objects with his hands, feed himself and use language to express simple needs and rejections. This normal development has been well described. It varies in time of maturation but happens in more or less the same sequence. The mother delights and reacts to every step of her child's growth. She will play with his hands and feel his grasp; he will touch his own face and her breast, and she will give him a rattle to play with and later a biscuit to chew or a spoon to hold. She will pull him up by his hands and, as he raises his head to look at her, she will talk to him. She will prop him up to sitting so that he is able to look around and when he pushes himself on to his knees, and soon after to his feet, she will assist him and let him have space and opportunity to move around the floor safely. Soon he will be taken by the hands for his first steps.

The mother reacts intuitively to her baby's stage of development and so is able to further his physical and emotional growth. She follows his cues all the way and it can be said that she is the pupil of her baby. By the time the second or third year has been reached and the child can walk and talk, he will have developed an awareness of himself as separate from his mother, an important step in growing up.

Let us turn to the mother of the cerebral palsied baby. He may have been born prematurely, or the birth may have been prolonged and complicated. She may not be able to hold him in her arms to wonder at and admire, and most likely he is whisked away to the special care unit. Her baby is to be labelled 'at risk'. Anxiety, worry and guilt replace joy, pride and contentment.

Day by day, she will experience problems she never imagined. As she picks him up he may be very stiff or floppy and he will cry a great deal by day and night. Feeding will be difficult as he may not be able to suck. She cannot cuddle him for mutual comfort as he stiffens when she picks him up, and she may feel rejected.

A mother follows the cues given by her baby, but what happens when the mother follows the cues of her cerebral palsied baby? She will support his back and head but this increases his extensor spasm and his body will stiffen. She will now be unable to bend his hips for sitting on her lap or carrying around. The very hypotonic baby will be easier to handle, but she has to support him totally and must continue to do so even when months have passed. Her baby's hands will remain fisted and his arms retracted and flexed at the elbow.

In the normal baby, the hands soon move to midline to touch each other, his face, his blanket or the mother's breast.

The cerebral palsied baby is unable to see his hands as his arms remain flexed and retracted. These retracted arms are part of his total extensor pattern. Should the mother pull his arms forward and touch his hands it may cause discomfort, and increase the retraction of his arms and with it the extension of his back and legs.

The mother will be inclined to leave well alone so as not to upset her baby. The hands will be 'forgotten' and the baby will be denied their use. Without hand function there is no way of pulling up to sitting and standing, or of feeding and dressing and playing with toys.

When the baby is propped up for sitting, his hips will resist flexion and his back become rounded. When held up for standing, he will rise on his toes, Handled from behind, which is easiest for the mother, he is unable to look at her. As he does not respond to her, all verbal communication dries up.

Physical and emotional growth go together. The cerebral palsied baby, unable to move on his own and dependent for all his needs, becomes very demanding and clings to his mother. At times he may use his disability to get attention and is likely to throw himself backwards or sideways off his seat. Using only the stereotyped patterns available to him, they increase in strength and may produce contractures and deformities.

The mother, in her anxiety, responds by following his wishes at all times. Her feeling of guilt and her sorrow prevent her from limiting her child's demands and she cannot deny him immediate gratification. This interaction prevents her child from growing up both physically and emotionally. The discrepancy between his chronological age and his performance widens. The parents' heavy burden receives no relief; their expectation dwindles and their hope fades, only to be revived by a visiting team, possibly consisting of health visitor, physiotherapist, social worker and community nurse who give their advice and, to complicate matters further, friends, neighbours and members of the family are also likely to add their comments.

It is unlikely that the counsel of such diverse, though well-meaning, people will be uniform. The parents' anxiety will increase, and as they are vulnerable to suggestions, they become confused and feel even more inadequate to bring up their own child.

A mother is the most important person in her child's life. She transmits her feelings to her baby and she has the most intimate knowledge of him. There is a bond between them that nobody can enter.

At the Watford Centre for Spastic Children we respect this bond and aim to prepare the mother to become the best possible mother for her cerebral palsied child. She should be the one to teach him the functions of daily living.

If we succeed, the baby will then have uniform handling throughout, and his mother will be able to structure his day to his best advantage by reinforcing the abilities he has learnt. In the normal situation this happens naturally because the mother reacts to her own child, but instead of reacting, the mother must *teach* her cerebral palsied child. Ester Cotton (1980) says: 'What the normal child learns by assimilation the cerebral palsied child must be taught as a skill'. To enable the mother to do this, she has to learn how her child's development differs from the normal. She has to understand how he can be guided, stage by stage, towards his highest potential. If she can do this herself, she may regain some of the joys of motherhood and her baby will be spared the trauma of separation.

We choose to teach this in a totally practical way by encouraging the mother to experience the child's problems, step by step, and finding her own solution. Learning must be active, and only by doing will the mother be able to know how to guide her baby towards a more active participation in their daily life.

Learning is best done in a group as this relieves the pressure on the individual. The mother is not observed, singled out and criticized, but is joined by other mothers and babies with problems and difficulties very similar to her own. They can support each other and learn from each other.

To give a purposeful atmosphere, the work of the group has to be well structured. We need a quiet room, and each mother and baby should have their own plinth, which becomes their space on which to work. Each child has a ladder-back chair to grip the bars in sitting and standing and a baby walker for his first steps.

One person, the Conductor, will plan the work of the group and write a programme to be followed at each session. The same movements, the same language, rhyme or song will be used each time, as only by repetition do we acquire skills. The programme is also the means by which the mother learns. If she can learn through the contents of the programme, so much the better and instruction and advisory talk become unnecessary and she will be more self reliant.

The movements given in the programme are the basic requirements for function and have been called The Basic Motor Pattern (BMP) by Ester Cotton (1980).

The Basic Motor Pattern explains that the child's basic needs for function are:
1   mobility of hips;
2   extended elbows;
3   symmetry;
4   fixation;
5   grasp and release.

These essentials are divided into a series of tasks, which make up the programme and replace the cerebral palsied child's innate patterns.

What actually happens when mother and baby join the group? The mother will sit on a plinth and she will be asked to help her baby to take off his socks in preparation for our work together. Most mothers will sit behind their child so that he leans against her. His arms appear too short to reach his feet as he is unable to bend his hips and lean forward, and his arms are retracted and flexed at the elbow.

The newcomer will watch other mothers and their babies to observe those that succeed in the task. She will see how mothers move their children's arms forward in extension, which makes it possible for them to bend their children's hips to place children's hands on their feet. She may notice in this position the baby's head comes to midline (Fig. 7.1 shows the BMP used for taking off socks). Some mothers will say to their babies 'look at your socks', 'grasp', 'pull', 'open your hands', 'give me the sock'. This immediately sets the scene to connect movement, function and language.

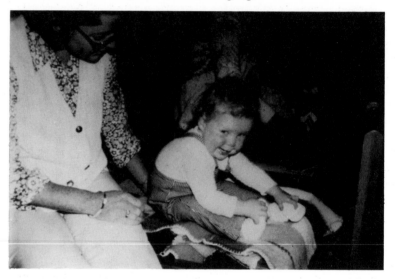

Fig. 7.1

The goal is that the child should take off his own socks, and each mother will get him to do it in her own way. Some children are more difficult, some mothers more anxious. Removing socks is a daily occurrence, it can be repeated every time the baby has to be undressed. The child learns to sit, to use his hands, to look at what he is doing and so becomes aware of his feet. The mother will appreciate that she can teach her child through everyday situations.

We have described the mother as sitting behind her baby. It is preferable, however, to face him so as to have eye contact and thus better communication. We create that situation by giving each child a ball to hold in both hands and asking him to push it. It is now natural to face the child, so as to receive the ball and push it back. It is difficult to control the baby from the front and few mothers do it, but by watching each other they can learn how it can be done. Some will sit by their child's side, others will find a way to hold their child from the front by giving fixation to one or both legs, or by grasping his elbows or shirt. The child's hands should be left free to push the ball. Fixation is essential for movement and, through achieving fixation, action, however simple, can be realized.

Having shown the importance of fixation for movement, we now want to teach the child the use of his hands to hold himself for sitting and standing. He is given a stick to grip with both hands and to move his arms in sitting and in supine. In sitting he pushes the stick down to his feet, up to his knees; in supine the stick is directed to the ceiling, above his head and down to his tummy. By moving the child's arms the mother notices that his shoulders are tight and, as his arms move up, so his grip on the stick loosens.

In giving the task at each session we repeat the same instructions which include concepts of space and body image. First, directions are given and then the movement is practised with a suitable song or rhyme, which gives rhythm to the movement. Using the same songs or rhymes, mother and baby become conditioned to the task and can repeat it at home as a game. By stating the task and then singing to it, the mother encourages her baby and so avoids individual nagging. All of us doing the same thing at the same time creates a group situation. Repeating the same programme at each session relieves the mother's tension. Anything the child cannot achieve at one session may be achieved at the next. If a child becomes distressed, we ask the mother to nurse him and let him watch. That too is a learning situation and he will soon want to join in again.

The programme must include the variety of movements which the child needs at this stage of development. We give him a stick to grasp and he is pulled up to sitting. This demands an ability to bend his hips and keep a grasp on the stick. He is slowly moved back to lying again, and learns to right his head.

Lying on his back, he lifts his legs and tries to hold his feet (Fig. 7.2). He sees his feet, and we play 'Little Piggy went to Market' with his toes. He is once again in the position of flexed hips with extended arms. Holding his hands and feet together, his mother pulls him up to sitting, and she learns how the same movement patterns can be practised in different situations. This can be a suitable game at home every time she changes his nappy.

The mother helps him to turn from supine to prone. As he gets on his tummy we say: 'I stretch my arms, I stretch my legs, I lie still,' and we sing a song to encourage them to keep their position of extension in prone. They are then asked to lift their heads and look up in different directions. 'I look at the ceiling, I look at the floor, I look at the window, I look at the door, I look in the middle and what do I see, two little hands belonging to me.' The mother will notice that the head does not move in isolation but that lifting and turning causes a reaction throughout the child's body. She can help him by fixing his hips.

With the child in the prone position lying on the plinth the mother helps her child to push down and off the plinth to the floor. At the point where his legs are over the edge of the plinth, he is in a posture of flexed hips with arms stretched forward, as in sitting, as in holding his toes in supine. It is now easy to extend the knees and dorsiflex the feet (Fig. 7.3). Once his feet are on the

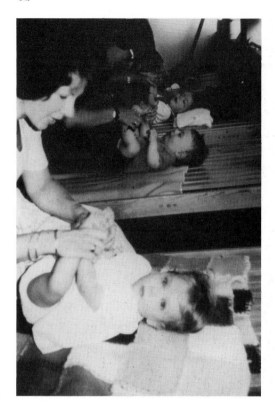

Fig. 7.2

floor he will push with his hands against the plinth to stand upright (Fig. 7.4). In time the child will push himself out of his bed in the same way, and once again he can learn from the daily living situation.

We started the session with long sitting on the plinth, introducing a basic motor pattern of mobile hips with extended arms and knees. We repeated this pattern in different situations. The programme also teaches sitting on a chair with legs down and feet on the floor. Now the child holds on to a bar of a chair in front. To start, the mother extends his elbows, which helps him to sit upright. Fixing his feet on the floor and his hands on a bar, the child finds his balance. Again rhymes make him turn his head and look in different directions, as was done in prone. Figure 7.5 shows a seat designed by a parent, which incorporates the principles that teach sitting. It also enables the mother to look at her child while still controlling him safely. Another parent adapted this seat to a 'potty seat', so transferring a learning situation from our session to everyday life at home.

Next in the programme, we sit round the table and play with toys, and learn to hold and eat a biscuit, and hold and drink from a cup. We encourage the mothers to help their children to participate and be active in all tasks. We stress that all situations can be used for learning. It follows, therefore, that the children are not picked up and carried to the table at the other end of the

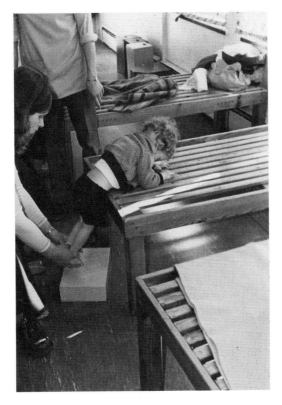

Fig. 7.3

room, but this is now an opportunity for walking assisted by a baby walker (Fig. 7.6). In all the tasks in the programme the children have used their hands for grasping, releasing, holding or pushing. It now becomes natural for the mother to let her child grip the bar of the baby walker. Feet must be flat on the floor, as in standing. They may start by pushing and pulling the walker to and fro. To control walking is difficult with some children and the conductor may help until the mother can manage it on her own. The children who can take steps and push the walker enjoy it very much, which encourages those who still have problems.

Eventually, and in her own time, each mother guides her child to the table, sits him on a box and stretches his arms forward on the table. Some children, especially the athetoids, will throw themselves backwards, and most mothers will have learned that supporting their child's back or holding his head will make matters worse. This can be corrected by the mother stretching her child's arms forward. (Fig. 7.7).

We stress that the child's feet must be firmly on the ground and those that cannot reach the floor will be given supporting boxes. A basic motor pattern of flexed hips and extended arms forward is again apparent. Any child that can stretch his arms on to the table and fix his feet on the floor will now sit on his

Fig. 7.4

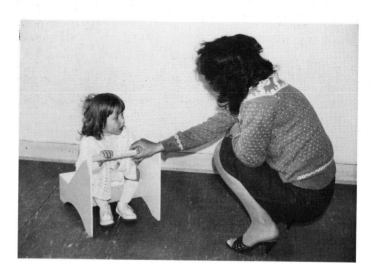

Fig. 7.5

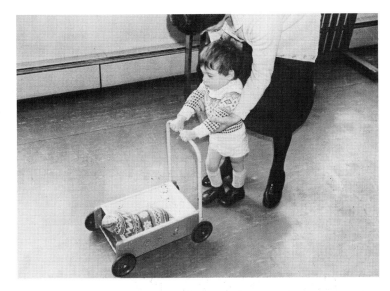

Fig. 7.6

Fig. 7.7

own. Often this is the first time that the mother need not hold her baby, and this is an important step forward for both of them.

Once settled round the table, we make it a very sociable event. We sing nursery rhymes with finger play, such as shutting and opening hands, counting fingers, clapping, finding 'Tommy thumb' and 'Peter pointer' and a variety of games which familiarize the children with their hands. This is followed by rolling a colourful toy along the table, and the children are helped to push it from one to the other. This makes them use their hands and stretch their arms. It also encourages them to look at the toy, follow it with their eyes and wait for their turn to push it along.

Next we introduce listening. The conductor produces a sound from a bell, a rattle or a squeaky toy held under the table. The children listen, wait for it to be shown and to have their turn to produce the sound. Many cerebral palsied children are classified as distractable and unattentive because they have not yet learned to look and listen. Looking and listening precede speech and are essential for learning. Mothers experience with us how looking and listening can be stimulated, and that waiting patiently for the child's response can bring results. Playtime at home may be oriented towards the goal of looking and listening.

We finish the session with eating and drinking. The mother finds out how her child can assist in feeding. They are given a two-handled mug, which the child is made to hold and a sponge finger that he can grip. Once again he is using his hands and the mother guides them to his mouth. Problems of mouth closure and tongue thrust can now be discussed and advice can often be given by a mother who has learned from her own experience.

Our sessions have been called 'mother and baby groups' but they often include fathers, who join us whenever they have time. Equally welcome are siblings, who enjoy the singing and the games we play.

The task series in the programme sets out the pattern of development for the cerebral palsied child. Each task is part of an active movement that can be used in everyday life and integrated into the family situation. The children in the group are all diagnosed as cerebral palsied, but they are, of course, different in their abilities and potential achievement. No two children are alike. However, the tasks which are basic for function are relevant to each of them; for example, the task of holding on to a bar with both hands for safe sitting will benefit equally the athetoid, spastic or hemiplegic child.

The athetoid has to learn to grasp and hold on, which will help him to control his tonic neck reflex and extensor thrust.

The spastic child may have a good grasp, but he must learn to extend his elbows, while holding on, or else he will collapse in flexion.

The hemiplegic child will learn to use both hands simultaneously and achieve symmetry.

The length of stay of each child in the group varies according to age and ability, and also the confidence of the mother in helping him.

The next step for the child is to tolerate short periods of separation from his mother. He is by now familiar with the environment and the staff of the centre. The transition to a learning situation without his mother, but still within the centre, will be easier to accept.

We must have realistic goals and value each child's progress accordingly. The mother who is actively engaged in teaching her child will be sensitive to any progress, however small, when and as it happens. She is better equipped to appreciate small changes in her child than she would have been as a mere observer. As they work together and support each other, the success of any child is of value to all. It helps us to create a hopeful and positive atmosphere.

The groups have been conducted for about ten years. The children participating, using movement, function and language, are prepared for further learning. It is not possible at this early stage to know how far each child will go, but we feel we have given mothers and children a useful start which may lead the child to some degree of independence and an opportunity to develop potential abilities.

The child profits by his mother's ability to teach him in the daily living situation. This gives him the repetition necessary for learning and the opportunity to use any skill he may have acquired.

The mother involved in the work of the group becomes increasingly self-reliant and confident and gains a deeper understanding of the problems and their possible solutions.

At the start of this chapter I remarked how early intervention can help to normalize patterns of posture and movement in the cerebral palsied child. But how best to intervene? Perhaps by teaching the mother along the principles of Dr F. Froebel, the educational reformer of the 19th century. 'Hearing is forgetting, seeing is remembering, doing is understanding', and all my working experience leads me to share that conclusion.

REFERENCES

COTTON E. (1980) *The Basic Motor Pattern.* The Spastics Society, London.

FURTHER READING

COTTON E. (1974) *Conductive Education and Cerebral Palsy.* The Spastics Society, London.
COTTON E. (1981) *The Hand as a Guide to Learning.* The Spastics Society, London.
MATTERSON E. (1969) *This Little Puffin, Nursery Songs and Rhymes.* Puffin Books, Penguin Books Ltd., Harmondsworth.
SUTTON ANDREW (1980) *Backward Children in the U.S.S.R.* George Allen and Unwin, London.

For anyone wishing to know more about Professor Andras Peto's system of teaching called Conductive Education, the address is: The Institute of the Motor Disabled, Villânyi Ut 67, Budapest XI, Hungary.

CHAPTER 8

PHYSIOTHERAPY FOR SEVERELY MENTALLY HANDICAPPED CHILDREN

Susan Rushfirth

'...the young child at first senses the world in fugitive and fluctuating blotches... Sounds may likewise be heard as shreds of wavering distinctness against a neutral background of silence or of continuous undertone. Doubtless he feels the pressure of his six or seven pounds weight...Perhaps this island of pressure sensation is the very core of his vague and intermittent awareness of self' (Gesell *et al.* 1975).

This description of the imagined experience of the newborn infant could serve to describe the meaningless and confusing world of the profoundly and severely mentally handicapped child. For some it will be their entire world, for others one from which they will emerge slowly and possibly only in part. They will not, in intellectual terms, develop beyond an average 5 year old.

Why do we aim to supply more than just love and basic care?

We are concerned simply because they are alive and amongst us. We want to help them learn even the most basic responses so that they may enjoy their world as far as possible. The less handicapped the child the more sophisticated and participatory this enjoyment will be; but even the most handicapped will find a degree of pleasure in comfort, order and consistent sensory experience. There is no such pleasure in chaos, isolation and deformity. In addition, the demand for assistance in the care of the older mentally handicapped person voiced by strained parents and overworked care staffs should prompt us to ensure that our emphasis on self help, functional mobility and above all, the prevention of deformity is appropriate and insistent.

Our involvement should persist long beyond childhood, but it is during childhood that the developmental 'blind alleys' are entered and it is to the avoidance of these that we should look.

We know that the inability of all physically impaired babies to form a sensory-motor base may affect their learning potential; but whereas the physically handicapped child will to an extent enjoy an *awareness* of his surroundings, a degree of *motivation* , a desire to *co-operate* and the *intention* to perform, the mentally handicapped child, lacking this spontaneity, will not be making the same *sense* of his environment. A distorted or diminished world will *not motivate* him to respond in a predictable manner, he will *not* necessarily find any *reason* to move in it and thus will *not intend* to do so.

We will be considering three basic areas where effective help can be provided:

1 the making of sense;
2 motivation;
3 general management.

THE MAKING OF SENSE

Studies by Saint-Anne Dargassies (1968) have shown that a fetus is sensitive to pain even before it is capable of sustaining independent life. Sensitivity to touch develops next and with the early myelination of the trigeminal nerve the sense of smell. Movement first occurs during the fifth month and as early as the seventh month the fetus is briefly sucking his fingers.

Reactions to sound are measurable between 32 and 34 weeks but sight develops only after term. The sense of taste is present at birth and some newborn babies demonstrate a preference for a certain milk food. A mature and completely organized central nervous system is not of course a prerequisite for an ability to move or respond. Indeed it has been frequently demonstrated that a child will react to basic stimuli even when suffering gross anencephaly (Murphy 1980, personal communication).

The stimuli to which the child reacts are the first point for consideration. Reactions are dependent upon the degree of maturation (or damage) of the central nervous system. The significance for us lies in the fact that what a child appreciates he may well enjoy, and what he enjoys he will also find *rewarding* (see Rewards or Reinforcers, p.94).

The premature infant briefly sucking his fingers is one of the earliest signs not only of an appreciation but also of a purposeful movement in response to a *meaningful* stimulus. The initially reflex activities of the neonate are superseded by the increasingly complicated action schemes and behaviour patterns of early childhood — all born of an increasing ability to integrate and learn from sensory stimuli. From birth to 16 weeks the tactile sense will be all pervasive. The vegetative life turns around sleep, waking, food and warm supportive handling. As the visual sense improves he will become increasingly able not only to see but to watch what he feels and manipulates. Murphy notes that if noise is added it will be neither blended nor separated. It is not until 32 weeks that the infant can choose to select auditory attention focus in the presence of any or all of the other sensory modalities.

Why is it important that we consider this so closely? Imagine learning to walk a narrow beam which has been placed high enough from the ground to cause anxiety. Arms will be held wide for balance, eyes will be fixed on a point ahead, there will be total focus on the feel of the beam beneath our feet and an acute awareness of our body position in space. Imagine now being asked to read the time from a small clock on the wall. For many of the less well co-ordinated of us there could be three possibilities — to ignore the request and stay on; to obey and fall off; or to maintain balance, look briefly at the clock and tell the wrong time. Now relate this to the profoundly affected spastic child who is required to develop, say, a head raise from prone. He has been placed carefully into a position which he has rarely experienced and in which he is vulnerable. Not only is he experiencing a rare tactile and proprioceptive input, but in all probability is the subject of some distinct facilitatory handling and much 'encouraging' noise-making from a source he cannot locate and the meaning of which he does not understand. Rather like the incompetent gymnast his behaviour may not prove efficient. Where we ignored the request the child may seemingly fail to respond or reject the prompt. Where we responded and fell he may similarly attempt to concentrate on a sensory input whilst suffering a corresponding failure of motor performance. Where we fail to see the correct time; he may seemingly fail to 'see' anything and is thus unlikely to repeat the move. The child crying on the treatment mat may indeed lift his head, and experience the *feel* of the movement. But has he *really* learnt from it? Is he likely to repeat it? As Kephart (1971) says, 'The skill level of performance is less relevant than the readiness level to perform'. Whereas the mentally more able baby may well eventually enjoy and thus desire to lift his head, the mentally handicapped child may possibly find the 'sensory overload' too great and thus stressful.

The effects of stress on motor performance and indeed the stressful effects of an impaired motor performance are well known to be detrimental. When assessing the motor development of the mentally handicapped child it is necessary to consider in fine detail not only the level of performance but also the effects upon it of sensory stimulation. As with all work with these children, the steps must be small. Assessment on a wider scale would result in inappropriate intervention and unmeasurable progress.

When approaching the children there are certain assumptions that we cannot make:

1 that apparent blindness/deafness is real and not developmental (EEG testing may be indicated);

2 that the stages of sensory development and integration have proceeded evenly and sequentially;

3 that what may seem to us to be a stimulating environment is not, in fact, a highly confusing bombardment;

4 that the child's visual, auditory, and tactile attention will remain measurably the same in all positions. (Hendley and Robinson (1973, unpublished report) states this is not the case.)

5 that associated reactions and increased hypertonia are due primarily to a motor dysfunction;

6 that a lack of consistent response is due to mental impairment.

An assumption of competence can never be made. We must assess every area and ensure that our therapy does not in fact *contribute* to an *incompetence.*

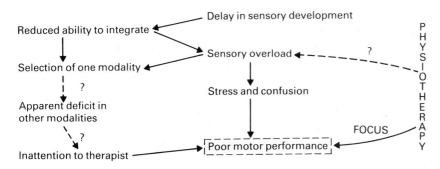

Fig. 8.1.

SOME ABNORMALITIES OF SENSORY DEVELOPMENT

(a) Tactile and kinaesthetic

Hypersensitivity around the mouth demonstrated by some children is well known. Less frequently considered is the effect of more generalized hypersensitivity. It has been clearly shown that stimulation to various aspects of the body, e.g. frontal, palms, produces such strong reactions that the effects of spasticity and reflex activity are increased. Conversely a reduced reaction to touch may often be displayed by those with no clear diagnosis or demonstrating low muscle tone. Kirman (1972) reports studies which note that people with Down's syndrome performed badly on kinaesthetic testing and that this deficit was linked with their low tonal state. In my experience youngsters with problems of clumsiness, poor adaptive balance reactions and poor locomotion demonstrate marked diminution of tactile responses (notably on *the soles of the feet*).

It is fair to surmise that the effects of reduced tactile competence combined with limited experience of self exploration and kinaesthetic stimulation will result in very limited or bizarre self image and level of body awareness.

The retention of the introverting basic senses of touch, taste and smell may well result in excessive self stimulation. This combines with a lack of appreciation of sight and sound to impair the development of an active response to the world. (Of course if, the child has not developed to a point where he is mouthing, self exploring, etc., we should ensure that he is aided in doing so.)

(b) Poor oculo motor function, eye contact and visual impairment

The effects of impaired vision on child development are of increasing interest and discussed in Chapter 14. When we consider that all early attention and thus early learning is dependent on sight, this deficit is particularly significant for the mentally handicapped as any compensation may not occur and certain deficiency persist. The normal eye contact made between mother and baby is a means of communication, a pathway to bonding and a focus of concentration. It is often avoided by those children and should always be sought before activity commences (see also pp.54, 64–6 and visual development pp. 218–20).

If a child has poor control of eye muscles, potential problems of attention and vision may occur with the need to turn or move his head. Posture and equilibrium are affected. Alternatively he may choose not to move his head and thus diminish his essential visible world. A hyperactive child who turns his head excessively and who demonstrates pronounced righting reactions will be constantly moving in the direction of visual stimuli.

(c) Abnormalities of vestibular response

The vestibular system demonstrates prenatal maturation in preparation for later anti-gravity activity. After birth it provides initial information regarding the position of the head in space and forms the basis for the development of adaptive movements of body and limbs. The degree of activity of the system is measured by the duration of the post-rotary nystagmus which occurs after the body has been spun. The duration of the nystagmus will normally diminish as the child matures and the initially excitable activity of the vestibular mechanisms are diminished and absorbed into the developing nervous system. If, as is the case with, for example, Down's syndrome, the mechanism remains uninhibited, the nystagmus and thus the instability of visual background described by Kantner *et al.* (1976) will remain marked. His studies with groups of normal and Down's syndrome children have shown that specific stimulation of the semicircular canals by controlled spinning in a rotary chair with velocity indicator reduced the excitability of the vestibular system. Measurement of both post-rotary nystagmus and rate of motor development revealed marked improvement of performance of the experimental group in relation to the control group.

Spinning, swinging and rolling can usefully be emphasized both to stimulate the possibly underdeveloped system and to habituate the hyperexcitable one.

(d) Delayed response

EEG testing has revealed that some children suffer such severe delay in the transmission of auditory or visual impulses to the cortex that they are in essence seeing or hearing objects or sounds that are no longer presented to them. Their delay in response although not of major significance to the physiotherapist should be considered when seeking attention or attempting to stimulate. A prolonged use of items may be necessary.

Children's perception of the world depends upon effective interrelationships between the main sensory pathways. These are poor or defective in the majority of mentally handicapped children. Therefore the possibilities of performing well-organized, purposeful movements are severely impaired. The physiotherapist's temptation to regard the sensory aspect solely as the responsibility of the occupational therapist or the teacher should be resisted. The sensory cannot be dissociated from the motor when considering such early stages of development.

Methods of improving sensory function in relation to motor learning vary according to the preference of the therapist. Some will favour the structured approaches of Temple Fay and Doman-Delacato with a strict sequence of phylogenetic movement patterns linked to a specific sensory combination. The majority would probably prefer to select from the more traditional approaches (Bobath, Rood, Vojta, Peto) combined with the relationship play described by Veronica Sherbourne (1979). To this I would add the necessity to adopt a *flexible* attitude to the following:

— direct tactile (rubbing, stroking, brushing) sensitization or desensitization;
— oculomotor training (teaching binocular and monocular fixation, tracking, convergence, divergence) in the presence ultimately of other stimulation;
— the possibility that motor performance may be best improved by concentration on the sensory;
— vestibular stimulation.

MOTIVATION

One of the factors that so clearly distinguishes mentally handicapped children from their contemporaries is the inconsistency of their responses to the world around them. We know that these children will not respond *simply because we ask them to*. It may be that they do not understand; or it may be that our approval or disapproval is a matter of supreme indifference to them. Alternatively, another course of action (or indeed of inaction) may be altogether more enjoyable and rewarding to them. The facilitation of a pattern of movement may well produce the desired effect. However, the more retarded the child the less likely it is that a movement experienced just once will be repeated quickly, or, more importantly, consistently. *An action, which is observed to occur regularly but not invariably, cannot be credited as a motor skill.*

The problem experienced when assessing some children is that the description of motor ability is frequently subjective and is thus invalid; for example, a boy suffering hydocephalus, blindness, spastic quadriplegia and severe mental impairment is observed to lift his head from time to time when sitting and in prone. He reputedly 'likes music' and occasionally lifts his head when a music box is played. We cannot begin to describe in general terms the ability that he obviously possesses. The fact that the action is possible is irrefutable; our task lies in making *it more likely to occur.*

THE RELEVANCE OF THE BEHAVIOURAL APPROACH

This method of teaching the severly mentally handicapped will be familiar to all those working in the field. As a teaching method its effectiveness depends upon assessment, structure, teamwork and no little talent on the part of the teacher. It must be emphasized that it cannot be undertaken by someone working alone or without specific training. There is a need for physiotherapists to acquaint themselves with this strategy if they are to motivate these children. Relatively minor adjustments in our approach may significantly improve the children's performance.

Behaviourism is a doctrine that, given adequate knowledge, all human actions admit of analysis into stimulus and response. All behaviour is learned and follows an increasingly complex pattern the development of which is largely dependent upon the stage that preceded it. Whenever we behave in a certain way something happens; for example, a baby cries and his mother attends; a boy scores a goal and his team cheers. Both children will strive to repeat the action because the results are rewarding. That is, the behaviours are *reinforced*, in a positive manner.

THE REWARDS OR REINFORCERS

Reinforcers are described by Perkins *et al.* (1976) as *always* strengthening the action they *follow*. If they do not make that action *more likely to be repeated*, they cannot be described as reinforcers. They follow *immediately after* the desired activity. The selection of a reward must be considered and identified as exactly as possible and *no assumptions of what is rewarding* can be made, they vary from person to person.

In general terms reinforcers are listed under four headings. The selection will be determined by the child's positive, pleasurable reaction.

Sensory reward

The child's ability to enjoy sensory stimuli is dependent upon the degree of maturity or of damage to his central nervous system. The more handicapped the child the less likely he is to enjoy a wide range of rewarding experiences. He will most certainly not understand the meaning of 'good' or 'bad', although tone of voice may have an effect. Food and drink are often given as examples of reinforcers but this largely demonstrates the assumed ability level of the subjects even in articles relating to the most handicapped. Therapists will commonly meet children who do not enjoy the process of eating and drinking. Their pathological reflex activities of bite and gag or their inability to retain food or avoid choking, frequently deny them the normal childhood preference for foods. The fact that recent work (Baily *et al.* 1969; Johnson *et al.* 1978; Byrne & Stevens 1980; Jones 1980; Carrington 1981, personal communication) has shown vibration to be a most effective stimulation and potential reward for those whose mental and sensory abilities are limited, enables us to encourage a group who have been previously very difficult to motivate. Vibration equipment should be used in the range 20–100 Hertz (Carrington 1981 personal communication) and has the advantage that it can be stopped and started at will. This latter point is important as the immediacy and duration of a rewarding stimulus is crucial. Unless it occurs immediately after the activity, the child will not associate the two. If it continues for too long, the child will accommodate and cease to find it rewarding.

In these days of increasing technology, bright screens of light and mobile attractive toys are increasingly available. If a child does appear to enjoy visual reward, we must not assume that it will be so enjoyable if linked to sound, i.e. if he is not yet able to integrate the two he may well drop his head when both are produced and seem to withdraw. If, say, light alone is offered, he may reveal interest and enjoyment.

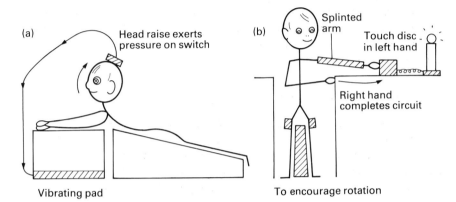

Fig. 8.2

Mentally handicapped children who also have visual impairment may not be able to compensate with other senses. Should myopia or partial sight be evident it is important to give appropriate visual rewards so that both mental and visual problems are not compounded (see Chapter 14). Although sounds are enjoyed by many, Byrne and Stevens (1980) have found auditory stimulation to be the least effective source of reinforcement for a group of multiply impaired children. We should be mindful of this when depending for encouragement on that much used tool of the trade, the voice. For the more development child, however, the tone, pace, emphasis and rhythm of the human voice provide the source of many auditory clues. Skilled musical accompaniment or well-timed spoken words frequently provoke a motor response.

Social reward.

Social reward is that which comes from other people. That is affection, attention and verbal praise. Praise is not in itself meaningful to a small child. When a baby interrelates with his mother he is rewarded physically *and* verbally. The child comes to associate phrases such as 'Good boy' with a kiss or a hug which he directly enjoys. In time he will not always need to receive the physical reward to appreciate the value of the verbal version.

We are all rather liberal with our verbal praise but not always very specific in its usage. The warmth of our voice, the smile on our face and the certainty that the child associates this with a positive reward are three aspects of which we must be mindful. Remember that our words will have no meaning but our tone will. Attention should be reserved for the desirable not the avoidable; for example, for the straight sitter not the habitual 'leaner', for the completed task of walking to the bathroom not the tendency to drop to the floor.

Activity reward

Activity reward is used when the child will work for the reward of doing something such as using a swing, riding a bike or seeing mummy. If offered, it must be supplied. A sudden addition of extra tasks or a forgotten promise will only confuse or alienate.

Token reward

A token reward that can be made to represent some form of currency (social or financial) is of value to the less mentally impaired. As workers in the field we should be aware of any token economy both as it affects our approach and as a therapeutic tool.

Example A mentally handicapped spastic diplegic girl is being encouraged to walk an increasingly distance to use the toilet when taken, and to feed herself with a spoon. For each walk to and correct use of the toilet, and for each completed meal she is rewarded with a gold star. Each time she hits her head a star is removed. At the end of the day the stars are added and she is given a chocolate piece for each star.

Points for consideration

1   Rewards must be specific to the child.
2   We must not assume that our mentally handicapped clients will find our praise alone sufficient or that adult esteem is of any value. Does a child who sees a therapist twice a week really care what this semi-stranger thinks of him? The person whose approval he is most likely to seek is his mother and it is she who in many ways is the least likely to vary her tone whether her child succeeds or fails. We must encourage a *significant* use of voice and as far as it is possible a distinct difference in tone.
3   The reward must be given immediately the desired task is completed. We must, for example, reward with our attention the rise to standing and not the drop that may follow.
4   Consistency is imperative. If the same behaviour does not provoke the same response, the child will become confused and fail to learn. As far as is possible all those who know the child should be persuaded to participate and to learn that we are neither being cruel to withold reward nor are we bribing these children if we supply one.
     Three further terms *Prompting, Chaining* and *Shaping* serve to describe the manner in which we present the task, the way in which the skill components are linked and the method by which we guide emerging behaviour. Verbal or

physical assistance will *prompt* the child to perform. Depending on the task and the child, it may be easier to teach the final stage first (*backward chaining*) as when teaching self-feeding, when spoon to mouth will be the first achievement, or to prompt and reward the first stage as when we teach postural fixation by grasping a bar in mid-line (*forward chaining*). The latter also demonstrates how the task will be *shaped* from an initial acceptance of touch to a firm grasp.

Assessment is alway an important part of our work and record keeping should be as exact as time and staffing levels allow. The only objective way in which we can evaluate change is by counting the number of times the child succeeds and whether there is an increase in his success rate over a period of time. A *baseline* of how much of the task could be performed originally should first be established. If the child does not increase the performance level or if we are not succeeding in making the desired behaviour *more likely to* occur, then we must look critically at our technique and at the effectiveness of our reinforcers.

INTENTION AND IMITATION

It has been stated that *the intention* to perform is frequently absent in the case of a child who seemingly finds no reason to do so. The intention to perform movements may also be lacking because comprehension is low and the child does not understand the meaning of the directive. The absence of *imitation* is a third major factor. A small baby who would not understand the meaning of 'Clap hands' will at an early stage imitate another doing so.

In the more specific routines of teaching individual skills, the effectiveness of group activities in which imitation and participation play so major a part will be eliminated. Children are handled in groups for a variety of reasons which will vary from Centre to Centre and will depend upon the aim of the activities and the purpose of the grouping. For the severely mentally handicapped the rewards of imitating a colleague and succeeding as he has succeeded in the initiation and ultimate acquisition of skill may not be available. Therefore the exceedingly attractive concept of Conductive Education, for example, with its grouping of children according to disability, its emphasis on rhythmical intention and the identification of a basic motor pattern cannot be easily introduced where the children have a low comprehension level, poor powers of concentration, little imitative ability and absolutely no intention of acceding to our desire that they should 'Hold their stick with two hands'.

An alternative, but in essence a no less structured approach, is based on exact *Repetition*. If an activity is repeated in the same order and with the same sensory and personal structure the child will, in time, begin to *Anticipate* the activity. A chain of reaction is then provoked:

REPETITION → ANTICIPATION → INTENTION AMBITION → INITIATION → PARTICIPATION.

Where possible the child's partners should remain constant so that sensitivity to the child's actions is developed and degree of assistance appropriately reduced.

Use of voice is repetitious and directing; rhythms are simple be they sung or spoken and activities must occur in the same order. Changing the routines to engage the attention of the staff is not desirable. We become bored long before the children have learned the routine. It is very necessary that skillful group leading maintains levels of interest, fun and ambition even within the essential setting of routine and repetition.

GENERAL MANAGEMENT

SIGNIFICANT ABNORMALITIES OF MOTOR PERFORMANCE

Abnormalities of motor performance and the development of deformity are common among all physically handicapped children. These are discussed in other chapters, particularly Chapter 2 and 9. The difficulties frequently found in severely mentally handicapped children in my experience are mentioned below.

Persistence of preferred head turning

Figure 8.3a and b show how persistent head turning can, in the long term, be associated with the devastating Windswept Deformities. Other relationships are discussed on pages 114–17 which make these problems particularly need management in these children. Figure 8.4 (a-f) presents some suggestions, and includes asymmetry due to leg shortening which may also be a feature.

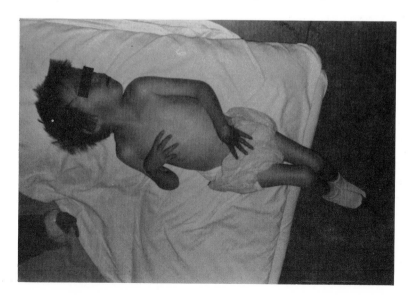

Fig. 8.3 (a) Six-year old boy demonstrating preferred head turn to left.

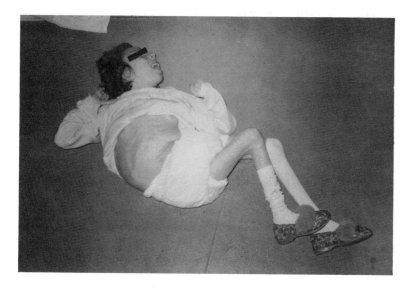

Fig. 8.3 (b) Adult woman demonstrating severe wind-sweeping to left.

Scrutton (1978 a and b) has described a method of correcting asymmetric hip deformity in sitting. He advocates the exertion of a horizontal pressure along the abducting, externally rotating femur. This pressure is given horizontally through the front of the knee over the edge of the chair and towards the firm back rest. This is combined with passive abduction and external rotation of the other leg which was previously held in adduction, internal rotation and extension. The pelvis is thus placed in a symmetrical position and pelvic rotation corrected. Further padding is added to prevent a sideways shift of the pelvis.

The use of neck retraction.

In the absence of vertical head control some children fixate their heads by the use of neck retraction. They thereby demonstrate the strange picture of independent sitting without apparently having head control. They are frequently hypotonic with a genetic abnormality. They balance themselves on wide-based hips, flexed, externally rotated knees and prop their hypotonic trunk on their hands and are able only to use their upper visual fields.
The effects of neck retraction are:
1   deformity of the neck and thoracic kyphosis;
2   the over use of the sitting posture increases the already existing tendency towards flexion and abduction of the hips;
3   children thus affected demonstrate poor hand function and exhibit poor balance reactions, both in sitting and in prone positions;
4   in the prone position the abnormal neck posture seemingly blocks the development of spinal extension and limb abduction necessary for reaching and balance;
5   feeding and respiratory problems are common and abasia is a feature.

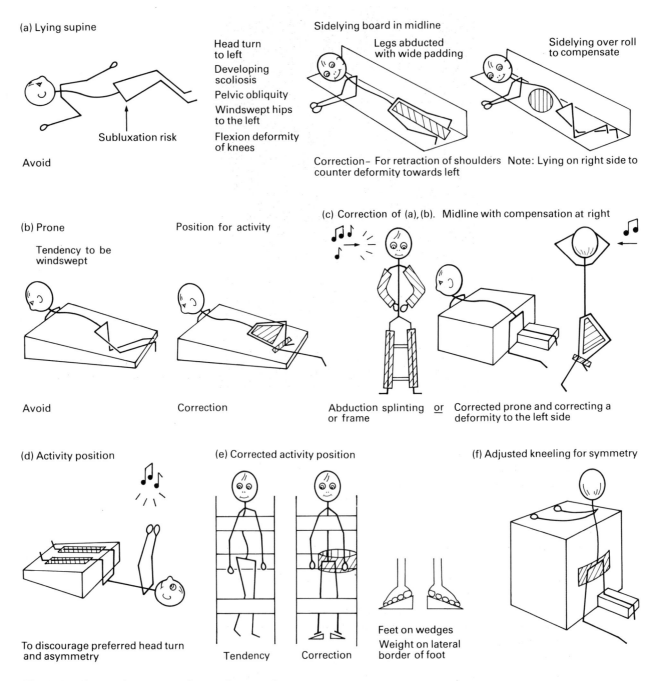

(a) Lying supine

Sidelying board in midline

Head turn
to left

Developing
scoliosis

Pelvic obliquity

Windswept hips
to the left

Flexion deformity
of knees

Legs abducted
with wide padding

Sidelying over roll
to compensate

Subluxation risk

Avoid

Correction– For retraction of shoulders Note: Lying on right side to
counter deformity towards left

(b) Prone

Position for activity

(c) Correction of (a), (b). Midline with compensation at right

Tendency to be
windswept

Avoid

Correction

Abduction splinting or Corrected prone and correcting a
or frame   deformity to the left side

(d) Activity position

(e) Corrected activity position

(f) Adjusted kneeling for symmetry

To discourage preferred head turn
and asymmetry

Tendency   Correction

Feet on wedges
Weight on lateral
border of foot

Fig. 8.4 Abnormal postures and corrective procedures.

Fig. 8.5   Three-year-old with genetic abnormality. Note neck retraction and asymmetry.

Persistent abasia

The inability to bear weight through the feet has a long-term significance in terms of management in later life. With the exception of those children for whom weight-bearing increases the likelihood of asymmetry (that is, those cerebral-palsied children who require skilful and gradual introduction if damaging, spastic patterns are to be avoided), early weight bearing is always encouraged.

The generally flexed, hypotonic child who *will not* bear weight, the developmentally slow child who *cannot*, or the sensorily impaired child who shows little awareness of the fact that he has legs at all will benefit from the massive proprioceptive stimulation of strong weight-bearing through the hips? The beneficial effects on postural tone, head control, symmetry and hip stability are powerful in themselves and even if the child fails to walk they should be actively sought (Fig. 8.6).

Many children have not developed the ability to bear weight until their early teens and thus long-term persistence is required, particularly if we value the care advantages this produces in later life.

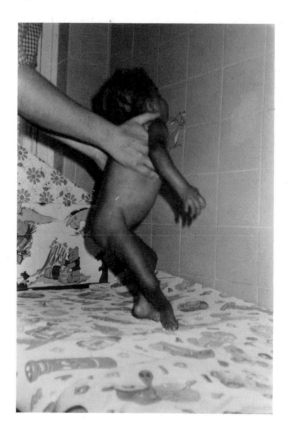

Fig. 8.6   Abasia. Note risk of anterior subluxation and primitive position of feet.

Primitive positioning of hips and feet

Hypotonic children frequently demonstrate 'frogging' of the legs in the primitive pattern of abduction of the hips, flexion of the knees and dorsiflexion of the feet. If allowed to persist, bilateral anterior subluxation of the femoral heads will occur, combined with fixed flexion of the knees.

The neonatal mobility of the foot or the infantile tendency to flat feet (Scrutton & Gilbertson 1975) have been known to persist and to interfere with stable weight bearing. If corrective footwear proves unsuccessful, surgery is indicated in the form of fusion or tendon transplant. Any child who has a delayed or abnormal weight bearing opportunity will experience problems, e.g. deficit of posture, balance and speed. Slenderness of foot, poor arch formation, abnormal weight distribution and, of course, tightened tendo achilles and equinus deformities can be considered likely and early intervention is indicated.

Failure of prone development

Although head control, mid-line orientation and wide-based sitting frequently emerge, experience suggests that a failure to tolerate the prone position has a significant influence on further development, and that certain motor deficits are associated with this failure.

There are specific children with a marked preference for the supine position into which they will thrust or fall. They are usually hypotonic or mildly hypertonic, are frequently microcephalic and commonly epileptic. Wide-based sitting is tolerated but they do not move out of this position and show reduced or absent parachute reactions, preferring, when tipped, to utilize trunk and hip flexion combined with hand clasp in mid-line to stabilize themselves.

The effects of these actions will be:

1 kyphosis and spinal rigidity;
2 when placed on their feet, demonstration of flexor withdrawal or abasia;
3 others will bear weight with help but have no equilibrium or saving reactions;
4 automatic stepping is retained by a small number but most show a complete *lack of reciprocal movement*.

Questioning reveals that these children will not tolerate the prone position and have not therefore propped on elbows, crept or crawled. No rolling beyond that from prone to supine has occurred and they are commonly very adept at rising directly to sitting (albeit without a marked degree of trunk rotation). Whilst accepting that a percentage of the normal population has never crawled, crept or shuffled, the lack of this development in the case of the mentally handicapped has more profound effects (Fig. 8.7).

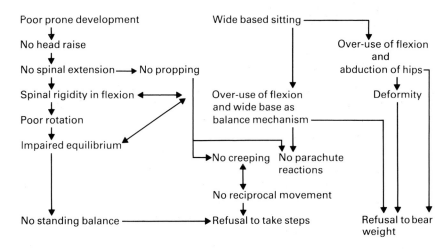

Fig. 8.7

BEHAVIOUR AFFECTING MOTOR PERFORMANCE

Withdrawn or self-stimulatory behaviour

'Tactile defensiveness' manifested by the withdrawn child is a significant block to our handling and thus to our ability to facilitate, prompt and shape the desired activity. The child tends to avoid physical contact and will withdraw into a private world of rocking, hand flapping, etc. It is not surprising that a child who does not and cannot seek tactile stimulation will avoid it. Unresponsive to his mother he may well not be handled freely and positively. The saddened family may regard the child as delicate (as he may well be if other organic deficiencies are present). The heart defects of Down's Syndrome or the atresias of some other genetic abnormalities are the cause of great anxiety. Epilepsy, particularly if believed to be triggered by strong stimulation, will also deter some adults from playing in the warm, physical manner which is normally instinctive.

Self-stimulatory behaviour is frequently regarded as caused by environmental deprivation, but some very young babies who live with their loving families and who enjoy a rich sensory and emotional opportunity have been seen to commence this flapping, rocking behaviour as early as a few months old. The reason for this behaviour makes interesting study but for our purpose its significance lies in its blocking effect on further development.

Poor prone development is frequently a feature of the 'flappers'. They will not tolerate the position (see p. 14) and one can only guess at which came first — the inability to lift the head and thus the absence of any rewards in prone, or the preference for flapping in supine and thus no desire to adopt or perform in prone. Rocking children also fail to demonstrate a wide range of alternative motor behaviours. They are often unable to change from one position to another and even in later life when they are able to 'rock' in standing can, on assessment, be seen to walk alone yet always require assistance to stand.

The more choices a child has, the more alternative behaviours he can perform. The more options open to him, the more easily he will learn. Alternative rewards must be established if we are to reinforce varied motor behaviour. Vibration, for example, may be a useful modality. Children treated on a vibration mattress can receive instant reward for lifting the head, for example, or remaining in the prone position.

Destructive behaviour — self, others, property

For various reasons, pathological, physiological or acquired (learned), some children demonstrate the distressing habit of self mutilation. In some cases the children have apparently no control, in others, the behaviour has developed as a means by which the child exerts control over the amount of attention paid to and the activity demanded from it. Some children will attempt to withdraw from a situation which they find stressful, tiring or unrewarding by the use of destructive habits.

The assessment of sensory ability and particular attention to the behavioural approach are both necessary in these cases. We must avoid undue sensory confusion and should not render a child anxious by requesting a task which is too far beyond his ability level. An allowance must also be made for reduced concentration and tolerance span, the appropriate behaviour must be rewarded *fully* and the undesirable must be ignored, i.e. not cajoled or persuaded.

Splinting or other restraints may help to reduce distracting or damaging mannerisms and actions but should never by used in isolation. The splinted part should, if possible, be in a position for activity or experience; for example, if arms are to be restrained this should be done in functional elbow flexion to allow joining of hands and meaningful mid-line activity (not simply held straight by application of rigid tubes). The degree of restraint should also be variable to allow gradual reduction.

Disinclination to adopt posture

This problem has been included because if falls between the two areas of motor and problematic behaviour. The distinctly negative reaction to certain positioning is so marked in some cases that parents become fearful that the child is experiencing severe discomfort and do not persist with that position. The number of times the child is required to, say, lie on his stomach is reduced and the resultant effects on general development are blamed on handicap rather than lack of persistence.

What is the reason for the dislike? (Fig. 8.8) Is it fear or vulnerability? Prone and standing positions may be particular problems. In the former an inability to free the nose or the effects on respiration of the surface pressure may cause anxiety. In the latter, an obvious fear of falling may persist. Children who lack the intellectual capacity to respond to reassurance or to rationalize their fear will require lengthy teaching; for example, a gradual reduction of support from holding a bar, then a taut rope, then a slack rope,etc., may prove effective.

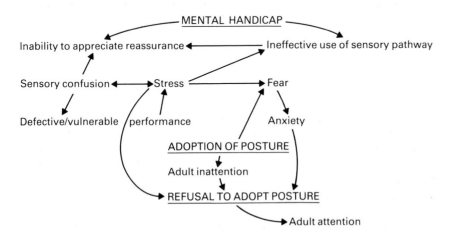

Fig. 8.8

Is it sensory confusion resulting from, or in itself causing, distress? Is it because the refusal attracts adult attention?

MANAGEMENT BY PHYSIOTHERAPY

Our physiotherapy centres are enviroments which we affect and control. The ability of more able patients to *transfer* the skills experienced and learned in these centres will not necessarily be shared by the severely handicapped. Therefore, whether it be as members of an early intervention team, a school staff or a residential establishment we should be prepared to visit and influence the everyday physical environment of the children so that they are more likely to achieve and less likely to deteriorate. Chapter 1 describes our relationships with parents and with our colleagues. The need for close family support and detailed interdisciplinary work is never more necessary than for the mentally handicapped.

Physiotherapists will be working with parents, some of whom are facing the devastating fact of having produced a severely handicapped child. Others may be experiencing the gradual realization that their slow baby is becoming relatively more retarded as time passes. Extremes of bad behaviour, poor sleeping patterns, a refusal to eat well and a failure to relate to the parents are just some examples of the extra strains that can be experienced. These families face a difficult future and will require time to express their fears, and honest and practical guidance and assistance in developing a realistic approach without being overwhelmed by their child's potential problems.

This section has dealt with the clinical aspects of stimulus and response: loving stimulation and responsiveness should perhaps be used as frequently. The consistent motor response is often the action or reaction that the parents long to see. The suitable stimulation and appropriate reward could be, in the classroom, the positions into which the children are placed by their teacher, the motor activity she is encouraged to seek and the sensory reward she knows to supply.

The method of achieving the stated aims will vary with staffing levels and experience. It is beyond the scope of this chapter to describe all the methods and equipment available. However, it is possible to list those aspects of total care that the therapist's expertise enables her to influence:

1   the attitude of family, care (night and day) and educational staff to the development of postural symmetry, and sensory and motor development as they affect care, need, self help, communication, locomotion;

2   the degree of knowledge gained by this group in relation to same;

3   the manner in which the desired postures and activities are integrated into the waking and sleeping day;

4   the means (equipment, splinting) by which they can be achieved.

Points **1** and **2** depend on direct teaching and demonstration. The percentage of time spent on teaching rather than treating will vary. However, we should say that the effectiveness of a therapist is measured not by what happens in her presence but by that which occurs in her absence.

Point **3** is dependent on close interdisciplinary cooperation. It involves the description of correct handling, positioning (activity and rest), and the establishment of play and eductional routines likely to promote postural symmetry, a range of movement opportunities, increased body awareness and those significant motor and sensory areas identified as deficient. Most importantly the postures and movements to avoid must be described and communicated. Correct positioning must become a way of life not a periodic luxury. Fig. 8.4 (a-f; see p.99) for example is from information sheets for care staff. Fig. 8.9 demonstrates the means by which a child lacking head control gains extra play positions.

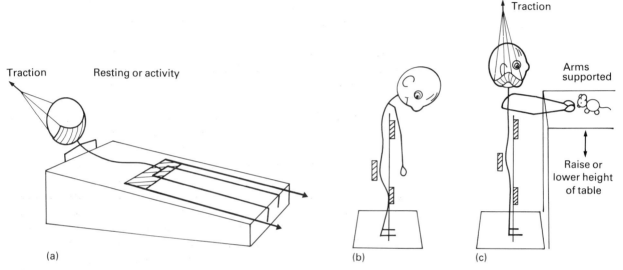

Fig. 8.9   Corrective procedures for head control.

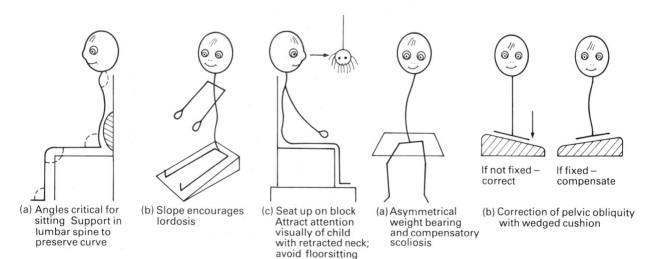

(a) Angles critical for sitting Support in lumbar spine to preserve curve

(b) Slope encourages lordosis

(c) Seat up on block Attract attention visually of child with retracted neck; avoid floorsitting

(a) Asymmetrical weight bearing and compensatory scoliosis

(b) Correction of pelvic obliquity with wedged cushion

Fig. 8.10   Abnormal sitting postures and corrective procedures.

Point **4** is an aspect shared with occupational therapists. In essence it is the supply of equipment or splinting (including spinal support and footwear) likely to facilitate treatment and management aims. As such it must be a structural interpretation of these aims.

The largest area is seating and the design of support from simple strapping to total moulding is a growing field. Figure 8.10 (a-e) shows some points for consideration in the prevention of or compensation for skeletal asymmetry and loss of normal spinal curves. The prevention of pressure sores as described by Nelham (1981) is also considered.

REFERENCES

BAILEY J. & MEYERSON L. (1969) Vibration as a reinforcer with a profoundly handicapped child. *Journal of Applied Behavioural Analysis* **2**, 135–70.

BYRNE D.J. & STEVENS C.P. (1980) Mentally handicapped children's responses to vibrotactile and other stimuli as evidence of the existence of a sensory hierarchy. *Apex British Institute for the Mentally Handicapped* **8** (3) 96–8.

GESELL A., ILG F. & AMES L. (1975) *Infant and Child in the Culture of Today,* revised edition. Hamish Hamilton, London.

JOHNSON D., FIRTH H. & DAVEY G.C.L. (1978) Vibration and praise as reinforcers for mentally handicapped people. *Mental Retardation* **16**, 339–42.

JONES C. (1980) The uses of mechanical vibration with the severely mentally handicapped. *Apex British Institute for the Mentally Handicapped* **17** (4) 112–14.

KANTNER R., CLARK D., ALLEN L. & CHASE M. (1976) Effects of vestibular stimulation on nystagmus response and motor performances in the developmentally delayed infant. *Physical Therapy* **56** (4), 414–21.

KEPHART N.C. (1971) *The Slow Learner in the Classroom.* Charles Merrill, Columbus, Ohio

KIRMAN B. (1972) *The Mentally Handicapped Child.* Thomas Nelson, London

NELHAM R.L. (1981) Seating for the chairbound disabled person — a survey of seating equipment in the UK, *Journal of Biomedical Engineering* **13**, 267–70.

PERKINS E.A., CAPIE A.C.M. & TAYLOR P.D. (1976) *Helping the Retarded.* Institute of Mental Handicap Publications, Kidderminster

SAINT-ANNE DARGASSIES A. (1968) The development of the nervous system in the fetus. *Documents Scientifique Guigoz* 75–6.

SCRUTTON D.R. (1978a) Development deformity and the profoundly retarded child. In *Care of the Handicapped Child* (ed. Apley J.). Spastics International Medical Publications Ltd, Heinemann, London.

SCRUTTON D.R. (1978b) Seating for asymmetric hip deformity in non-ambulant multiply handicapped children. In *Orthopaedic Engineering* (eds Harris J.D. & Copeland K.). Biological Engineering Society, London.

SCRUTTON D.R. & GILBERTSON M. (1975) *Physiotherapy in Paediatric Practice.* Butterworths, Sevenoaks.

SHERBOURNE V. (1979) The significance of movement experiences in the development of mentally handicapped children — content of a developmental movement programme. In *Physical and Creative Acitivities for the Mentally Handicapped* (ed. Upton G.). Cambridge University Press, Cambridge.

FURTHER READING

GENERAL

Cotton E. (1975) *Conductive Education and Cerebral Palsy*. The Spastics Society, London.

Cunningham C. & Sloper P. (1978) *Helping Your Handicapped Baby*. Heinemann, London.

Devereux K. (1979) In *Physical and Creative Activities for the Mentally Handicapped* (ed. Upton G.). Cambridge University Press, Cambridge.

Finnie N.R. (1974) *Handling the Young Cerebral Palsied Child at Home*. Heinemann, London.

Groves L. (ed.) (1979) *Physical Education for Special Needs*. Cambridge University Press, Cambridge.

Holle B. (1976) *Motor Development in Children Normal and Retarded*. Blackwell Scientific Publications, Oxford.

Levitt S. (1982) *Treatment of Cerebral Palsy and Motor Delay* 2e. Blackwell Scientific Publications, Oxford.

Piaget J. (1953) *The Origins of Intelligence in the Child*. Routledge & Kegan Paul, London.

Upton G. (1979) *Phyical and Creative Activities for the Mentally Handicapped*. Cambridge University Press, Cambridge.

SENSORY DEVELOPMENT

Ayres A.J. (1972) *Sensory Integration and Learning Disorders*. Western Psychological Services, California.

Klaus M., Kennell J., Plumb N. & Zuehlke S. (1970) Human maternal behaviour on first contact with her young. *Paediatrics* **46**, 187.

DOMAN AND DELACATO

Thomas E.W. (1968) *Brain Injured Children*. Charles C. Thomas, Springfield, Illinois.

Wolf. J. (1968) *Temple Fay M.D. Progenitor of the Doman & Delacato Treatment Procedure*. Charles C. Thomas, Springfield, Illinois.

BEHAVIOUR MODIFICATION

Capie A.C.M., Taylor P.D. & Perkins E.A. (1980) *Teaching Basic Behaviour Modification*. Institute of Mental Handicap Publications, Kidderminster.

Hester S. (1981) Effects of behaviour modification on standing and walking deficiencies of a profoundly retarded child. *Physical Therapy* **61** (6), 907–11.

Kiernan C. & Woodford F. (1975) *Behaviour Modification with the Severely Retarded*. Excepta Medica Publishing Co., London.

PARENTS AND HANDICAPPED CHILDREN

Schaefer N. (1979) *Does She Know She's There?* Harper and Row, London.

CHAPTER 9
THE CEREBRAL PALSIES

Sophie Levitt

The history of the assessment and treatment of the group of conditions called the cerebral palsies, or cerebral palsy, is of interest to all therapists in paediatrics. It reveals the evolution of the viewpoints underlying therapy of most developmental disabilities.

The focus on the 'palsy' or motor problems has particularly affected physiotherapists. Traditionally trained by orthopaedic surgeons and others preoccupied with muscle and joint actions, it was not surprising that the early treatment of cerebral palsied children was primarily orthopaedic. Phelps, an orthopaedic surgeon, was the pioneer in cerebral palsy habilitation. Although other aspects of these children were considered, most of the approach was concerned with various 'muscle pictures' and bracing. Other therapy approaches soon appeared devised by Temple Fay, Kabat and Knott, and the Bobaths, which were neurological, claiming that the cerebral cortex knew nothing of muscles but rather of movement patterns. The selection of movement patterns for therapy was, and still is, controversial. Vojta, more recently recognized, also adds to the controversy with his own system of reflex creeping patterns and reflex rolling (Phelps 1952; Fay 1954; Bobath 1969, 1980; Knott & Voss 1969; Vojta 1974).

Collis (1953) as well as the Bobaths also pointed out the importance of motor development in therapy. Rood, who contributed the use of sensory stimuli and particular muscle work, also saw her system in an 'ontogenetic skeletal sequence of development' (Rood 1956). Fay, Vojta and others have set developmental sequences only in the prone position. I have used Kabat and Knott together with Bobath ideas in a motor developmental framework (Levitt 1968, 1970).

All neurological systems use sensory stimuli of touch, proprioception and vestibular input. Auditory and visual stimuli are also mentioned but do not always receive as much emphasis. The touch, temperature and proprioception seem more related to treatment of abnormal tone and defective motor patterns.

Facilitation of movement and posture on an automatic level so that the child need not formally cooperate is possible. The different treatment systems have created a variety of 'facilitation methods' to do this. (Pearson & Williams 1978).

110

The Peto approach, introduced to Britain from studies by Cotton (1975) in Hungary, concentrates on the child's conscious and not automatic levels. Learning techniques in an educational setting of groups of children are preferred. There is much less 'laying on of hands' to facilitate motor control, which would also be difficult in group work in classrooms. Motor patterns are analysed in relation to what the child should learn as part of a task. Chapters 7 and 16 discuss further aspects of this view.

The different systems are reviewed in other publications (Decker 1962; Gillette 1969; Levitt 1976). I have always desired to be eclectic, and select from the different systems according to each child's problems. The rationale and the practical application for the eclectic approach can be read elsewhere (Levitt 1962, 1982). Although therapists may still wish to confine themselves to any one system, many of them do come to modify this 'system' with years of experience. Other ideas and methods are incorporated into the system first studied so that it changes and becomes eclectic. As long as therapists assess the child's problems from observation and not from an unproven hypothesis, then techniques which may help can be chosen from any system.

No one system has, as yet, been scientifically proved to be the best, as research designs are very difficult to formulate for this purpose. As children are so individual and as their needs change from age to age, a broadminded view is essential. The therapist is then able to increase her repertoire of methods for all children. In addition, more methods that can be shared with other disciplines and parents become available to suit different situations and countries.

This chapter overlaps with various other chapters in this book as many of the ideas in the field of cerebral palsy are applicable to other developmental therapy problems. This chapter will, therefore, be relatively brief.

NATURE OF THE CONDITIONS

The cerebral palsies are a group of conditions due to non-progressive damage to the brain before, during or after birth. There are many causes, but by the time the therapist is expected to deal with the child the causes have little influence on the treatment programmes.

Although the brain damage itself does not change nor is it curable, the symptoms may change with time. The brain and nervous system are maturing in the presence of the damage and this cannot take place in a vacuum. The way the baby is handled and the attitudes that surround the baby influence how the maturation expresses itself in the subsequent child's and adult's ultimate function.

Although the motor delay and dysfunctions are the main problems in the cerebral palsies there is the possibility of other handicaps. The brain damage itself can be diffuse enough to affect speech and hearing, vision, perceptual function, mental ability and general behaviour. Epilepsy may occur. There may also be other associated handicaps which are due to lack of motor experiences in physically disabled children. Lack of motor exploration affects development of sensations, perceptions, mental abilities and speech. Emotional and social skills are also hampered. Parent–child interaction is not always easy and may create emotional problems.

Early therapy is advisable to minimize the degree of motor handicap and of the secondary development handicaps.

There are still medical practitioners who hesitate about the referral of cerebral-palsied babies for therapy. This may be due to the fact that some babies improve and even become normal without any treatment. Unfortunately we do not yet know definitely which neurologically damaged babies will become cerebral palsied and which will not. It is best to give each child the benefit of developmental therapy, and his parents practical guidance in his daily care, by a therapist who can also detect motor patterns of cerebral palsy. Every chance for the baby's damaged nervous system to develop is offered by early treatment of this kind. We know that the human nervous system when damaged has powers of compensation. In addition, the baby and young child are still maturing and dormant abilities can be activated. In cerebral palsy there is a potential for abnormal patterns of movement and posture to become habitual and deformities can occur and become fixed. Prevention of deformities is possible to a large degree and often completely with early treatment. If deformities are allowed to develop, then secondary deformities may also be promoted in other parts of the child's body. This handicaps him even more.

Early treatment also decreases the associated handicaps which need specific therapy. The associated handicaps have also been known to become more severe than the motor problems. Handicaps interact with one another and the cerebral-palsied child must be considered as a multiply handicapped child. Not all cerebral-palsied children have multiple handicaps, but today there seem to be increasing numbers referred for therapy who are mentally and multiply handicapped.

DIAGNOSTIC TYPES OF CEREBRAL PALSY

There are many medical publications which describe the types of cerebral palsy. Classifications vary in different clinics and countries. Usually there is the spastic, the athetoid and the ataxic type. The diagnostic classification may not play a directly significant role in the therapy plans. Diagnostic types are based on the *predominant* symptoms and there may be symptoms of the other types. The therapist must observe all the signs and symptoms which disrupt the function or the emergence of any function of the child. It can be surprisingly encouraging to see children with a variety of diagnostic symptoms who will nevertheless function independently. Training function in as normal a motor pattern as possible should be the aim of therapy.

In order to plan such training or therapy, assessments of function must be given more priority than the detection of abnormal symptoms; for example, the assessment should consider what elements the child can do as part of any motor ability and also what he can do in total motor abilities. What he cannot do is closely related to this. Whenever possible the reasons for his not being able to do any motor act should be found. The pattern of performance of each motor action is also assessed.

Recognition of spasticity, involuntary movements, low tone and ataxia is made during the functional assessment of any type of cerebral palsy. The medical picture is thus appreciated in terms of the child's everyday functions. Progress is really of value to the child and his family not as improvements of medical symptoms as such, but as improvements in the child's performance.

Deformities are more likely to occur in spastic children, but athetoids with rigidity and hypotonic ataxics also show deformities. Abnormal tone is associated with the genesis of deformity. Abnormal tone may not prevent function in moderately affected children although motor patterns may look abnormal.

Classifications into the hemiplegias, quadriplegias, diplegias and triplegias are also guidelines for therapists. However, the therapist must still observe whether there are other problems in the so-called 'uninvolved' limbs.

OTHER HANDICAPS

It is important to plan the child's therapy and educational programme so that speech, mental development, sensory-motor and perceptual activities are integrated. Other handicaps may increase the motor handicap. However, assets in other areas of the child's function can be used to decrease the motor problems. Improved motor function, conversely, helps improve the other handicaps as well as the developmental problems.

Analyses of any task a cerebral-palsied child must learn will have to include all the child's assets and defects which affect the task. A multidisciplinary team is usually needed and is discussed in Chapter 1.

DEVELOPMENT OF THE DIFFERENT TYPES OF CEREBRAL PALSY

The motor problems which are the primary problems in these children have been studied at different ages. The motor patterns have been described for each type of cerebral palsy at different developmental levels (Bobath & Bobath 1975). The division into types does, however, cloud the fact that there are motor patterns commonly seen in all types of cerebral palsy. Although each child is an individual whose handicap differs in severity and function from the next, the following are problems frequently observed in all children with cerebral palsy:

1 asymmetry;
2 recurring abnormal motor patterns;
3 deformities;
4 abnormal reflex reactions.

1 ASYMMETRY (Figs 9.1, 9.2 and 9.3)

When considering the spastic hemiplegic child one uses many bilateral, reciprocal, alternate and unilateral movements which can be applied to all children. It is rare to find an absolutely symmetrical involvement in quadriplegic, diplegic and triplegic children, One limb is often worse than the other. The head and trunk control is not always symmetrically developed. Many athetoids and ataxics as well as spastics have similar asymmetries which are mentioned below.

(a) *Weight bearing (stability)* is greater on one side when the child is leaning on forearms, on hands or on hands and knees. The child may sit more on one buttock or take weight more through one knee or foot in positions of sitting, kneeling and standing when symmetrical weight bearing is normal.

(b) *Counterpoising is unequal* on each side. This may be due to poor movement of one limb which is associated with inadequate trunk adjustment counterpoising that limb. The trunk may be adequate but disused on the one side. Other children may already have inadequate weight bearing on the one side of their bodies so that they tend not to use that side. Counterpoising would then be secondarily diminished as well.

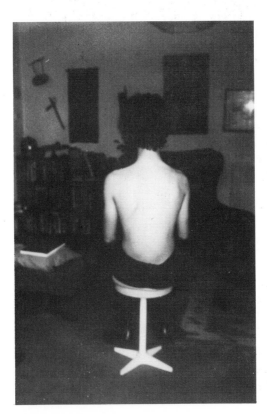

Fig. 9.1

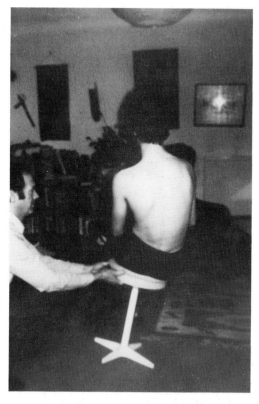

Fig. 9.2 Tilt reaction.

(c) *Rising (righting) reactions* may be better towards one side. This could be due to better arm propping on one side which helps the child rise from lying to other positions. It may be due to a deformity blocking hand support or foot placement within any of the phases of rising from one position to the next. It may be neurological damage that has prevented the rising reaction from developing and the child is only able to get into any position by using a good hand grasp on one side. This creates an asymmetrical pattern of rising preventing activity on the other side. Activity involving rising is one way of decreasing hypertonus, particularly if rotation is part of the child's rising pattern. Hypertonus, therefore, remains greater on one side.

(d) *Tilt reactions may be asymmetrical.* This has been observed not only in hemiplegics but in all types of cerebral palsy. It is particularly evident if there is also a visual field or acuity defect on one side.

(e) *Saving including parachute reactions* may also be better on one side.

(f) *Visual handicap which is greater on one side* may create asymmetry in all the above postural reactions. Unequal acuity, especially if extreme such as blindness in one eye, and field defects delay the development of the postural reactions on the affected side.

Fig. 9.3

(g) *Deafness on one side* may lead to communication and play towards the better side. If this is associated with other handicaps on the same side, then asymmetry may be established.

(h) *Pathological reflex reactions* may be more active on one side of the child. Preferred head turning to one side is linked with the asymmetrical tonic neck reflex in some children. The asymmetrical tonic neck reaction, flexor spasms, extensor spasms, withdrawal reactions of foot or hand and other reactions may be more active on one side of the child's body.

(i) *Asymmetrical distribution* of hypertonus or athetosis occurs in individual children.

(j) *Emotional satisfactions and rewards* may be given to the child on one side more than on his other side. It may be because of his immobility, vision, a better arm and hand or other physical reason that adults approach him from one side. This serves to reinforce his existing asymmetry.

(k) *Growth of limbs* may be unequal. This results in secondary abnormal postures; for example, a shorter leg results in plantar flexion in that foot in order to reach the ground. There may be secondary pelvic tilt, scoliosis or lateral lean of the trunk in sitting but more so in standing and gait.

Therapy for asymmetry

The causes of the child's asymmetry should be investigated. The asymmetry should be persistent for it to be abnormal as there are asymmetries which are normal. Methods are selected according to the causes above; for example, everyone taking care of the child should approach him in the midline. If he needs to catch sight of the motivating stimulus on his better side, it should then be moved to the centre. Training of head and trunk control in midline and equal weight distribution through both hips, knees and feet should be emphasized. Symmetrical postures should be the starting positions for symmetrical movements. There will also be movements which involve each limb doing a different pattern at the same time. One hand may hold the toy whilst the other manipulates it or one hand turns a screw one way whilst the other hand turns it the opposite way. Maintenance of head, trunk and pelvis in the starting position of symmetry can be continued if both arms and hands are used together in bilateral, alternate or reciprocal actions.

It will also be necessary to train movements and positions using the less habitual patterns. Looking and turning to each side, reaching to each side and many other activities have to be devised to obtain action on both sides of the child.

Chairs and tables, the position of the furniture at home and in classrooms and equipment have to be checked. The child should be reminded to maintain symmetrical positions in all equipment as well as during his activities without equipment. Chapter 8 discusses the 'wind blown' position of legs, pelvis and trunk asymmetry and how to correct this problem.

Compensatory raises of a shoe, or placing small sandbags under a shorter thigh, is used in positions where unequal growth of limbs creates asymmetric postures (see Fig. 8.4).

2 RECURRING ABNORMAL MOTOR PATTERNS

The voluntary movements and postures vary from one cerebral-palsied child to the next. However, there are some abnormal patterns which may be seen in many children and relate to:

1   persistence of infantile postures and movement patterns;
2   pathological motor patterns;
3   compensatory motor patterns.

These patterns have already been discussed in Chapter 2. There are motor patterns characteristic of particular types of cerebral palsy as well as those seen in all types of cerebral palsy. Asymmetries have already been mentioned above and other examples are shown in Figs 9.4, 9.5 and 9.6. which may occur in spastics or athetoids and especially in mixed types of cerebral palsy.

Arm habitual synergy

Shoulder: adduction, internal rotation

Elbow: pronation

Wrist: flexion

Hand: flexion

Thumb: adduction

Some corrective synergies

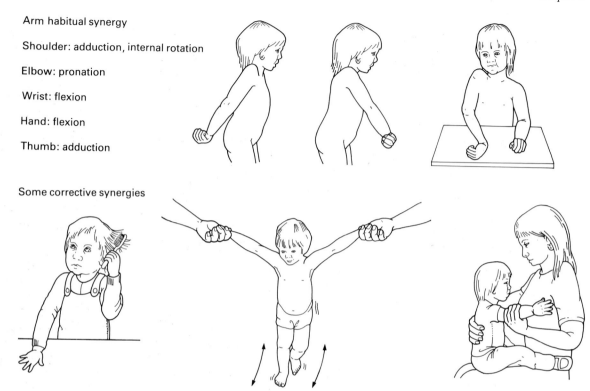

Fig. 9.4 Some corrective motor patterns for the arm and hand.

The therapist must assess each child's motor patterns not in one position but in every motor ability that the child is attempting or carrying out reliably.

Although many of the abnormal patterns are called 'spastic patterns' it is possible to observe these patterns in other types of cerebral palsy and also in severely mentally handicapped children without spasticity. Some blind babies without neurological handicap retain some of the primitive patterns also seen in cerebral-palsied children. Some normal children use 'spastic' synergies as part of a great variety of synergies. Abnormality is only confirmed if the particular synergies are recurring, as there are no other synergies but these few stereotyped patterns.

Repetition of a few synergies of posture and movement may lead to deformities into these patterns. Abnormal tone also reinforces a recurring synergic movement pattern and creates deformities.

Associated reactions are seen in cerebral-palsied children. When the child uses his hands, especially with effort, he may also increase tension in his legs or trunk or head. Athetoids may not keep still in one part of their body whilst they use another part. It is possible that grasping with one hand associates with clenching unnecessarily with the other hand.

Observation of associated abnormal 'overflow' in other parts of the body should be made when the child speaks as well as when he moves and balances.

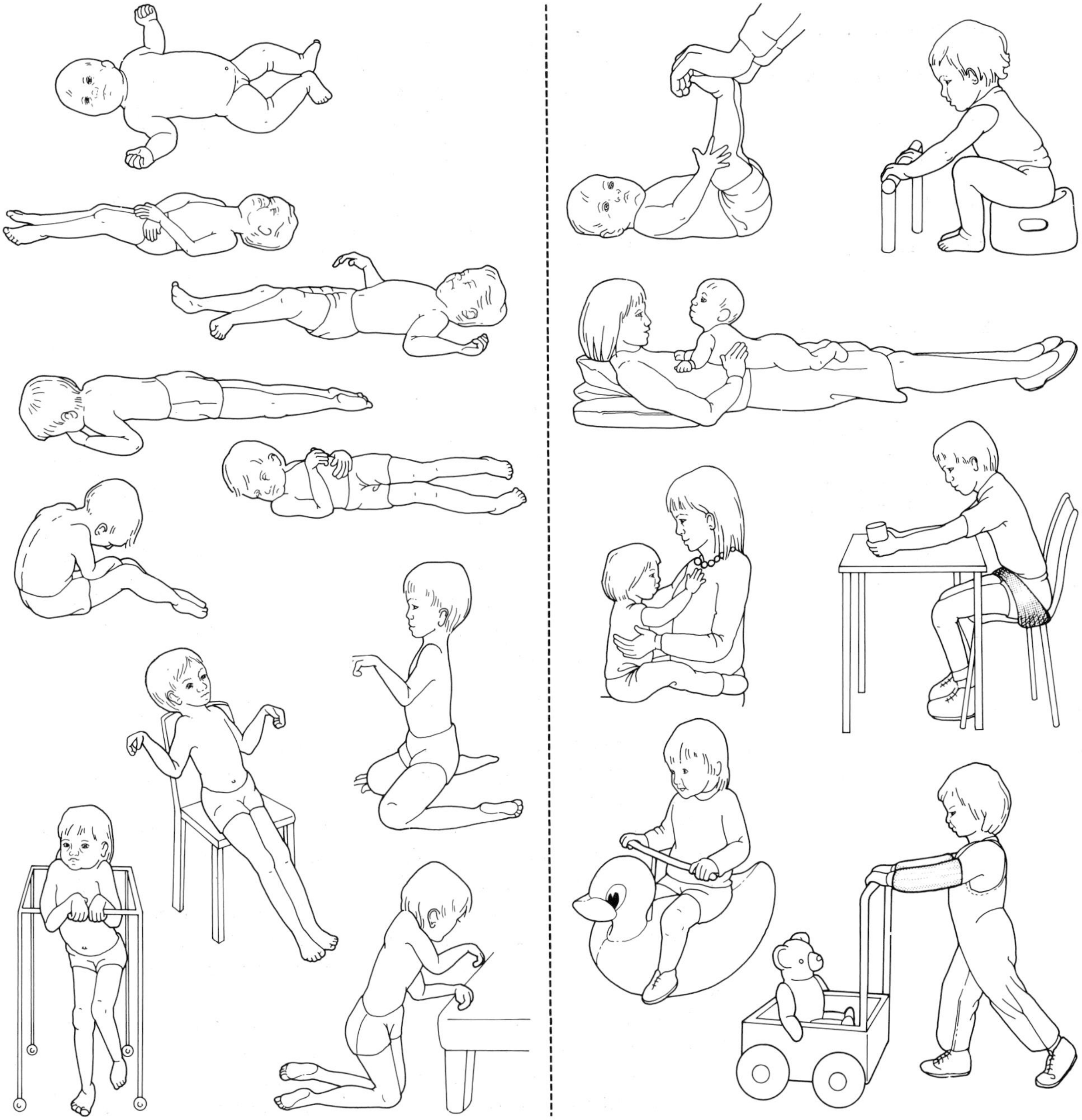

Fig. 9.5 Examples of motor patterns which are corrected within the child's developmental levels. *Left* some abnormal motor patterns. *Right* some corrective motor patterns.

Therapy for abnormal motor patterns

This has also been discussed in Chapters 2, elsewhere in this book and in other publications quoted by the authors.

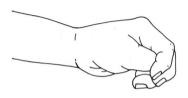

Fig. 9.6a Some abnormal motor patterns of the hand.

Therapy principles involve:

1 correction of abnormal motor patterns within developmental motor abilities and skills;

2 increasing the variety of movement synergies; emphasizing specific corrective motor activities and specialized neuromuscular techniques in physiotherapy (Bobath 1969; Knott & Voss 1969; Stockmeyer 1967; Cotton 1974; Vojta 1974; Rood 1956).

3 selection of equipment, toys and playthings;

4 positioning to facilitate corrective motor patterns in and out of special equipment;

5 procedures to counteract deformities which include the above.

3 DEFORMITIES

Abnormal motor patterns which recur cause the deformities in cerebral palsy. The cause of the abnormal motor patterns is controversial, and thus so is the cause of deformity.

Traditionally the hypertonus is associated with tight, shortened muscles which hold the joints in abnormal positions. The antagonists to the spastic tight muscles are weak or, if normal, cannot work against the tight pull of the spasticity or rigidity. The patterns of these abnormal limb and trunk positions are considered to be due to the distribution of the hypertonus.

This is not the full story. The child may make various biomechanical compensations to function in the presence of his abnormal tone; for instance, if he is 'on toes' because of tight, hypertonic, plantar flexors, he may hyperextend his knees to push his heels down to the ground for better balance control. Some children flex hips and knees and manage to obtain balance for walking in this pattern. Hypertonus is rarely present in only one muscle group. It is thus difficult to analyse which abnormal joint position is due to hypertonus and which to secondary biomechanical adjustment.

Another view which I recommend is to assess which normal postural reactions are deficient and what compensations the child must use to overcome these deficiencies. The biomechanical patterns can be seen in normal people standing and walking in situations where balance is threatened, e.g. on ice, on skis or across dangerous ground. When hypertonus is present or when the damaged central nervous system has a potential for spastic mechanisms, then the child activates his hypertonus. He 'stands on spasm' instead of standing using his normal postural mechanisms.

Once again repeated use of hypertonus shortens muscle groups and they contribute to deformities.

Therapy to prevent and correct deformities

The development of the postural reactions in symmetrical patterns prevents deformities. In addition, special neuromuscular techniques used by physiotherapists to activate or to augment the postural reactions are indicated in selected children.

Should abnormal tone be present, this is largely counteracted by correct training of the motor abilities. However, many physiotherapists find that there is still a need for specific treatment for the hypertonus.

Treatment for hypertonus includes many methods; for example the following are used with individual children:

(a) rotation movements of trunk and shoulder and pelvic girdles;

(b) ice applications for 3–4 minutes to the limb or to the most spastic muscle groups;

(c) activation of the apparently weak antagonists to spastic muscle groups;

(d) use of warmth with slow movement;

(e) slow passive stretching manually or with plasters or splints;

(f) rhythmical shaking of the whole limb;

(g) deep pressures to tendons at muscle insertions;

(h) physiotherapists may find certain drugs helpful for muscular relaxation.

It is important to recognize that simply keeping hypertonic children mobile will reduce the hypertonia. Mobility must use the variety of synergic patterns and rotation in these patterns seen in normal motor development as far as possible.

Treatment principles for deformities and the prevention of deformities discussed in Chapter 2 also apply to the cerebral-palsied children. Prolonged positions or repeated abnormal movements are particularly evident in these children.

ABNORMAL REFLEX REACTIONS

There are abnormal reactions which distinguish the different types of cerebral palsy. There are many reactions which are found in all types. They are usually the infantile neurological reactions of reflex stepping, Moro, grasp reflexes, primitive supporting, infantile feeding reflexes, neck righting and asymmetrical tonic neck reaction. In practice, therapy suggestions are made to decrease these reactions when the child has matured beyond developmental ages when these reactions are no longer expected. Each child will differ according to the potential in his nervous system.

Pathological reactions such as the tonic labyrinthine and symmetrical tonic neck reflexes are rare in cerebral palsy. Some observe elements of these reflexes or intermingling of these reflexes. It is not helpful for the therapist to try and detect these reflexes. They may be stimulated one day in a specially structured test and not appear on the next occasion. If they do exist in the children, they will be detected only as part of the many possible abnormal patterns used in the developmental motor abilities.

It is also worth observing whether the position of the child's head or his total body position increases any abnormal patterns of posture and movement. This may occur, mainly in spastics, and frequently does not correlate with any preconceived reflex patterns of the tonic reactions.

The reflex reactions that affect the child's progress are the mature postural reactions which appear with neuromotor development. These reactions are not maturational only. They can be learned. In other words, the child learns

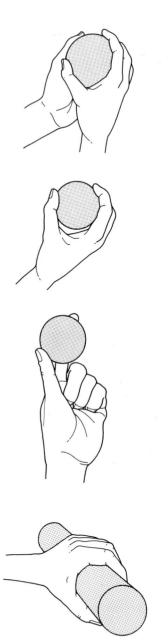

Fig. 9.6b Some corrective motor patterns of the hand.

to activate and use postural reactions in the context of sensory-motor or perceptual-motor activities. Speech, if relevant to the child's understanding, is also used to activate these postural reactions; for example, in training a blind, moderately spastic child to save himself, I have said repeatedly 'hand down' as this is facilitated. The additional verbal instruction seems to improve results.

Therapy for counteracting abnormal reactions

Building up the normal postural reactions will simultaneously suppress and integrate the primitive reactions. There are also special methods to decrease the Moro, asymmetrical tonic neck, reflex stepping and other abnormal reflex reactions (Levitt 1982). Correct positioning also decreases the activity of reflex reactions. Avoidance of the known stimuli which produce any abnormal reflex is also important in handling the child.

SPLINTS, CALIPERS AND PLASTERS

Differing viewpoints exist about the use of these aids. It is helpful to use some form of splintage or special plasters or equipment such as standing frames, prone boards, chairs and wedges to correct one part of the child's body whilst he uses another part actively. It follows teaching principles which break down a task into elements that the child can achieve whilst other elements are given assistance until the child can cope with them.

If feet are held plantigrade, then the child can activate his head and trunk control in sitting. If his feet are held plantigrade in standing, he may be able to actively practise head, trunk and pelvic stabilization. Should all these elements be too difficult, then knee splints may be used alone or with his feet held in calipers. The child can then hold himself better in alignment and activate his head, trunk and pelvic girdle muscles with hips straight. Some children are frequently using adducted legs which create too small a base for balance in sitting, kneeling or standing. By training abduction or abducting the child's legs in abduction pants, or in a standing frame, postural stabilization of his head, trunk and hips becomes possible. Elbow splints also help a child keep his bent arms straight so that he can take weight through his hands and activate his shoulder stabilizers and his head and trunk control. Grasping with both hands with elbows held straight is yet another technique to achieve stability of shoulder girdles and head and trunk control in sitting. In standing and walking, elbow splints help the child grasp or lean on to his aid whilst activating postural mechanisms for these activities. There are many other possibilities where splintage is used in a dynamic way rather than in a totally passive approach. Assessment of each child affects how splintage is used or may show it is not indicated at all.

In splints, postural stability is progressed to weight shift or body sway and counterpoising. Rising, tilt and saving are not as easily achieved with splintage of knees and hips, as mobility is then restricted. Rising from sitting to standing is very well facilitated if the child's feet are held in plasters or below-knee calipers.

Voluntary movement for feeding, dressing, play and other daily activities may also be restricted in splints placed on the child's arms. However, the splintage may be used to stabilize an athetoid arm or lower limbs whilst the other hand and arm are used in an activity.

Use of splintage is well known for correction of deformities, but this aim must not be carried out in practice without concern for the child's active postural and movement control. As improved postural reactions are facilitated with minimal splintage, then prevention of deformities as mentioned above, can also take place.

SURGERY

Correction of deformities is not always possible in every child. Besides the factors creating deformity already mentioned, there are unknown factors which still seem to generate deformities in some children. It may be due to unequal growth of bones and muscles, increased weight and height of a child or other features such as adolescent deterioration which is not fully explained

Surgery should be carefully considered for selected children. Pre- and post-operative physiotherapy must include training of the postural reactions to make full use of the surgical corrections. Timing according to the child's neurological development rather than according to his chronological age is essential. Teamwork between surgeon, physiotherapist and nurses is necessary for good results once thoughtful selection of children for surgery has been made.

SPECIFIC SYMPTOMS OF TYPES
OF CEREBRAL PALSY

Hypertonus has already been discussed above. Involuntary movements including intermittent spasms are usually associated with the athetoid type of cerebral palsy. These are of various kinds. They may be controlled by the child as he carries out a purposeful motion. They seem to be better controlled in prone or other specific positions in different children. Postural stabilization and couterpoising activities within the developmental motor skills do seem to decrease some involuntary motions. The child may also work well against graded manual resistance, weights or heavy toys.

The arousal of athetoid movements in other parts of the child's body whilst he uses his arms or his legs or speaks can be controlled. The child can consciously train himself to keep his feet still or to grasp to keep his trunk still or use other ways of self-control. Focusing on a visual point during training helps athetoids control themselves when sitting, standing, kneeling upright or walking. Athetoid children with their attention held by any auditory or visual stimuli such as television often show marked decrease of involuntary movements of their heads and trunks.

There are still many athetoid movements which are beyond our understanding and beyond treatment methods today. The increasing development of electronic aids has, therefore, been a great help to such athetoids as well as to all other severely handicapped cerebral-palsied people.

Dystonia is also seen in athetoids and is treated much like other hypertonus. There is special emphasis on symmetry as dystonia may involve tense twisting of the head and body to one side.

Ataxia and hypotonus in a pure form are rare. However, poor balance and incoordination have to be treated in all forms of cerebral palsy. Eyé-hand incoordination and fine finger manipulations also need training in all cerebral-palsied children though the ataxics have special problems within these areas.

Slow rising reactions from one position to another help athetoids, ataxics and spastics develop stabilization of shoulder, pelvic and trunk muscles. If rising reactions are carried out quickly with a momentum, they may be acquired but the postural stability and counterpoising can remain inadequate in the transitional positions used in the rising patterns. Rising slowly counteracts low tone and some involuntary movements in head, trunk, shoulders and hips. Slow-graded limb movements against gravity or against resistance of a heavy toy or manual resistance not only increase control of involuntary movements but decrease hypotonia.

Tilt and saving reactions are usually better in many athetoids and some ataxics. However, they must be trained in all cerebral-palsied children if they are absent or abnormal.

CONCLUSION

An outline of some current thinking in cerebral palsy therapy has been given. The general approach is to assess and plan procedures for the child's daily function. Medical symptoms of hypertonus, hypotonus and involuntary movements are considered within the different levels of functional development of the child. Improved motor function involves activation and practice of the postural reactions of stability, counterpoising, rising, tilt and saving. Correction of deformities with corrective motor patterns and splintage or surgery forms part of the total motor programme.

The contributions of the speech therapist and occupational therapists are given in other chapters although their work includes consideration of the factors discussed above. Chapter 2 offers additional viewpoints on the cerebral palsies.

Techniques of treatment have been given in many other publications and cannot be discussed in only one chapter. General suggestions for therapy have been made which the physiotherapist will adapt for each child.

REFERENCES

BOBATH B. (1969) Treatment of neuromuscular disorders by improving patterns of coordination. *Physiotherapy* **55**, 1.

BOBATH K. (1980) *A Neurophysiological Basis for the Treatment of Cerebral Palsy.* William Heinemann Medical Books, London.

Bobath B. & Bobath K. (1975) *Motor Development in the Different Types of Cerebral Palsy.* Heinemann Medical Books, London.

Collis E. (1953) Management of cerebral palsy in children. *Medical Illustration 7.*

Cotton E. (1974) *The Basic Motor Pattern.* The Spastics Society, London.

Cotton E. (1975) *Conductive Education and Cerebral Palsy.* The Spastics Society, London.

Decker R. (1962) *Motor Integration.* Charles C. Thomas, Springfield, Illinois.

Fay T. (1954) Rehabilitation of patients with spastic paralysis. *Journal of the International College of Surgeons* **22**, 200.

Gillette H.E. (1969) *Systems of Therapy in Cerebral Palsy.* Charles C. Thomas, Springfield, Illinois.

Knott M. & Voss D. (1969) *Proprioceptive Neuromuscular Facilitation,* 2e. Harper and Row, New York.

Levitt S. (1962) *Physiotherapy in Cerebral Palsy.* Charles C. Thomas, Springfield, Illinois.

Levitt S. (1968) The treatment of cerebral palsy and proprioceptive neuromuscular facilitation techniques. *Sjukgymnasten* **27**,3.

Levitt S. (1970) *The adaptation of PNF for cerebral palsy.* In the Proceedings of the Sixth International Congress of the World Confederation for Physical Therapy, Amsterdam.

Levitt S. (1976) Stimulation of movement. In *Early Management of Handicapping Disorders,* (eds Oppé T.E. & Woodford F.P.), Elsevier Scientific, Amsterdam.

Levitt S. (1982) *Treatment of Cerebral Palsy and Motor Delay,* 2e. Blackwell Scientific Publications, Oxford.

Pearson H.P. & Williams C.E. (eds) (1978) *Physical Therapy Services in the Developmental Disabilities.* Charles C. Thomas, Springfield, Illinois.

Phelps W.M. (1952) The role of physical therapy in cerebral palsy and bracing. In *Orthopaedic Appliances Atlas* Vol. 1, pp. 251–522. Edwards, Ann Arbor.

Rood M.S. (1956) Neurophysiological mechanisms utilized in the treatment of neuromuscular dysfunction. *American Journal of Occupational Therapy* **10** (4) 220, part 2.

Stockmeyer S.A. (1967) The Rood Approach. *American Journal of Physical Medicine* **46**, 1900.

Voljta V. (1974) *Die Cerebralen Bewegungsstörungen im Säuglingsalter.* Ferdinand Enke Verlag, Stuttgart.

FURTHER READING

Bobath B. (1971) *Abnormal Postural Reflex Activity Caused By Brain Lesions,* 2e. William Heinemann Medical Books, London.

Brereton B. Le G. & Sattler J. (1967) *Cerebral Palsy: Basic Abilities.* Spastic Centre of NSW, Sydney.

Finnie N. (1974) *Handling the Young Cerebral Palsied Child at Home,* 2e, William Heinemann Medical Books, London.

Foley J. (1965) Treatment of cerebral palsy and allied disorders. In *Physical Medicine in Paediatrics.* (ed. Kiermander B.). Butterworths, London.

Holt K.S. (1965) *The Assessment of Cerebral Palsy,* vol. I. Lloyd Luke, London.

KABAT H., McCLEOD M. & HOLT C. (1959) The practical application of Proprioceptive Neuromuscular Facilitation. *Physiotherapy* **45**, 87.

LEVITT S. & MILLER C. (1973) The inter-relationships of speech therapy and physiotherapy in children with neuro-developmental disorders. *Developmental Medicine and Child Neurology* **15**, 2.

SAMILSON R.L. (1975) *Orthopaedic Aspects of Cerebral Palsy.* Spastics International Medical Publications, London.

SHEPHERD R.B. (1974) *Physiotherapy in Paediatrics.* William Heinemann Medical Books, London.

TWITCHELL T.E. (1959) On the motor deficit in congenital bilateral athetosis. *Journal of Nervous and Mental Disorders* **129**, 105.

WOLF J.M. (1969) *The Results of Treatment in Cerebral Palsy.* Charles C. Thomas, Springfield, Illinois.

For anyone wishing to know more about Professor Andras Peto's system of teaching called Condutive Education, the address is: The Institute of the Motor Disabled, Villânyi U + 67, Budapest XI, Hungary.

CHAPTER 10

PERCEPTUAL MOTOR DISORDERS

PART 1   Clumsiness in Childhood

Lorraine A. Burr

Many people are clumsy but when this clumsiness disturbs efficiency in function it can rightly be called a disablement. The social and emotional stresses that incoordination can invite have been used throughout the ages as a basis for comedy. Yet for those whose clumsiness causes isolation and rejection the offer of remediation can be a lifeline.

In recent years children with perceptual motor disorders have been recognized and allocated diagnoses such as minimal brain damage. Recent critical opinion, however, suggests the symptoms are so varied and of such obscure aetiology that the 'Clumsy Child Syndrome' probably does not exist as such.

Nevertheless there are numbers of children whose movements do not provide the effective function that they and others would wish. This is most evident in education where writing ability dictates the level of academic opportunities available.

APPROACHES

Varied theories of both neurological and educational basis have been presented as treatment for these conditions. Their value lies only in the provision of a framework for the development of treatment programmes. All these approaches claim equal success for their methods.

Claims that sensory motor techniques can influence visual and motor perception are questionable and unproven. However, disability of the apparently neurodevelopmental type as opposed to brain damage appear to be able to respond to the opportunity to extend perceptual experiences. The level of intellectual capacity also seems to influence this ability.

Treatment can only in truth be aimed at an improvement in self-confidence and self-image with the resultant change in attitudes to learning.

REVIEW OF THEORIES AND TREATMENT METHODS (MAINLY TAKEN FROM ABBIE 1974)

McKinlay and Gordon (1980)

Theory   Neurodevelopmental problem affecting brain growth development including maturational rate. There is a possible disruption in the dendrites essential for the interconnection between nerve cells, glial cell production of myelia (myelination of neurone sheaths) that allow the rapid conduction of electrical impulses. Since the cerebellum is particularly vulnerable to processes affecting brain growth in late pregnancy and early infancy (Dobbing & Smart 1973) there is a resulting immaturity of motor development.

Treatment   Since the disturbance of brain development during the growth spurt may lead to limitation in the number of dendrites or glial cells then a physical remedial style of management may be more appropriate than purely psychosocial analysis or remedy.

Ayres

Theory   Rood Basis — Learning and behavioural problems in many children may be due to inadequate sensory integration at a subcortical level. It is assumed that in normal sensory motor development there is a sequence of development in which the tactile and vestibular mechanisms play an important primary role. Later-developing sensory systems are dependant on adequate integration of these earlier ones.

Treatment   By providing and reinforcing sensory information, in particular, tactile and vestibular, the inadequate integrating mechanisms will be stimulated to a normal response level. By assuming the total interrelationship of all areas of the brain it is possible to influence a poorly functioning area by increasing the information to the competent areas. Reading, numeracy and emotional response are therefore considered in relationship to movement.

Standardized tests are available but require certifiction for their administration.

Doman and Delacato

Theory   Phylogenic recapitulation — All human development relates to phylogenic stages of fish (spinal cord, medullary level), amphibian (posture), reptile (mid-brain) and mammal (bipedal). Difficulties with reading and higher levels of learning are related to injury at a level in an earlier stage.

Treatment   The child is taken back to the level at which his development progress has stopped and is passively exercised in movement appropriate to this stage. Each level is established in progression until a level of cortical dominance is achieved. The programme is extremely intensive and requires total committment from all the family.

Kephart

Theory This is a combined neurodevelopmental and Piaget-based approach by an educationalist and psychologist. Learning can occur by accumulation according to the normative approach until a sufficient quantity of information has ben amassed? At this point a jump to a new stage of educational generalization will occur. Thus development will be seen as a series of step-like processes. Learning disability is seen as a breakdown at one of these stages due to possible neurological disfunctioning.

Treatment The importance within the classroom of input (perception), output (motor ability), feedback and matching are an integral part of this programme. Exercises to develop body awareness, perceptual and motor skills and occular control form part, and use is made of physical education equipment and classroom remedial activity.

Naville and De Ajuriaguerra — Psychomotricity (Naville 1970 a and b)

Theory A Piaget-based therapy. Incoordination is seen as having both physical and social and psychological causes and treatment is aimed at influencing deficits in all these area.

Treatment A highly intensive course for therapists of mainly psychological and educational background. There are four main groupings in treatment, namely gross motor skills, exercises, disassociation, coordination and relaxation. Body image, laterality, awareness of time and space, auditory and visual memory are trained. The aim of treatment is sensory integration and emotional adjustment of the total child. Literature is mainly in French or German.

Mesker, (Maastricht, Holland)

Theory Learning disabilities are disorders of communication. Poor maternal bonding or environmental disruption result in poor processing of all language abilities. Immature cerebral integration increases this disability and disturbs the development of perceptual processes. Importance is given to the correct progress of neurological development from a primitive corkscrew state to symmetrical integration then to laterality and thus to the development of dominance via integration. The perception of primary, secondary and tertiary word images is delayed by immature sensory motor experience.

Use is made of the EEG to recognize cases of subcortical epilepsy.

Treatment Mainly carried out by speech therapists and sometimes physiotherapists. The method of maternal voice filtration of Thomastis is used extensively. This is accompanied by exercises to encourage the development of dominance and later by the psychomotor dominance board to remedy writing difficulties.

Frostig

Theory A child's early skill development will depend upon his visual perceptual proficiency, i.e. recognition and interpretation of visual stimuli.

Treatment An eductional programme based upon visual perceptual abilities. These are space, spatial relationships, form constancy, visuo-motor coordination and figure ground discrimination. There is a closed standardized test available. Gross motor training is Piaget based but is not seen as forming the basis of perception. Studies of this programme have noted increase in perceptual skills but other studies suggest this is not maintained (Barlow 1971).

SIGNS, SYMPTOMS AND ASSESSMENT

The difference between the words dyspraxia and apraxia is essential to the problems faced by the 'clumsy child'. He is able, yet not able (Mesker 1979). He can often perform all tasks required yet does so with inefficiency. His movements are correct yet their quality (Naville 1970a,b,) is very poor. An assessment form must allow for the question of, How? not, What? So ticks are uninformative and observations are essential. A correlation of all difficulties and their related functional implications — for example, poor head control plus poor body awareness, plus poor visuomotor efficiency equal poor writing ability — is the best way to draw up a profile. The interrelation of sensory and motor deficits and psychoperceptual problems can equal a handicap of enormous proportion, whilst each area has only minor poverty in itself.

   For medically trained professions the initial assessment of neurological development is comparatively straightforward. However, if this expertise is not available then observation of functional aptitudes must suffice. Non-medical personnel can comment on areas of apparently poor function which can later be translated for a treatment programme. All assessment sheets used should take account of the following factors.

GENERAL PHYSICAL INTEGRATION

Shoulder and Hip Stability Problems can be evident through excessive propping and leaning.
Value and Quality of Movement Rhythmic and smooth coordinated presentation in movement.

Cerebral Integration   Ability to perform reflective, organized movements in unison and in opposing patterns.

Associated Movements   Facial grimacing, posturing of the hands, etc.

Trunk Rotation   Fluid efficient movements in rolling or when twisting across the body midline.

Predominance of flexion patterns or overuse of extensor patterns.

SENSORY AND PSYCHOMOTOR FUNCTION

The body reflects the mind and the mind affects the body. The term sensory motor refers to the unconscious functioning self. Psychomotor relates self to the environment through thought and action (Naville 1970).

Body Perception   Overall awareness of body parts, their movement, potential and possibilities in a kinaesthetic, proprioceptive and tactile sense. Axis movement appreciation. Projection of self-image. Man drawing.

Finger Recognition   Rhythmic sequencing and efficient proprioceptive selection of individual fingers.

Laterality and Cerebral Dominance   Family history and repeated observations of presented body side for activities.

Midline-crossing   Overall ability to function with one body half in the space of the other body side in an effective manner without necessarily turning the body.

Functional Use of Vision   Focus, following and scanning in visual organisation of tasks.

Hand-eye Coordination   Hand-eye link and pattern of interaction in planning activity.

Auditory Response   Listening ability and apparent comprehension.

Perceptual Motor Skills   Judgements of body in space. Judgement of distance, time and velocity of objects moving away from and towards the body.

Visuospatial Skills   Projection of judgements and anticipation of interactions of objects. Recognition of relationship of objects in terms of shape and form.

Language   Language organization. Ability to self monitor using internal language. Phonetic recognition. Sequential organization. Spelling ability. Content of language.

Writing praxis Body position. Hand position. Observation of writing disabilities, repetitions of movement, mirror imaging and organization upon the work page. Appreciation of sensory motor modules (writing with eyes closed).

Constructional praxis Creation of 3D free form in imaginative projection of constructional concepts, e.g. brick building, constructional toys, etc.

Quality sense Number and quantity concepts (body rhythm).

Emotional behaviour Attitudes, presenting and reported behaviour and response to stress, communicative patterns and self projection.

TESTS

Stott/Henderson A British standardized test of physical proficiency aimed at delineating areas of disability in referred children. Whilst excellent as a screening test (based on Osteretsky) it does not provide a grading system for improvements as it has a pass/fail criteria.

Aston Index A screen test for teachers developed at Aston University. A profile of abilities in both body awareness (Goodenough), motor efficiency, visuospatial concepts and academic skills. It can provide a clear picture of areas of deficiency in children failing in class. There is a related therapeutic programme for teachers use.

Ayres Test A battery of tests standardized on American children. Certification is necessary in order to acquire this test.

Frostig A visuospatial, visuomotor test of basic developmental proficiency. Restricted.

Goodenough (Part of Aston Index) Ostensibly a test of intellectual capacity but relevant to give a developmental age in body perception.

Illinois Test of Psycholinguistic Abilities A closed diagnostic test of communication abilities. The aim is to specify areas of deficit in order that a remediation programme can be devised.

Bender — Visual Motor Gestalt Test Relevant mainly to children with a mental age over eight years (Mellor 1980). Helpful in analysis of manner of pencil reproductions rather than pass or fail score.

Advocators of differing theories will offer alternative explanations for presenting signs and symptoms. An assessment form will no doubt be related to the specific profession of an individual therapist. Table 10.1 offer Signs and

Symptoms with their functional implications according to some of the present theories. The items in Table 10.1 can provide a basis for the formulation of an assessment chart. The specific tests which can be used are noted and references given wherever possible.

Table 10.1

Symptoms	Presenting signs	Reference	Tests	Functional implications
Diminished or poorly integrated basic reflexes	Predominance of flexion patterns in all activities	Ayres 1972	Ayres	Inefficient movements. Poor PE performance. Poor body language. In school head turning creates attention disturbance (reflex response)
	Decrease in extensor tone for achievement	Illingworth 1972		
Poorly integrated vestibular reflexes.	Apparent poor balance response. Over or under reaction to vestibular stimulation	Ayres 1972	Ayres Dizziness in rolling	Clumsiness of movements. Poor self-orientation in space. Apparent poor balance
Tactile defensiveness	Hyper-responsiveness to tactile stimuli. (Overticklish)	Ayres 1972	Dislike of touch, especially head and neck	Poor concentration and attention span. Fidgeting. Emotional withdrawal from touch. Objection to neckties and top shirt buttons
Poor symmetrical cerebral integration	Lack of ability to perform. Symmetrical rhythmic mirrored movements. Unilateral presentation to activities	Mesker 1972	Throwing 2 bean bags. Jumping 2 feet together	Overall disturbance of sense of movement. Disturbance of body language. Poor rhythmic sense
Poor lateralization of cerebral hemispheres	Poor directional sense. Poor appreciation of both body sides	Mesker 1972	Unable to jump sideways rhythmically or perform opposing movements. Psychomotor Dominance Board test	Problems with tying laces, knife and fork, writing — mirror images, directional problems, organisational problems in movements
Cerebral hemisphere suppression	Unilateral disregard. Unilateral presentation. Artificial dominance (Non-integrated)	Ayres 1972 Mesker 1972	Unilateral. Presentation (observation). Man-drawing presentation (reduction in image of one side)	Problems in: writing directional sense, writing down one side of page, movements efficiency, team games
Poor head control	Poor movement patterns. Poor ocular motor control	Ayres 1972	Observation. Ability to focus in gross motor activities	Problems in: copying from blackboard, PE activities, body language

Table 10.1   *continued*

Symptoms	Presenting signs	Reference	Tests	Functional implications
Limb girdle instability and poor muscle co-contraction	Poor proprioceptive awareness of limb positioning in space. 'Wheelbarrows' collapse	Baker 1981 Ayres 1972	Ability to perform smooth movements (push/pull) or bear weight through arms. Ability to stand on one leg	Poor pencil control. Poor PE performance. Clumsy hand interaction. Poor writing presentation
Poor trunk rotation	Rigid body presentation	Baker 1981	Rolling in fluid manner	Midline cross problems. Body language problems. Poor appreciation of lateral space
Low proprioceptive body awareness	Inability to reproduce demonstrated gestures, unilateral, bilateral and cross. Poorly projected drawn self image	Bergeres and Lezine 1965	Bergeres and Lezine gestures Goodenough test (Aston index)	Dressing problems. Emotional self-identity problems. Immature behaviour and aggresive playground behaviour. Poor movements efficiency
Poor facial gesture copying	Complex grimacing when trying to copy one specific movement. Wooden face		Ability to copy facial grimaces	Disturbed presentation of self to peers. Sometimes poor sensory feedback in phonetic selection of sounds. Messy eating
Poor proprioceptive recognition of body axis	Poor awareness of movement — unable to project sense of turning self to corners in pencil tasks, etc.	Laban 1975	Ability to turn on axis with eyes closed in precise manner	Pencil skills poor in mazes, dot to dot, etc., writing — poor letter formations. Inability to copy geometric shapes. Inefficient movement ability
Poor proprioceptive finger recognition and sequential coordination	Incoordinate hand movements	Burr 1979 Baker 1981 Ayres 1972	Tactile recognition sequencing and opposition of fingers in unilateral and symmetrical presentation (note need to use vision or tactile reinforcement)	Disturbance in quantity sense. Poor manipulative skills. Poor pencil control
Poor midline crossing ability	Disorganisation of perceptual motor skills	Ayres 1972 Bergeres Lezine 1965	Aiming across the body with feet together Cross-gesture copying	Poor organization of written work. Poor perceptual motor function in games. Poor directional sense
Poor visual focus and following	Erratic eye movements Poor hand–eye link	Ayres 1972 Kephart 1971 Burr 1980	Ayres Kephart Abercrombie 1963	Poor planning of activities gross and fine. Poor eye contact and resulting emotional difficulties. Poor visual switching from blackboard to book when copying

Table 10.1 *continued*

Symptons	Presenting signs	Reference	Tests	Functional implications
Poor visuomotor-and perceptual-motor judgements (hand-eye coordination)	Ineffective judgements in: graded movements, aiming, catching, organization of tasks, hand–eye tasks	Ayres 1972 Frostig 1964 Burr 1980 Naville 1970 a & b	Frostig Aston index Ability to catch and throw a ball Aiming skills Pencil mazes	Problems with: control of tools, pencil control (mazes, dot to dot), ball games, skipping, writing, buttons, laces, etc.
Poor motor planning (sequential organization)	Inability to memorize and carry out a sequential task	Ayres 1972 Baker 1981	Obstacle courses Sequential toy construction (set of barrels)	Problems with: self-monitoring through internal language, task organization, essay or story construction, spelling
Poor selective responses	Poor attention and concentration	Ayres 1972 Baker 1981	Observation	Problems with: classroom behaviour, team games, road crossing
Poor auditory response	Queried hearing loss. Poor use of language. Disturbance of listening	Ayres 1972 Mesker 1972	Observation of listening ability	Problems with: development of internal language. Inappropriate behaviour, poor listening and interpretation of requests
Poor organization of language abilities	Educational problems of reading and writing	Bradley 1980	ITPA Aston index Observation of sequential behaviour	Problems with: spelling, work construction, internal language
Constructional dyspraxia	Inability to create projective 3D forms	Ironside 1980	Brick building	Problems with: mathematics, geometry, projective imagery
Writing dysgraphia	Poor writing ability and low output. Mirror imagery. Repetitions of letter formations	Mesker 1972	Observation psychomotor dominance test. Aston index (Graphometer test)	Visual over-monitoring of written work. Poor sensory module appreciation. Messy written work. Low writing output
Poor emotional projection of attitudes. Low confidence	Loner in school. Agressive behaviour		By report	Fidgeting and poor concentration. Withdrawal from social and learning experiences. Disturbed behaviour in class and/or at home

A RATIONALE FOR TREATMENT

1   The problem lies with self-awareness, both physical and psychological.
2   Development of the psychological self begins with communication.
3   Development of the physical self begins with movement and touch.
4   Self-identity depends upon good feedback from the environment.
5   Immature neurological patterns interfere with learning.

6   Over-reliance on inefficient visual organization increases the inefficiency of function.

7   Selection of appropriate attention is essential to learning.

8   Listening is essential to comprehension.

9   Internal language is needed to organize and plan tasks.

10   Attitudes to learning determine the outcome of eduction.

11   Training in specific depressed skills could increase stress and anxiety of failure.

12   Behavioural anticipation depends upon the ability to project an image of self on to other people.

TREATMENT PROGRAMME FOR A CHILD WITH PERCEPTUAL MOTOR DEVELOPMENTAL DISORDER

The programme has developed from the practice of several different approaches (Ayres, Mesker, Naville, Kephart). It provides techniques for achievement which allow stable reference points to be established. These provide a foundation for efficient function. Imaginative (projective) techniques have been used throughout as these are the most appealing to children and the most relaxed media for therapy.

If the child feels in control of the session at all times he is then able to accept responsibility for progress and to improve in confidence. Equally the therapist must feel at home with the media and technique. This will be related to their own original specific discipline.

Plateaux of progress will occur at intervals of approximately 2–3 months and rests from treatment for consolidation are advisable.

School and family need to be kept aware of the treatment and progress. Their cooperation and support for the child is essential to its value. Advice to school to reduce the interferance of poorly integrated reflex patterns, and to achieve the highest level of attention ability, is treatment in itself. Explanation of the disability will also improve communcation between teacher and child and modify expectations.

Aim of treatment   To develop a good physical and psychological image of the moving self in order to improve functional efficiency and social skills.

Note   If facilities are available, an initial physiotherapy course using sensory motor techniques is recommended.

ATTENTION AND LISTENING

Listening is essential to normal learning. The effect of sudden silence can be dramatic.

1   Listening should begin from a symmetrical posture.

2   The speaker should always face the child before speaking.

3 The child should focus on the face before the speaker says words other than the listener's name.

4 When the eyes wander from speaker's face, stop speaking, in midword if necessary.

5 Allow pauses for listening comprehension.

6 Encourage verbalization of activities.

7 Encourage repetition of therapist's requests for encouragement of internal language.

8 Encourage verbal analysis of tasks, 'Why did it go wrong?'.

9 Encourage learning to stop moving when a noise such as a drum ceases. (Being still is more difficult than moving.)

10 Use tambourine rhythms to recognize and associate different sound patterns, e.g. fast running or slow walking, and to carry out these movements, changing when appropriate.

11 When the child has gained confidence make very simple, very obvious verbal mistakes occasionally and draw attention to the occurrences — ask the child to note and correct you just for fun. (Care must be taken not to confuse, only surprise.)

12 Above all listen to yourself all the time and analyse what you say and the instruction that you give.

13 Play a game in which the therapist first tells the child how to carry out a simple domestic task step by step. When the idea is established the child must tell the therapist what to do. The instructions must be carried out literally. The fun that ensues draws attention to the language and sequence of words: 'it', 'in there', 'do it', should be discouraged and correct wording sequence structures developed. The aim is to develop internal language structure and listening ability, and task organization.

VISUAL ORGANIZATION

Many dyspraxic children rely on their vision to provide information that their proprioceptive knowledge cannot give. This tends to encourage an overuse of this already inefficient sense. Ocular motor control being disturbed, scanning and organization are equally disorganized. Ayres' theories suggest a neurological link between the trapezius, sternocleidomastoid and the extra-ocular muscles, therefore, theoretically input into head control may improve ocular motor control.

1 The eyes should always be focused before an activity commences. This should be on a point or goal which begins large at the start of treatment and diminishes in size and definition as the session progresses. Initially the mirrored self or preferably the therapist can provide this goal especially with verbal reinforcement. The reflex body/head (tilt) righting patterns can be elicited in this way and the success in control encourages voluntary repetition.

2 Reference at later stages to 'look' can help facilitate involuntary normal patterns of efficient movement.

3   Kephart's eye-training technique often proves helpful but needs to be carried out by the parents every day.
4   Visual tracking during daily routine can be encouraged by parents.
5   Visual scanning of a task can be encouraged by activities which verbalize planning.

FACIAL GRIMACING AND ASSOCIATED MOVEMENTS

Poverty of gross motor skills can be reflected in poor facial control. Increase in grimacing or lack of facial gestures can lead to disruption of interpersonal relationships. Poor sensory control of facial musculature can increase inability to appreciate sound formations. Emotional withdrawal can be reflected in refusal to examine the personal face.

Treatment

Sitting in front of a mirror, parts of the face are isolated in movements; e.g. wriggle nose, wink one eye, upper lip raise. Attention is drawn to the other involvements of the face.

During body-awareness sessions and activities in general, voluntary attempts should be made to control facial grimacing. A deep exhalation can be helpful in relaxing body tensions.

Playing at home with mother's make up or 'face paint' can increase facial awareness.

It is possible that facial tensions reflect neck and shoulder tensions and, therefore, transfer to pencil control. Conscious ability to relax these body parts could help fluency of written work.

BODY AWARENESS

In all activities it is important to draw attention to the body parts involved and their behaviour. It can help to halt an activity, that is inefficient, to discuss the cause of the problem, e.g. why did a 'wheelbarrow' collapse — flexion of arms — (induced possibly by poorly integrated ATNR or poor muscle co-contraction). The next attempt can aim to consciously control the flexion. The child needs to concentrate on his whole body to memorize effective patterns, and to analyse and control ineffective ones. This same analysis can later be extended to functional, object-related activities.

Technique

Proprioceptive awareness

Relaxation technique — lying on a firm surface with the eyes open each body part is isolated in limited movement, e.g. 'wiggle one foot'. This technique

Fig. 10.1 Group therapy session.

consists initially of unilateral recognition of body parts, then symmetrical. First, the large body parts are named and isolated, then the fingers. These follow the developmental pattern of thumb, little, index, middle and ring.

Kinaesthetic awareness

When all body parts are recognised, with vision excluded, then the planes of movement can be introduced, e.g. 'hands up'. The opportunity should be given to experience these movements in prone and supine and attention drawn to the verbal directional change, e.g. 'head up' is opposite in prone and supine.

Push/pull games increase joint awareness and co-contraction. These should be voluntarily controlled by the child. Smooth rhythmic movements are often difficult and assistance by verbalizing may be necessary.

Tactile awareness

Tactile input is available in many forms. Handling, confining experiences such as rolling in a blanket, rolling in tyres, on varied surfaces all provide touch information which the therapist can use. Touching is a very emotive experience and to many tactile defensive (Ayres) children it is frightening. The mother is most able to handle the child and her cooperation in verbal reinforcement of touch can be invaluable. Firm handling and touching can reduce tactile defensiveness considerably. Withdrawal of touch experience tends to increase the condition and the subsequent process of breaking down the touch barriers can be very stressful.

Emotional withdrawal often manifests itself in tactile defensiveness and projective techniques are the most appropriate, e.g. a cat that wants to be stroked or a cat washing itself.

AXIS APPRECIATION

Awareness of the body axis seems essential to the perceptual sense of self (Laban 1975). We are able through our cerebral integration to move ourselves without vision through 360°, 180°, or 90° in any plane precisely as we wish. Our control of direction, turn right, turn left, is probably based upon this appreciation, as is possibly our understanding of encircling form as in the drawn circle. The ability to stand still with the eyes closed requires a high level of proprioceptive body perception and voluntary adjustment. Once this task is mastered perception of movement can begin. Many children, whose body perception is very poor, cannot initially even stand with their eyes closed. Again imaginative projection can assist therapy.

Technique

Ask the child to perform turning movements very precisely on command with the eyes open. Start with 'turn right round and back again'. Next an 'about turn', then a quarter turn. Once this has been appreciated with visual focus and clues, then it is repeated with the eyes closed. The turn must be a spin not a shuffle.

Five-year-old childen appear to manage this quite well. For many children the use of left or right should be avoided as being abstract. Holding an object one in each hand can overcome this problem and assist the sense of alternate space. The next stage is to introduce directional movement; for example, two steps forward ($\frac{1}{4}$) turn to the 'brick'. When this ability has been visually established the same movements can be carried out with the eyes closed. Therefore all floor plan turns should be 90°, etc., precisely on corners to appreciate the movements involved. A blackboard can then be introduced relating the turns to the drawn line and recognition given to the differences in movement (see Writing Therapy).

Alternative planes of movement can be introduced using an Ayres Scooter Board or crawling.

MOVEMENT AWARENESS

Following body awareness the sense of the moving body can be experienced and understood. It is then possible to voluntarily control the pattern of a movement by analysis. Children of 5 years upwards are capable of this process, the level depending much upon their emotional state rather than intelligence.

Technique

1   Stand in front of a mirror beside the child and shake self about gently like a 'jelly on a plate'. Swing the arms 'like a gorilla'. Alternate with being stiff 'like celery or a carrot' and wobbly like a jelly. Next introduce jumping — the 'jelly' from 'plate to plate'. As individual jumps are achieved introduce more 'plates'. When a fluid and rhythmic jump can be achieved, with feet always landing together, hoops to represent 'plates' can be brought in. This increases the perceptual judgements required. 'Hot' plates encourage rhythmic fluidity.

2   There can then be a steady progression to integrated sideways movements and integrated rhythmic movements.

3   The use of projection as in 'umbrellas opening and closing', 'storks getting muddy feet, so they change legs' and general stories for the younger children provide an interesting and relaxed media for therapy.

4   Rabbits jumping, bears walking, fish swimming (on Scooter Board) can all be 'input' increased by 'looking' turning head from side to side to watch out for trouble.

5   Rolling over the sea to collect fish and return to the 'mermaid' represented by Mum seems to improve rolling performance, failure to arrive at 'the rock' can then be analysed as to why this was not achieved (visual, directional organization, axis and head control) and a repeat attempt may be successful. Verbalization by the therapist during the repeated action is essential.

PROJECTION OF MOVEMENT

Directional Appreciation

Once an appreciation of the body axis and the body moving have been established the use of obstacle courses, floor plans and mazes can introduce precision in the sense of direction.

Obstacle courses giving verbal directions such as around, under, over, etc., provide the earliest reinforcement of the body's deliberate movements through space. They can be expanded as the child progresses to include specific auditory appreciation, motor planning, sequential memory and organization of internal language.

A map drawn on the floor of the roads from 'house' to 'school' plus divergences such as the 'sweet shop' helps to project the concept of turning in a meaningful manner. The child must work out how to get from 'home' to the 'goal' walking along the roads (between the lines) and turning correctly at the corners according to the direction drawn on the floor. Later he is encouraged to plan these mazes himself, giving the therapist directions which must be carried out exactly as the child directs. The language factor is made evident by the 'errors' made by the therapist at the child's instruction. At a higher level a plan drawn on a floor or wall or blackboard can use projections of self to plan the route. This should have been already walked through on the floor-drawn map.

Appreciating corner turning when actually walking from 'home' to 'school' helps to project to reality.

These activities are very helpful in developing the use of internal language organization and self-monitoring.

PERCEPTION OF MOVEMENT OF OBJECTS IN SPACE

Recognition of the properties of the moving self are transcribed to the movements of objects relating to the body.

1   This can begin with judging the movements required to jump forwards over a rope on the floor (feet together) and over other varied objects. The rope can be lifted to introduce varied heights, swung for timing and wiggled for orientation. A good pattern of movement is important at all times. Judging the likelihood of being able to climb through different size spaces in advance helps projection of shape and form. Controlling the body through skittle spaces on a scooter board without knocking them over changes the plane.

2   Being pulled by a rope on a scooter board along a long corridor can give experience of adjusting the body in space on a moving object. Lying or sitting on the board provides alternative planes for adjustment. Sitting on a 4 ft (1.2 m) beach ball or Theraflatable (B. Knickerbocker) shape whilst throwing and catching a ball or varied bean bags increases the need for self-orientation whilst making perceptual and motor judgements.

3   Pointing with one hand whilst aiming with the other appears to improve hand–eye judgements of space. Aiming games which use varied objects, distances and heights that are initially unpredictable help to develop judgements of grading, value and distance.

4   Hoop aiming, floor darts and bean bag boules using varied weight bags are usually popular games. Progress to games such as croquet then bat and ball. These can be easily learnt skills and the aim is to give as much opportunity as possible for varied judgements.

5   Analysis of failure in terms of 'too high', 'too short', help focus concentration on the need for judgements. These games require concentration and can provide an opportunity genuinely to win as well as to accept minor failure. Progress is rewarding in self-image and some learnt skills are to be encouraged for this very reason.

PERCEPTION OF THE MOVEMENT OF OBJECTS AND PEOPLE

This section of the programme can only be carried out in a group setting. The emphasis is on judgements not only of an uncontrolled moving object but anticipation of the behaviour of others. It stresses cause and effect in terms of movement and relies upon awareness of people in space and a high level of selective response.

All team races require anticipation of sequence/rhythm and appropriate response. Team games are at an even higher level. If the group is stable, analysis of the problems that the others present is possible. A good group identity means that mutual support can be very rewarding. If, however, there is little group identification the a token economy system may be necessary to control behaviour. Naturally, the games must be chosen for each member to achieve at some point in the session and equally to fail. Road crossings can present a problem to the children and a session recognizing this difficulty is useful. The major problem is anticipation and projection and sometimes figure ground selection. Each child here needs to be treated as an individual with the group and again analysis training can be exploited.

CONSTRUCTIONAL DYSPRAXIA

Constructional dyspraxia shows itself in the inability to build projected ideas such as garages, houses, etc., in free-form bricks (Lego has reference points on base-boards, etc., so these can usually be used quite well and therefore mask the problem.) Poverty of internal language monitoring is often the root cause in the projection of concepts of structure and form. Treatment should follow the developmental sequences (Sheridan). Initially a 'tower' becomes on the floor a 'train' which snakes around to become a circle. From this basic shape further ideas of angles, spaces, heights can be developed.

Plain-coloured, multisized bricks should be used with farm animals to aid projection.

PENCIL SKILLS AND WRITING

PENCIL CONTROL

Although the dynamic tripod is the usual method of adult pencil grip many and varied finger patterns can be noticed. Poor finger control may disturb fluency and the use of Taskmaster Pencil Grips can often improve efficiency.

Changing a pencil holding position can often add to the stress experienced by the child. Analysis of the grasp is important but only to consider the reason for that particular position. Commonly poor coordination of the fingers results in a thumb/4/5 grasp but this can be more effective when the joint ligaments are lax than the dynamic tripod (thumb/1/2).

Pencil control stems from the shoulder so poor shoulder control will result in poor handwriting presentation.

WRITING

Therapeutic programme for appreciation of movements in relation to writing; age — pre-writing approximately under 8 years of age. The programme will move at a pace acceptable to the child. It passes through the appreciation of movement and its related spatial 'trail' to projection of the 'trail' in writing patterns. The teaching of writing is the speciality of the teacher but the early pencil skills are not established in the dyspraxic child and remediation is necessary at this basic level. Children taken on for this programme should have already received basic therapy as described above.

The progress of treatment is as follows.

1   Body awareness — check.

2   Axis appreciation — treatment usually begins at this stage.

3   Movement trails — several large toy animals are put in a line along the floor and the child is asked to walk past them in a straight line looking at their heads and then return past their tails (Fig. 10.2). The same animals are retained throughout.

Fig. 10.2   Psychomotor therapy for writing dyspraxia.

4   This activity is projected on to a blackboard with simple line drawings of animals and the child is asked to draw a line to show where he walked.

5   The child is then asked to walk in and out of the animals checking their noses are clean and their tails in order. This is then drawn on the blackboard. The animals are wiped away and recognition given to the line remaining, i.e. curvy

Sometimes it is necessary for the therapist to follow the child walking along by trailing a chalk behind him to draw the pattern described by him on the floor. This then relates to the blackboard. This technique can be effective at any stage.

6   The next writing pattern

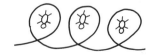

is walked by the child checking each animal's nose and tail all round, tails first, then moving on to the next animal. This is transcribed to the board.

7   The patterns of

are followed by

turning the corners correctly at 90°. After approximately 6 sessions the child is usually ready to progress to the next stage.

Hand–eye coordination in pencil skills

Materials required:
      1 Blackboard approximately 2.6 ft (.75 m) square
      1 Set miniature farm animals
      Coloured chalks.

The blackboard is placed on the floor and the child kneels in front of it. He is told it is a large page on a book and we are going to draw across it. One farm animal is placed on the right and the farmer on the left, directly opposite. The child is then asked to draw from farmer to animal in a straight line. He must put his chalk by the farmer but look at the animal. This ensures the beginnings of the correct hand–eye pattern. Further animals are then placed on the right and the pattern repeated.

Following this, 3 or 4 animals are placed randomly on the board and lines drawn from farmer to animal. As the number of animals increases, the figure ground selection becomes more difficult but if correct eye–hand correlation has been established this is not disturbing.

Once several animals have been introduced the number of points of visit can be increased to encourage planning sequential organization and internal language development. This can be helped by verbalization.

A return is now made to the movement directions of 'inspecting animals'

and the patterns appreciated in the gross projected movement and reduced to fine movements.

Symmetrical movements of the hands which project to writing movements can be used to help directional appreciation (Mesker). This can progress to simple words on the Psychomotor Dominance Board if some writing ability has already been established.

Psychomotor Dominance Board — Mesker and Hofjuizen Hagemejer

The theory of the use of this board is based upon Dr Mesker's principles of cerebral integration through symmetry to laterality, then integration and dominance. The written word is seen as the motor expression of communication so words are total concepts rather than a disjointed collection of letters. Cursive writing is encouraged. He places emphasis on the importance of sensory motor modules having a meaning in experience sound and movement.

Words have Primary (sense recognition), Secondary (word sound) and Tertiary (written module) forms. The Psychomotor Dominance Board treatment relies upon these first two being sensorily meaningful. Although Dr Mesker requires full words to be written immediately in treatment it has been found in practice that unless there is a secure appreciation of letter formation this is impossible.

The Board is placed upon a normal-height table and the child sits with his nose against the joint edges of the upright Board holding a 2.5cm chalk in each hand. This allows visual monitoring of the hand (hand–eye link). Initially a check is made of appreciation of the task and directional efficiency. The patterns

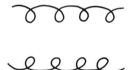

then

are used for familiarization.

Stage One — Symmetry

A check is made of the letter formation taught in school, each letter of the alphabet is written with both hands on the board in the writing direction. Help is given by the therapists writing the letters on the lower blackboard.

Joining up sections of the alphabet such as, abcd, or defg, etc., encourages fluidity. Once all the alphabetical letters have been established as correct formations, progress is made to short words.

Dr Mesker directs that the child should think of these words and their meaning for himself as far as possible. Use is made of the letters that gave the greatest difficulty in the letter formation check. Words such as cat, bed, dog, etc., are used.

The next stage increases the length of the words and begins short sentences, also mainly suggested by the child. Conversations can provide a good basis. Before progress can be made to the establishment of dominance by visual reinforcement the following factors must be established:

1   fluidity of all word formations;
2   good word spacing;

3   symmetrical interaction of both hands;
4   equal appearance of word forms on both sides of the blackboard;
5   good sentence structure.

Stage two — **writing dominance**

Seated in the same position the child is now allowed to bring his head around to the side of chosen dominance as practised. The vision is allowed to monitor this side whilst both hands continue to write sentences on the board.

Dr Mesker's therapists would return then to exercises for cerebral integration before returning to the board. However, it has been found possible to use the board very effectively if attention is given to the initial letter sensory module formation.

Guidelines for use of psychomotor dominance board

Dr P. Mesker, Maastricht, Holland — as interpreted and practiced by the Occupational Therapy Department, Northwick Park Hospital.

Materials

Double-sided Blackboard as Fig. 10.3 (angle exaggerated)

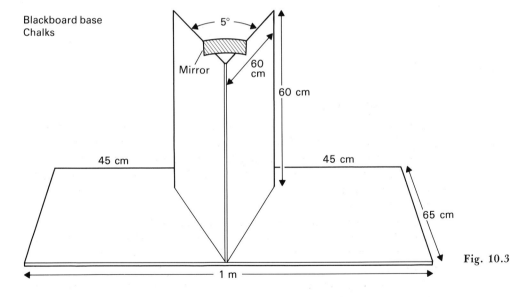

Blackboard base
Chalks

Fig. 10.3

Practice

Followng the psychomotor dominance test as described in English in *Die Menslke Hand* (Mesker 1972) the decision is made regarding the movement direction for treatment. This is normally the hand of choice for writing; left, (centripetal) towards the body, right, (centrifugal) away from the body.

For some children who rely too much on vision in writing, the transfer from symmetrical stage to visual reinforcement returns them to overmonitoring. It is helpful here to write the sentence in symmetry and then repeat it with visual reinforcement.

Another problem can arise with transfer from board to paper. This may be due to too short a time in symmetry or to emotional barriers to the writing task. Writing sentences from board to paper with eyes closed and then with eyes open can help to overcome this barrier.

This technique has been found most effective as it offers an alternative means of approaching a stressful task.

ALTERNATIVE TREATMENTS

Alternative treatments can be based upon movement therapies. The philosophy and science will be related to the media used. Since these children have such emotional distress, help given from any discipline must be effective unless the clumsiness is caused by an essential emotional need. Total lack of progress should be investigated by a psychologist or psychiatrist.

CONCLUSION

A clumsy child is not necessarily unhappy unless this disability is educationally unacceptable or associated with visuospatial perceptual difficulties. There are several theories of both neurological and educational origins, none of which have been proven effective. Treatment should always be based upon observation of the presenting symptoms. The necessary theoretical base will depend upon the original disciplinary training of the therapist. The importance of the total child should be considered at all times and the mind and body should be held as inseparable. Emotional factors have physical presentation and projective techniques provide an excellent medium for treatment.

REFERENCES

Abbie M. (1974) Treatment of minimal brain dysfunction. *Physiotherapy* **60** (7), 203–207.

Abercrombie M.L.J. (1963) Eye movements and perception and learning in visual handicap. In *Visual Disorders in Cerebral Palsy* (ed. Smith V.H.). London Spastics Society. Heinemann, London.

Ayres Jean (1972) *Sensory Integration and Learning disorders.* Western Psychological Services, Los Angeles.

Baker J. (1981) A psychomotor approach to the assessement and treatment of clumsy children. *Physiotherapy* **67** (12), 356–64.

Balow B. (1971) Perceptual motor activities in the treatment of severe reading disability. *The Reading Teacher* **24**, 513.

Bender L. (1938) *Visual Motor Gestalt Test and its Clinical Use.* American Orthopsychiatric Ass., New York.

Bergeres J. & Lezin I. (1965) *Imitation of Gestures.* Clinics in Developmental Medicine No. 18, London Spastics Society, Heinemann, London.

Bradley L. (1980) Reading, Spelling and writing problems: research on backward readers. In *Helping Clumsy Children* (eds McInlay I. & Gordon N.). Churchill Livingstone, Edinburgh.

Burr L. (1979) Treatment of the child with dyspraxia. *Br. J. Occup. Ther.* **42** (2), 34–9.

Burr L. (1980) Use of vision in hand-eye coordination. *Br. J. Occup. Ther.* **43** (2), 59–63.

Dobbing L. & Smart (1973). Early undernutrition, brain development and behaviour. In *Ethology and Development* (ed. Barnell S.A.) Clinics in Developmental medicine. No. 47. Heinemann, London.

Illingworth R.S. (1972) *The Development of the Infant and Young Child, Normal and Abnormal*, 5 ed. Churchill Livingstone, Edinburgh.

Ironside M., Sattler J. & Legay Brereton B. (1975) Cerebral Palsy — Basic Abilities, 2 ed. Spastics Centre, Mosman, NSW.

Kephart N.C. (1971) *The Slow Learner in the Classroom,* 2 ed. Charles Merrill, Columbus, Ohio.

Laban R. (1975) *Life for Dance.* Macdonald Evans, Plymouth.

Mellor R. (1980) *McKinlay and Gordon — Helping Clumsy Children.*

Mesker P. (1972) *Die Menslke Hand.* Dekker Van der Vegt, Nijregan, Nederlands.

Mesker P. (1979) *Kunnen en niet kunnen.* Van Corcum, Assen, Nederlands.

Naville S. (1970a) Psychomotor Therapy. *Remedial Education,* September, p.13.

Naville S. (1970b) Methodologic de la Réeducation Psychomotricité. *Psychomotricité* Geneva.

THEORY REFERENCES

McKinlay I. & Gordon N. (1980) *Helping Clumsy Children.* Churchill Livingstone, Edinburgh.

Delaçato C. (1963) *The Diagnosis and treatment of Speech and Reading problems.* Charles C. Thomas, Springfield, Illinois.

Naville S. & De Ajuriaguerra (1964) *Einture de l'enfant Neuchatel.*

Frostig M. & Horne D. (1964) *The Frostig Programme for the development of Visual Perception.* Follett Educational Corp, Chicago.

Test references

Aston Index. A Classroom test for screening and diagnosis of language difficulties. LDA — Park Works, Norwich Road, London.

Ayres Battery. Western Psychological Services — USA. 12031 Wilshire Boulevard, Los Angeles, California, 90025.

Frostig. *The Marianne Frostig Development Test of Visual Perception.* NFER Nelson Pub. Co. Ltd., Norville House, 2 Oxford Road East, Windsor, Berks.

Goodenough. Draw a Man Test. Part of the Aston Index.

ITPA — Illinois Test of Psycholinguistic Abilities, revised edition. S.A. Kirke, J.J. McCarthy, W.D. Kirk, Univ. of Illinois, Urbana, Ill. 61801 USA.

Mesker Psychomotor Dominance Test. Mesker P. and Hofhuzen Hagemejer J. Dekker, Van de Vegt. Mimogan, Nederland.

Stott D., Moyes F. & Henderson S. (1972) *Test of Motor Impairment.* British Standardised NFER. Pub. Co., Windsor.

FURTHER READING

ABERCROMBIE M.L.J. (1964) *Perceptual and Visuomotor Disorders in Cerebral Palsy.* Clinics in Development Medicine II, Heinemann, London.

CHAPMAN J., LEWIS A. & WEDELL K. (1972) Perceptive-motor abilities and reversal errors in children's handwriting. *J. Learn. Disabil.* **5**, 321–5.

COHN R. (1971) Arithmetic and learning disabilities. In *Progress in Learning Disabilities* (ed. Myklebust H.R.). Crane and Stratton, New York.

CRITCHLEY M (1964) *Developmental Dyslexia.* Charles C. Thomas, Springfield, Illinois.

GRIMSBURY H. (1977) *Children's Arithmetic — the Learning Process.* Harper and Row, New York.

GUBBAY S.S. (1975) *The Clumsy Child.* W.B. Saunders, London.

HASKELL S., BARRETT E. & TAYLOR H. (1977) *The Education of Motor and Neurologically Handicapped Children.* Croom Helm, London.

ILLINGWORTH R.S. (1963) The Clumsy Child. In *Minimal Cerebral Dysfunction* (eds Bax M. & McKeith R.). Little Club Clinics in Developmental Medicine No. 10, The Spastics Society, Heinemann, London.

MCCARTHY, MALI DE (1961) The itpa — an approach to differential diagnosis. *Am. J. Ment. Defic.* **66**, 399.

MILLICHAP J.G. (Ed.) (1977) *Learning Disabilities and Related Disorders.* Year Book Medical Publishers Inc, Chicago.

MCKEITH R. (1963) Defining the concept of minimal brain damage. In *Minimal Cerebral Dysfunction* (eds. Bax M. & McKeith R.). Little Club Clinics in Developmental Medicine No. 10, The Spastics Society, Heinemann, London.

ORTON S.I.T. (1937) *Reading, Writing and Speech Problems in Children.* Chapman and Hall, London.

PIAGET R.M. (1969) *An Outline of Piaget's Developmental Psychology for Students and Teachers.* Routledge and Kegan Paul, London.

ROBERTS A.S. (1968) Poverty of facial function associated with brain damage. *Arch. Gen. Psychiat.* **19**, 491–6.

STOTT D.H. (1977) A strategy for remedial handwriting. *Special Educational Forward Trends* **4**, 20–3.

STRAUSS A. (1947) *Psychopathology and Education of the Brain Injured Child*, vol.1. Grune and Stratton, New York.

TANSLEY A.E. (1974) *Reading and Remedial Reading*, 2ed. Routledge and Kegan Paul, London.

TOUWEN B., PRECHTL H. & BAX M. (1970) *The Neurological Examination of the Child with Minor Nervous Dysfunction.* Clinics in Developmental Medicine No. 38. Spastics International Med. Publications. W. Heinemann, Medical Books, London.

VAN WILSON B. (1967) *Perceptual Motor Training Activities Handbook.* Teachers College Press, Columbia Clinic, New York.

WALTON J. (1963) Clumsy children, p. 24–5. In *Minimal Cerebral Dysfunction* (eds Bax M. & McKeith R.). Little Club Clinics in Developmental Medicine No. 10, The Spastics Society, Heinemann, London.

EQUIPMENT

Ayres Equipment, Western Psychological Services, 12031 Wilshire Boulevard, Los Angeles, California 90025 U.S.A.

B. Knickerbocker, Theraflatables, The Princetown Centre for Learning Disorders, Inc. P.O. Box 6149, Lawrenceville, N.J. 08648 USA.

Vinyl Pencil Grips, Taskmaster Limited, Educational Supplies, Morris Road, Leicester LE2 6BR.

GAMES AND ACTIVITIES

BINDLEY W. & GRIFFITHS R. (1976) *Listening and Speaking Games and Activities to Develop Language Skills.* Nat. Ass. for Remedial Education, London.

COLLEGE OF SPEECH THERAPISTS, Material for Language stimulation, The College of Speech Therapists, 6 Lechmere Road, London, NW2 5BU.

NASH WARTHAN M. (1978) *Take Time.* A programme of activities for children with language problems, co-ordination problems and impaired sense of rhythm.

UPTON G. (Ed.) (1979) *Physical and Creative Activities for the Mentally Handicapped.* Cambridge University Press, Cambridge.

PART 2   Assessment for Neurodevelopmental Physiotherapy for Minimal Cerebral Dysfunction

Pauline Watter

The term *minimal cerebral dysfunction* (MCD) is used as an umbrella term to include that group of normally intelligent children variously described as being clumsy, having attention-deficit problems or sensory integrative disorders. Some, but not the majority of such children, exhibit hyperactivity, while approximately half of school-aged MCD children also have learning disabilities.

The physiotherapy neurodevelopmental assessment of these children should include examination for localizing signs of neurological dysfunction such as tremor, abnormal deep tendon reflexes, clonus, involuntary movements and associated reactions. In general, few of these signs are found to be abnormal in MCD. Additionally, examination for localizing signs of musculoskeletal abnormality should be included.

The examination for non-localizing signs is of utmost relevance in MCD, and should include: the assessment of primitive reflexes; postural and orientation reactions; tactile, vestibular and proprioceptive function; visual and auditory functions; gross and fine motor coordination; and motor planning. It is also useful to monitor the child's written work.

PRIMITIVE REFLEXES

The persistence of primitive reflexes beyond the age when they would normally be integrated is related to the production of abnormal patterns of increased tone in MCD children, and affects their posture and movement. Early in their development MCD infants may exhibit poor sucking or rooting, or strong tongue thrust, contributing to a history of feeding difficulties.

In the older preschool or school-age child with MCD those reflexes most likely to persist include the extensor thrust, the tonic labyrinthine reflex (TLR), the asymmetric tonic neck reflex (ATNR) and the symmetric tonic neck reflex (STNR). When testing these reflexes, the classic testing positions are frequently inadequate, and more subtle testing positions are required. The extensor thrust may only be evident once the child is weight-bearing, and may not be stimulated in supine lying. Similarly, the presence of TLR in MCD children frequently manifests itself in the supine position as a decrease in flexor tone, without an active increase in extensor tone, and the TLR influence is often stronger in supine than prone lying. The ATNR and STNR need to be examined in kneeling on all fours, and the upper limbs may be more affected than the lower limbs in MCD children.

Rather than actually limiting movement, the persistence of such reflex patterns in MCD children tends to affect the quality of movement, and may remain strong due to their compensatory use to provide stability when proprioceptive tone and balance problems exist. Therefore they may remain strong due to the child using them to provide a stable background posture, for example during reading and writing, or eating.

POSTURAL AND ORIENTATION REACTIONS

These reactions are adaptive and provide a positive reaction to influences which may disturb posture. They contribute to the child's ability and confidence in coping with his physical world. In children with MCD they are frequently inadequate being poorly developed or absent. The placing reaction may be difficult to elicit, and functionally may be inefficient. The positive supporting reaction tends to be poor, and can contribute to the motor difficulties of MCD children. The child does not laterally transfer weight well, partly due to poor positive supporting which makes the weight-bearing leg unstable. The child then uses protective reactions in the non-weight bearing (NWB) leg to maintain his one-legged stance, and not his (inadequate) equilibrium reactions in the weight-bearing side. The use of the NWB limb's protective reactions tends to transfer body weight away from the standing leg, further decreasing standing tone in the supposedly weight-bearing leg. The problems just cited also contribute to poor development of skills such as hopping, skipping and galloping in MCD children.

The optical head-righting may be inadequate in either vertical or horizontal suspension. As the body moves through space, a normal child maintains the head above the body midline in the direction against gravitational pull. In MCD children, the abnormal response can be at either of two extremes. It can involve a loss of body tone with the head dropping below the body midline. The child may then become quite difficult to hold since the loss of tone may increase with the length of time the child is suspended. At the other extreme, the child may build up tone and appear 'stiff' to handle, with the head being maintained rigidly in line with the body. Although this child may appear less affected than the other, he still does not adjust dynamically to changes in body position. The increase in tone is frequently an attempt to compensate for the loss of orientation by simply 'holding on' to the original position. Spatial fears of heights, movement or change in position are frequently noted during assessment of this reaction, as are compensations such as tapping the body or stroking the therapist in order to build up sensory clues regarding the body position. The horizontal suspension position is more discriminating than the vertical for MCD children.

Body-on-body righting reaction is generally normal for MCD children, with the exception of those who exhibit hypertonicity or rigidity. The body righting reaction in standing, where the child cannot rotate the head without also rotating the body demonstrates the lack of dissociation of movement in MCD children. Once again the high-toned children seem to show more problems here than do those with low tone. Protective extension of arms and legs is frequently inadequate.

As explained earlier, the normal response can be regarded as being in the middle range of responses, with MCD children exhibiting problems at both extremes of the range. In this case, the reactions can be too slow, being inadequate, poorly directed and coordinated, or non-functional. On the other hand, some MCD children exhibit too-fast protective reactions which may also be jerky and poorly controlled. These fast reactions may contribute to an anxious state of over-readiness in these children, and are their way of coping with their protective dysfunction.

Parachute reactions in both arms and legs are often absent or poorly developed. When the child is lowered quickly to a surface, the arms may flex followed by head and body flexion into almost a 'fetal curl' position. The legs do not automatically take weight, but as the feet hit the floor the child tends to either flex until he has landed in a sitting position, or to extend rigidly and abruptly. In both cases, the child's reaction is not functional and is maladaptive, and it is easy to perceive how this child falls so heavily in apparently harmless situations. Partly, the problem can be exacerbated by the fact that the child may not perceive his position in space or how high he is, and cannot spatially judge how fast he is moving towards the floor. Consequently he may withdraw from the situation (fetal curl) or produce a state of constant readiness (stiffened limbs) in an attempt at coping. Neither response is adaptive; both place the child at severe risk in situations such as school playgrounds.

Equilibrium reactions are learned, and in MCD children the position needed for the establishment of such reactions may not have been achieved. It has been noted that equilibrium reactions are generally inadequate, or may be absent, and when present may only be functional in inner range. Also their control may not have been relegated to sub-cortical centres in MCD children, so when the child ceases to concentrate on balancing, and has to combine tasks such as balancing and catching, then the balance may deteriorate rapidly. It is, therefore, important to assess individual reactions not only specifically but also in functional combinations.

TACTILE AREA

The tactile system is of major importance being the earliest maturing system. It has intermodal links with other systems developing at the same time such as the vestibular and proprioceptive systems, and low-level or early-developing visual and auditory functions. It also affects the level of arousal due to the number of its neurones terminating in the reticular activating system. Much of the infant's early learning is achieved through this system, and the information acquired compared with that from other early developing systems. Errors due to dysfunction in the basic systems can then be laid down, providing a faulty basis for comparison of later-acquired information. In this way tactile dysfunction may contribute to the development of error patterns in other sensory systems developing at the same time, or those which mature later from such a faulty basis. In MCD, dysfunction is likely to be multisensory. Where normal children with these problems may be able to compensate by using another sensory channel, the MCD child may not have any intact channel. His problems will, therefore, be compounded. When assessing tactile function it is important to be aware of the emotional reactions which may be associated with tactile stimulation. MCD children frequently exhibit immature giggling when touched, and less frequently strong negative reactions may be evident. The greatest care must be taken not to alienate children who may show tactile defensiveness, and timing of the tactile assessment will then be important.

Localization of touch over the whole body without using vision is frequently normal in MCD children, but its assessment may provoke frustration, negative or immature reactions. Sometimes, however, MCD children cannot localize touch appropriately for their age, and may not be able to show or name body parts.

Simultaneous touching of two points (without vision) may be poorly recognized but is frequently normal for MCD children. It is worth noting that children with attentional problems or hyperactivity may exhibit considerable tactile dysfunction. Its link with arousal mechanisms can be important in such children.

Localization of tactile stimuli (without vision) in the hands may be quite poor for many MCD children, even at older ages of 8 or 10 years.

When considering such an aspect of hand function, it is invaluable to consider also the proprioceptive components of stereognosis and finger position awareness. While many MCD children, even at preschool age, exhibit no difficulties with stereognosis, severe problems are usually encountered in recognition of finger position.

This involves the ability of a child to copy a finger posture without vision, once they have seen the therapist demonstrate the posture (an easier task) or have felt it demonstrated on their other hand (a harder task). This ability usually develops from about $5\frac{1}{2}$ years of age or during the first school year, and indicates that the child can then monitor finger position on his pencil by proprioceptive input, and does not need to use vision to continually check his finger position. In this way vision is freed for monitoring of writing and letter control.

In children with MCD, due to such tactile-proprioceptive dysfunction, vision is likely to remain tied to the manual act of pencil control, resulting in slow and untidy writing. The visual attention which should be directed to the writing will also be shared with pencil control and such constant shifts in visual focus may heighten problems with attention, making distraction of the child more likely.

PROPRIOCEPTIVE SYSTEM

The proprioceptive system is involved in maintenance of tone, monitoring of body position and has close links with arousal. Muscle tone at rest needs to be evaluated by passive resistance to movement. Many of the younger MCD children exhibit low tone, but the older children frequently exhibit hypertonicity or rigidity. This may sometimes be compensatory in nature, and overlie basic low tone. The high-toned children may also have a limited range of movements due to muscle shortening, and this is particularly noticeable in the hamstrings, hip adductors and internal hip rotators.

The maintenance of static postures without vision can be extremely difficult for MCD children, with tone changes, increased body sway and perhaps total loss of stability occurring. Compensatory input may also be evident. Automatic awareness of body position with subsequent adjustments for comfort are frequently poor, while non-visually directed duplication of demonstrated limb positions is also likely to be affected. Since this often affects arms more than legs, the upper limb may be unstable, contributing to the problems in writing or manipulative tasks. Reactions previously mentioned, such as the positive supporting reaction, are of course affected by proprioceptive dysfunction.

VESTIBULAR SYSTEM

Body tone, arousal, balance, the provision of a stable reference point (i.e. the body) for spatial judgements, and orientation of the body in space without vision are affected by vestibular functions.

The vestibular head-righting reaction is assessed in the same way as the optical head-righting reaction, but with eyes closed. Often the reaction seen in the latter is heightened once vision has been occluded, and fears of space, of heights or movement, as well as compensations to build sensory input for position clues may also be more evident. The basic types of abnormal reactions so common in MCD are also similar to those seen when assessing optical head-righting. The vestibular reaction is the earlier developed of the two.

Vestibular post-rotatory nystagmus, which should be assessed in both directions is also abnormal in many children with MCD. The duration of their nystagmus can be affected, being either too short or too long, while the pattern of beating can also be abnormal. It may be too easy to elicit (e.g. strong response after 3 or 4 spins) or too difficult to elicit (e.g. almost no response after 8 spins). In addition there may be abnormally strong changes in postural tone either during or after spinning, and the physiotherapist must be ready to inhibit negative reactions.

Spatial problems at a physical level can make the child appear clumsy, while at a conceptual level they can contribute to problems like reversals, poor letter shaping or shape copying, as well as conceptual problems in mathematics. Children with vestibular dysfunctions may avoid situations which prove to be disorganizing due to their vestibular effects, such as somersaults, carousels or swings.

VISUAL SYSTEM

Accurate assessment of oculomotor function depends upon adequate motivation of the child, and is affected by attention related factors. It has close connections with vestibular and spatial development, as well as contributing to writing and reading, and to motor factors such as eye–hand coordination and visually directed motor planning.

Optokinetic nystagmus should be assessed as it may be asymmetric in MCD children. Following with the eyes in all directions is frequently poor, as is the ability to fixate. While the latter may affect concentration and eye contact with people, poor eye-follow is associated with reading problems. The MCD child may exhibit visual difficulties such as jerkiness (especially on crossing his body midline), poor follow, either centrally or peripherally, or exaggerated end-point nystagmus, and seems to have more difficulty with composite diagonal movement than in a basic horizontal or vertical direction.

Convergence is frequently slow or incoordinated, and squint may be evident. The ability to fix on an object, then release and refix elsewhere is frequently slow in MCD children. This, for example, affects the ability to copy material from board to book, or to change visual attention from the teacher to a book. If this visual task requires much effort and is slow, consider how poor attention will heighten such problems. Scanning requires saccadic movement, but MCD children tend to have less regular saccades than do normal children. Since visual processing occurs during the saccadic movement (when no vision occurs) such irregularity affects the consistency of supply of visual information to the cortex. Further, the regressive phase of the saccades tend to be larger in MCD, so affected children may be slowed down by excessive re-reading of material. Evidently there are many combinations of visual dysfunctions which can have a variety of outcomes for children with MCD.

AUDITORY SYSTEM

During assessment, the child's ability to localize sounds should be briefly ascertained, as well as any history of middle ear infection. Since many MCD chidren may exhibit auditory discrimination problems, hearing loss from repeated infection, speech problems or aphasia in varying degrees, appropriate assessment by a speech therapist may be indicated.

Auditory sequencing may also be extremely poor, and with memory problems, seems to be associated with difficulties in spelling or recalling arithmetical tables.

MOTOR FUNCTION

As a result of factors such as poor balance, proprioceptive and spatial problems, general gross and fine motor coordination may be affected. In addition, poor rhythm and timing and poor control of speed and direction as well as effort flow, will all increase coordination problems in MCD children.

Coordination of gross and fine motor skills need to be evaluated with respect to the child's age and experience. The qualitative aspect of function is particularly relevant, since the therapist must perceive at which level the child is experiencing difficulty. It is not sufficient to merely note that he cannot hop.

The ability to plan movement appropriate to the situation is often poor in MCD children, and may occur at the fine or gross motor level. Fine motor apraxia affects the organization of activities such as writing and dressing, while gross apraxia will affect whole-body movement planning. Assessment should include the use of visual as well as verbal directions to establish the precise dysfunction. Compensations develop in many affected children; for example the child who cannot follow a visual clue for planning movement may verbally describe to himself what he sees, so transforming the prescribed visual direction into a verbal one, to which he may respond more easily. Unfortunately the child who copies others because he did not 'hear' what to do may get into trouble for 'cheating', and will certainly be slower to start work.

The ability to automatically cross the body midline with the arms is frequently poor, and may result in adjustments of the body or of a book to avoid the need to cross over. Diadochokinesia remains poor or immature in MCD children, with both the pattern of movement and the stability of proximal joints being affected. In general, since the MCD child frequently has not established automatic control of movements like hopping or astride jumping, more complex tasks involving two activities (such as jump and clap) are poorly controlled. As cortical control is used to monitor overlaid movement (e.g. clapping) it is no longer available for the more basic task (jumping) which consequently deteriorates due to the lack of lower level control.

If function in the areas discussed is assessed with respect to the child's age, then his particular dysfunctions and their effects on classroom function become clear. In addition, this provides the therapist with a basis for beginning treatment as well as revealing areas in which further specialist assessment may be necessary; for example, occupational or speech therapy, educational or behavioural assessment may be indicated. With accurate assessment, and active intervention, significant improvement in neurodevelopment function is evident in most children after six months. The use of home programmes with monthly review has emerged as a favoured regime suitable for most parents, with home programmes kept as brief as possible — usually 5 to 10 minutes a day, 5 days each week.

It is essential for the optimal improvement in the child's function that treatment, like assessment, be multidisciplinary, and dictated by the child's specific needs. At the same time the utmost care must be given to maintaining the integrity of the family and providing supportive measures where needed. Overloading the child and family by the involvement of too many professionals can be avoided by establishing the priority of the family's needs. Therapy should enable the family to cope better, and should never increase the stresses under which it operates.

FURTHER READING

AARON P.G. (1978) Dyslexia, an imbalance in cerebral information-processing strategies. *Perceptual & Motor Skills* **47**(3), 699–706.

ACKERMAN T., PETERS J. & DYKMAN A. (1971) Children with specific learning disabilities: Bender Gestalt test findings and other signs. *Journal of Learning Disabilities* **4**, 437–46.

ACKERMAN T., ROSCOE M.A., DYKMAN A. & PETERS J.E. (1977) Teenage status of hyperative and non-hyperactive learning disabled boys. *American Journal of Orthopsychiatry* **47**(4), 577.

ADAMS P.A. (1969) *Handwriting Disabilities in Educationally Handicapped Children; A Siblings Study*. Society for Research in Children's Development, Santa Monica, California.

AMAN M. & MAYHEW J. (1980) Consistency of cognitive and motor performance measures over two years in reading retarded children. *Perceptual & Motor Skills* **51**(3), 1059–65.

AYRES A.J. (1972a) *Sensory Motor Integration*. Western Psychological Services, Los Angeles.

AYRES A.J. (1972b) Improving academic scores through sensory integration. *Journal of Learning Disabilities* **5**(6), 338–43.

BANNATYNE A.D. & WICHIARAJOTE P. (1969) Relationship between written spelling, motor functioning and sequencing skills. *Journal of Learning Disabilities* **2**, 4–16.

BERLIN D., & LANGUIS M. (1980) Age and sex differences in measures of brain lateralization. *Perceptual & Motor Skills* **50**, 959–67.

BIBACE R & HANCOCK K. (1969) The relationship between perceptual, conceptual and cognitive processes. *Journal of Learning Disabilities* **2**(10), 17.

BIZZI E. (1974) Visual motor processing — inner ear: The coordination of eye–hand movements. *Scientific American* **231**, 100—106.

BJORKLAND D., BUTTER E. & WINGLES L (1978) Facilitative effects of haptic training on children's visual problem solving. *Perceptual & Motor Skills* **47**(3), 963–6.

BOLL T. & REITAN R.M. (1972) Motor and tactile perceptual deficits in brain-damaged children. *Perceptual & Motor Skills* **34**, 343–50.

BOND G.L. & TINKER M.A. (1967) *Reading Difficulties: Their Diagnosis and Correction*, 2e. Appleton-Century-Crofts, New York.

BRENNER M. & GILLMAN T. (1960). In *The Neuropsychology of Learning* (eds Knights R. and Bakker D.). University Park Press, Baltimore.

BULLOCK M.I. & WATTER P. (1978) The management of young children with minimal cerebral dysfunction. *Australian Journal of Physiotherapy* XXIV, **3**, 111–19.

BUTTER E. (1979) Visual and haptic training and gross modal transfer of reflectivity. *Journal of Educational Psychiatry* **71**, 2.

CLARK C., BRUININKS R. & GLAMAN G. (1978) Kindergarten predictors of three aspects of reading achievements. *Perceptual & Motor Skills* **46**(1–2), 411–19.

CRATTY B.J. (1974) *Motor Activity and the Education of Retardates*. Lea and Febiger, Philadelphia.

CRATTY B.J. (1975) *Remedial Motor Activity for Children*. Lea and Febiger, Philadelphia.

CRAWFORD J.E. (1966) *Children with Subtle Perceptual Motor Difficulties*. Stanwix House Inc., Pittsburgh.

DENHOFF E. (1968). The measurement of neurological factors contributing to learning efficiency. *Journal of Learning Disabilities* **1**(11), 636–44.

DENHOFF E. (1973) The best management of learning disabilities calls for paediatric skills of a special sort. *Clinical Paediatrics (Phila.)* **12**(7), 427.

DENHOFF E. (1981) Current status of infant stimulation or enrichment programs for children with developmental disabilities. *Paediatrics* **67**(1), 32–7.

DENKLA M. (1974) Development of motor coordination in children. *Developmental Medicine & Child Neurology* **16**, 729–41.

FERRY P. (1981) On growing nero neurongs: Are early intervention programs effective? *Paediatrics* **67**(1), 38.

FIDONE G. (1975) Recognizing the precursors of failure in schools. *Clinical Paediatric (Phila.)* **14**(8), 768.

FINLAYSON M.A. & RETAN R. (1976) Tactile function in relation to cognitive skills. *Developmental Medicine and Child Neurology* **18**, 442–6.

GALABURDA A.M., LE MAY M., KEMPER T.L. & GESCHWIND N. (1978) Right-left asymmetries in the brain. *Science* **199**, 852–6.

GAY A.J., NEWMAN N.M. KELPNEW J.L. & STROUD M.H. (1974) *Eye Movement Disorders*. C.V. Mosby Co., St. Louis.

GESELL A. & ARMATRUDA C. (1971) *The First Five Years of Life*. Methuen, London.

GIBSON J.J. (1966) *The Senses Considered as Perceptual Systems*. Houghton-Mifflin, Boston.

GOLDSTEIN E. (1974) A multidisciplinary evaluation of children with learning disabilities. *Child Psychiatry & Human Development* **5**(2), 95–107.

GRIFFIN D., WALTON H. & IVES V. (1974) Saccades as related to reading disorders. *Journal of Language Disorders* **7**, 310–16.

GRIFFITHS R. (1954) *The Abilities of Babies,* University Press, London.

HARRISON J.A. & BULLOCK M.I. (1978) Post-rotatory nystagmus in hyperactive children with spatial awareness problems. *Australian Journal of Physiotherapy* **24**, 173.

JACOBSON F.N. (1974) Learning disability and juvenile delinquency: A demonstrated relationship. In *Handbook on Learning Disability* (ed. Weber R.E). Prentice-Hall Inc., Englewood Cliffs, New Jersey.

JOHNSON R. & MAGRAB P. (Eds) (1976) *Developmental Disorders: Assessment, Treatment, Education*. University Park Press, Baltimore.

KEOGH B. (1972) Preschool children's performance on measures of spatial organization, lateral preference and lateral usage. *Perceptual & Motor Skills* **34**, 299–302.

KERR R. & BOOTH B. (1978) Specific and varied practice of motor skill. *Perceptual & Motor Skills* **46**, (1–2), 395–401

KNIGHTS R. & BAKKER D. (eds) (1976). *The Neuropsychology of Learning*. University Park Press, Baltimore.

LAMBERT N., WINDMILLER M., SANDOVAL J. & MOORE B. (1976) Hyperactive children and the efficacy of psychoactive drugs as a treatment intervention. *American Journal of Orthopsychiatry* **46**, 335.

LEIB S.A., BENFIELD D.G. & GUIDUBALDI S. (1980) Effects of early intervention and stimulation of the preterm infant. *Paediatrics* **66**(1), 83–90.

LEISMAN G. (1975) Characteristics of saccadic eye movements in attentionally handicapped patients. *Perceptual & Motor Skills* **40**, 803–9.

LEISMAN G. & Schwartz J. (1975) Ocularmotor function and information processing: Implications for the reading process. In *Promising New Methodological Approaches in Understanding the Reading/Language Process* (ed. Kling M.). International Reading Assoc., Newark.

LEVY J. & REID M. (1976) Variations in writing posture and cerebral organisation. *Science* **194**, 337–9.

McMAHON C. (1980) An Evaluation of the Effect of Neuro Sensori-Motor Therapy on the Presence of Behaviour Problems in Children with Minimal Cerebral Dysfunction. Honours Thesis, Department of Physiotherapy, University of Queensland.

MAKRIDES L., MOSHEN R. & REED A. (1980) Skeletal and central nervous system maturation in the child with minimal brain dysfunction. *Canadian Journal of Physiotherapy* **32**(1), 5–9.

MICCINATI J. (1979) The Fermould technique: Modifications increase the probability of success. *Journal of Learning Disabilities* **12**(3), 139–42.

MOSCOVITCH M. & SMITH L. (1979) Differences in neural organization between individuals with inverted and non-inverted hand postures during writing. *Science* **205**, 710–12.

OKE A., KELLER R. & MEFFORD I. (1978) Lateralization of norepinephrine in human thalamus. *Science* **200**, 1411–33.

PETERS M. (1977) Simultaneous performance of two motor activities: The factor of timing. *Neuropsychologia* **15**, 461–5.

PETERS J.E., RONINE J.S. & DYKMAN R.A. (1975) A special neurological examination of children with learning disabilities. *Developmental Medicine and Child Neurology* **17**, 63–78.

PIROZOLLO F. & Rayner K. (1980) Handedness, hemispheric specialisation and saccadic eye movement latencies. *Neurologia* **18**, 225–9.

REITAN R. (1971) Complex motor function of the preferred and non preferred hands in brain damaged and normal children. *Perceptual & Motor Skills* **33**, 671.

ROGERS D. & JONES D. (1980) Information-seeking behaviour in the tactile modality. *Perceptual & Motor Skills* **50**, 1179–91.

ROSSITER E. & LUCKIN J. (1981) Screening for learning problems in the first year at school. *Australian Journal of Physiology* **17**, 29–31.

RUDEL R.G., TEUBER H.L. & TWITCHELL T. (1974) Levels of impairment of sensorimotor functions in children with early brain damage. *Neuropsychologia* **12**, 95–108.

RUTTER M., GRAHAM P. & YULE W. (1970) *A Neuropsychiatric Study in Childhood*. Clins in Dev. Med. 35/36. Heinemann, London.

SCHAIN R.J. (1972) *Neurology of Childhood Learning Disorders*. Williams and Wilkins Co., Baltimore.

SCHUCKERT M., PETRICH J. & CHILES J. (1979) Hyperactivity: Diagnostic Confusion. Annual Progress in Child Psychiatry and Child Development.

SCOTT G.M. (1969) The contribution of physical activity to psychological development. *Research Quarterly* **31**, 307–17.

SEVINE M., RAUH J., LEVINE C. & RUBENSTEIN J. (1975) Adolescents with developmental disabilities: A survey of their problems and their management. *Clinical Paediatrics (Phila.)* **14**(1), 25–52.

SHERIDAN M. (1973) *Children's Developmental Progress from Birth to Five Years; the Stycar Sequences.* N.F.E.R, Windsor.

SILVER L. (1971) A proposed view on the aetiology of the neurological learning disability syndrome. *Journal of Learning Disabilities* **4**(3), 6–15.

TARNOPOL L. (1969) *Learning Disabilities.* Charles C. Thomas, Springfield, Illinois.

TUCKER D., ROTH R., ARNESON B. & BUCKINGHAM V. (1977) Right hemisphere activation during stress. *Neuropsychologia*, **15**, 697–700.

WEISS B., HECHTMAN L. & PERLMAN T. (1978) Hyperactive as young adults. *American Journal of Orthopsychiatry* **48**(3), 438.

WITELSON S.F. (1976) Sex and the single hemisphere: Specialisation of the right hemisphere for spatial processing. *Science* **193**, 425–7.

WITELSON S.F. (1977) Developmental dyslexia: Two right hemispheres and none left. *Science* **195**, 309–11.

ZIVIANI J., POULSEN A. & O'BRIEN A. (1982) Effect of a sensory integrative/neurodevelopmental programme on motor and academic performance of children with learning disabilities. *Australian Occupational Therapy Journal* **29**(1), 27–53.

CHAPTER 11

SPINA BIFIDA

Sophie Levitt

Spina bifida is one of the most common congenital abnormalities in the West. It is aetiologically associated with anencephaly and the encephalocele which are neural tube malformations. Spina bifida may occur with hydrocephalus, mental handicap, congenital deformities of legs, neck, trunk, cleft palate and hare lip as well as abnormalities of urinary tract. Visual handicap and cardiac problems may also be present amongst this multiplicity of defects.

The cause of these developmental defects is unknown but genetics, environment, diet and/or drugs may all play a part. The defect occurs in the early weeks of pregnancy when the development of the neural tube, later to become the spine and brain, occurs. Special tests may detect cases of anencephaly or spina bifida before the birth of the baby.

VARIETIES OF SPINA BIFIDA

Spina bifida occulta

The vertebral arches are unfused but there is no herniation of the spinal cord or its membranes. Skin changes, a hairy patch or unusual dimples or fat may appear over the defect. Nothing may be observed unless a spinal X-ray for some other reason is taken which reveals the split or bifid vertebra. Usually there are no neurological signs but some may occur especially after a growth spurt. There is often muscle imbalance in the feet, pes cavus or unusual foot growth in some of these children.

Spina bifida cystica

These include the children most handicapped as, besides the defective structure of the bones of the spine, there are also abnormalities of the spinal cord itself to a greater or lesser degree. There are two types
(a) Spina bifida with meningocele. Vertebral arches are unfused with a sac or lump of dura or meningeal membranes covered with skin herniating out of the spine. Nervous tissue is usually not present in the sac but, if it is, it does not create any neurological signs. Cervical meningoceles are the most frequent.

(b) Spina bifida with myelomeningocele. The herniation of the meninges contains nervous tissue creating abnormal neurological development and symptoms.

This chapter is mainly concerned with the child with myelomeningocele as his problems increasingly occupy paediatric therapists.

ASSOCIATED DEFECTS

Hydrocephalus is expected with 80% of myelomeningocele Hydrocephalus may also occur without spina bifida due to prematurity, precipitate birth, meningitis and other reasons. There is obstruction to the flow of the cerebrospinal fluid which circulates around the brain and spinal cord. Abnormal amounts of fluid collect within the cerebral ventricles leading to enlargement of the baby's head. The head may also be normal at birth but grows abnormally during the early months of life. Since 1956 neurosurgical valves and shunts for the fluid to control the hydrocephalus have been devised. Details of these procedures may be read in medical publications elsewhere (Durham-Smith 1965; Lorber 1970; Stark 1977).

Other defects include diastometamyelia in which a bony spur projects into the spinal canal splitting the cord in two. One side may remain normal while the other is paralysed in such a case. Hemivertebrae may occur and give rise to various scolioses, kyphoses or kypho-scoliosis. Syringocele or a cavity in the spinal cord may take place within the herniated sac. Syringomyelocele are cavities connected with the central canal and a distended canal of the spinal cord. Cranium bifidum or malformation of the occiput with a meningocele or encephalocele of brain tissue are also related defects. These additional defects occasionally cause death, if not some cases may become the brain damaged children seen in cerebral palsy units, severe mental handicap centres or who remain in spina bifida and neurological units. However many are only minimally handicapped.

Anencephaly or absence of the brain is incompatible with life.

Congenital Deformities. These are discussed below as they are common to the spina bifida child and form a large part of the therapy programme.

ASSESSMENT

Assessment will discover the neurosegmental level of the lesion. Most spina bifida children are affected in the lumbosacral area, but it can occur in all parts of the spine from cervical to sacral.

Sensory losses occur at all segmental levels corresponding closely to each level. Incontinence may also be a problem at each level.

CERVICAL SPINE

Assessment may reveal cervical scoliosis, torticollis or deformities of the shoulder girdle. Arm muscles and fine finger movements may be impaired.

The paralysis is rarely complete and the upper and lower limbs may be spastic as well. Control of urine and faeces may be absent. Cervical myelomeningocele is very rare.

THORACIC SPINE:UPPER LEVEL

Considerable deformity of the rib-cage may be common. Chest ailments are frequent, as is incontinence. Complete paralyses of the lower limbs may occur or paresis of varying degrees. Spasticity may be present. The child's weak trunk muscles make sitting unsupported impossible. If the arms are very weak they cannot be used to assist sitting, but with therapy some children acquire adequate strength to do so and use crutches. Their legs must be well splinted in appropriate orthoses (calipers). Although a few become ambulant in childhood, all become wheelchair users in their teens. Spinal and thoracic deformities often require special chairs or surgical intervention.

THORACIC SPINE:LOWER LEVEL

Some trunk muscle strength allows individual children of this group to achieve independent sitting. Their adequate arm strength makes it possible for them to cope well with wheelchairs and wheelchair transfers. A parapodium and crutches are used to walk around until wheelchairs are preferred in the child's teens.

UPPER LUMBAR SPINE

Hip flexors, adductors and, to a lesser extent, quadriceps are functional. Muscle imbalance around the hips often leads to dislocation. 70% of spina bifida patients have their last two thoracic segments and lumbar levels involved. They may achieve walking with long leg calipers (knee-ankle-foot orthoses) though wheelchairs may become preferred in adulthood. Incontinence of urine is present and circulatory problems as well as poor condition of their leg bones may often occur. As sensation is absent, fractures of their osteoporotic bones occur easily, remaining undetected. Care of their legs is important to prevent fractures, burns and other accidents.

LOWER LUMBAR SPINE

There is good function of hip flexors, adductors, quadriceps and some abductors and medial hamstring activity. Hip instability is again a problem as, besides the weak muscles, the hip joint is shallow without the tone to stabilize it. When legs are affected the feet may increase the problems if they are weak and deformed. Various deformities are common and splintage and surgery are necessary to obtain a plantigrade foot for walking. Below-knee calipers (ankle-foot orthoses) are usually worn.

SACRAL SPINE

Usually there is a mild paralysis with weak hip extensors and abductors. The feet are mainly affected, with pes cavus developing in many children. Incontinence is a major problem as nerve supply of the genito-urinary muscles comes largely from this part of the spine. Lack of sensation is a problem and circulation may also be affected.

TOTAL ASSESSMENT

Assessment of the child or baby will, therefore, consist of examinations of the following.

Muscle status which may be flaccid paralyses or weakness (see p. 181, Table 12.1).

Sensory loss: touch, pressure, temperature and proprioception.

Spasticity, which may be spinal if some reflexes remain, or cerebral if hydrocephalus has caused brain damage — both may occur.

Incontinence of urine and faeces or just urine.

Deformities of neck, trunk and especially of hips, knees and feet.

Circulation, especially of the child's legs.

Secondary osteoporoses with possibility of fractures. Secondary tissue trauma.

Developmental retardation of the child's mental, social, emotional and perceptual levels as well as his physical development. Locomotor disabilities cause the primary motor delay but hand skills can be affected (Rosenbaum *et al.* 1975). Speech and language handicaps associate more with hydrocephalus. Speech and language problems may exist due to developmental delays as well as specific syndromes such as the 'cocktail party' chatting associated with these usually lovable, happy children. The witty chatter often misleads others into thinking that many of the spina bifida children are brighter than they are. Intelligence varies from very bright to below normal.

Learning difficulties have been detected and need assessment by psychologists and teachers (Anderson & Spain 1977).

Comprehensive Assessment by a team of professionals is obviously needed.

MANAGEMENT

The management of the child with his individual set of problems requires a great number of people including the neurosurgeon, orthopaedic surgeon, urologist, bowel management specialist, nurses, physiotherapist, occupational therapist, social worker, teachers and others when appropriate. It is vital that this multifaceted care is coordinated and carefully controlled and integrated with the parents and their child. The cooperation of the child and his parents will be important and, at times, difficult because of the emotional stress and many practical problems which inevitably confront them. Teamwork with the parents is thus an essential part of the programme.

The physiotherapist who is in frequent contact with the child and his parents often develops close relationships with them, helping to allay some of the many anxieties and reporting specific concerns to other professionals more able to deal with them.

THE THERAPY PROGRAMME

It is impossible to isolate the therapy programme from the many other treatments needed for the child, as well as from the severe emotional factors which may arise at different stages. However, one can define the main objectives of the therapist as:

1   prevention and correction of deformities;
2   development of motor abilities, particularly locomotion;
3   development of body image, exploration of the environment and counteraction of secondary intellectual retardation; communication and social skills will be promoted;
4   prevention of skin and soft tissue trauma;
5   selection and supervision of equipment, especially of the fit and function of orthoses;
6   general encouragement and support of the child and his family. This includes help with physical and psychological aspects.

PREVENTION AND CORRECTION OF DEFORMITIES

The disrupted nerve supply from the spine results not only in paralyses but muscle imbalance. This leads to abnormal postures and movements. The abnormal postures or positions of the spine and joints of the limbs may also occur because of gravity when, for example, flail hips fall into flexed, abducted and externally rotated positions. The lack of sensation aggravates the situation as the child may not be stimulated to move out of prolonged positions even if some muscle power is present. Intensive physiotherapy linked with the orthopaedic management is required to correct or reduce existing deformities and to minimize the risk of further deformities occurring. The child will, therefore, be given maximum opportunity to progress through the developmental stages of childhood.

Treatment begins from the day the baby is born. Deformities may be present at birth. Most common of these is talipes equinovarus as well as dislocation of the hips. The orthopaedic surgeon decides the timing and extent of surgery and when to use conservative methods. Talipes equinovarus or other deformities may first be strapped, or serial plasters used. More care must be taken by the physiotherapist in using splints or strapping owing to the baby's loss of sensation, poor circulation and the condition of his legs. Different techniques of strapping and splinting are used by different orthopaedic teams.

In addition to the corrective strapping there will also be a need for the physiotherapist to passively stretch and correct the baby's feet. Maintenance of joint range continues up to about 3 – 4 months old when reassessment occurs. If correction has not been achieved, surgeons will select appropriate operations to establish a more normal posture of the feet. Orthoses may then be applied to ensure maintenance of the corrected positions. Numerous foot deformities may be seen at birth or develop when the child begins to take weight through his feet.

Hip dislocation may be a true congenital dislocation or due to muscle imbalance. The unopposed activity of the hip flexors and also of the adductors pulling the head of the femur partly or fully out of the shallow acetabulum may occur. Hips may merely be 'at risk' from birth. Different approaches are used by surgeons. Splints keeping the legs in corrective positions have been designed by different authorities. The physiotherapist and nurses will take care to prevent pressure and skin damage especially in the presence of wet, soiled nappies.

Surgery for the hip and the need to reduce dislocations is much discussed and different procedures planned. Correction by individual surgeons depends on when it is thought that the child has good potential for walking. Less extensive procedures such as soft tissue releases may be preferred for children who walk or who use a wheelchair as their prime means of mobility.

Deformities of the hip may occur without dislocation. Hip flexion is often present and with the surgeon's agreement, hip extension stretching can be started. The baby's hips are normally flexed at birth so that full range is only obtained after several weeks. The full extension is also developed by the nursing position in prone and later by placing the baby in the prone position for periods. Adductors also require attention to prevent shortening and deformity. As much hip mobility as possible is actively encouraged. If hip flexion persists, secondary lordosis of the lumbar spine is common.

Leg positions in children with total paralyses must be corrected, particularly if gravity throws them repeatedly into abnormal positions.

Besides corrective procedures for the child's hip and feet, knees may need treatment. Flexion, valgus or extension deformities of the knee occur. Flexion deformities may be the result of spasticity of the hamstrings. They may also develop when the child has a weak quadriceps and being unable to extend his knee sufficiently stands and walks with a flexed knee for a period of time.

Surgical intervention may be considered if the deformity is greater than 20 degrees. Valgus deformities usually seen in children with lower thoracic or upper lumbar lesions are considered to be the result of unopposed activity in the tensor fascia latae, or to arise following fractures of the femur or tibia close to the knee. This deformity may be corrected by supracondylar osteotomy of the femur and release of the tensor fascia latae. Knee extension deformities may be seen at birth in children with lower lumbar lesions causing unbalanced activity of the knee extensors. Serial plasters as well as various surgical operations may be used to correct these deformities.

Spinal deformities involve the original vertebral anomalies as well as those that develop due to muscle imbalance or paralyses. The presence of any spinal deformity will affect the baby's development of sitting comfortably or securely. It will also affect the child's ability to stand or walk in spite of good orthopaedic management of the lower limbs. Asymmetry and deformity may also lead to increased weight and pressure ulcers on one side of the child's body.

Careful positioning, training and surgical management are required. Some surgeons carry out extensive surgery involving fixation of the spine. Specially moulded and padded seats may be indicated and corrective therapy techniques used.

Prevention and correction of deformities is closely related to the varying degrees of muscle activity which can be obtained in each child. The development of motor abilities will, therefore, influence the results obtained.

DEVELOPMENT OF MOTOR ABILITIES

Motor abilities consist of the muscle actions which comprise the movements and postures seen at different stages of child development. The presence of paralyses and weakness as well as deformities leads to modifications of the normal motor developmental schedules. Should hydrocephalus also exist or have come under control, the bigger head, as well as the brain damage that may remain, require additional modifications as discussed in Chapters 2 and 9.

Developmental motor training for movement and postural balance mechanisms (Levitt 1982) as discussed in Chapter 2 will be used. Spina bifida children will require different orthoses to help them achieve the upright posture and increased mobility as soon as possible. This will also have a beneficial effect on their cardiovascular systems, kidney drainage and bone growth.

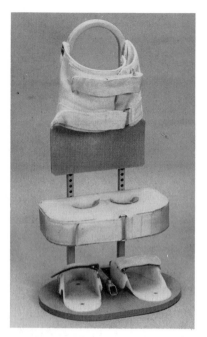

Fig 11.1   Standing brace.

Developmental physiotherapy for the infant begins in hospital and is of special importance as assessments of movement and sensation are simultaneous with treatment. Assessments and treatment use infantile reflexes and automatic movement reactions. The spontaneous movements and positions of the infant are studied as well as ranges of movement and deformities. Mothers are helped to handle their babies and bond with them (see Chapter 6). Passive stretching and positioning are patiently taught to mothers and fathers. Splints, which are carefully padded to prevent pressure, may be used. Parents will learn how to apply splints and how long to leave them on.

Developmental therapy at home.   Most therapy can be carried out at the child's home so that parent instruction and encouragement must continue. Motor developmental delay is common owing to many factors. The repeated hospitalization is particularly demanding in the life of a spina bifida child. Delay due to periods of immobilization is inevitable so that developmental therapy is needed to help these children. They also do not learn normally and in an uninhibited way and may lose motivation or become fatigued by their many handicaps. Nevertheless, there are children who will respond to, say, training of head control, sitting balance and pulling up to standing at normal developmental ages. Any obesity should be avoided as this also delays the development of locomotion.

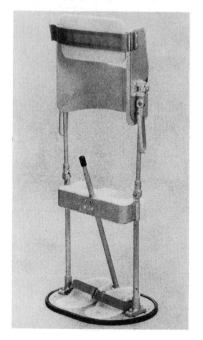

Fig. 11.2   Parapodium.

Orthoses.   Once pulling up to standing occurs, the child finds it very difficult to maintain standing with little if any muscle power in his legs. Most of his weight will be taken through his arms and he will need correctly selected orthoses to help him.

A standing brace may be given to aid standing if he shows an inclination to this. The brace has simple foot supports on a base plate, a frame with knee supports and an elasticized thoracic support (Fig. 11.1). Initially it can be used by the child at a sand or water tray to play with friends there or at a table. Many children have become mobile in the brace using walking aids such as rollators, parallel pusher, H-frame or elbow crutches. These children use a swivel, swing-to or swing-through action to achieve mobility.

Children with thoracic level lesions will continue to need extensive support similar to the standing brace. Progression to a parapodium will be considered after 4 years of age according to regimes in some centres. The parapodium incorporates hip and knee joints so that the child can sit down. A simple combined mechanism for locking and unlocking the hip and knee joints is located at the level of the hip joints. A knee extension pole, easily reached by the child, just above the knee support allows the child to manually extend the knees when moving from sitting to standing and when donning the parapodium (Ontario Crippled Children's Centre. Fig. 11.2). Mobility with aids described with the standing brace above may be used. Both these orthoses provide 'crutchless standing' as they supply complete support and leave the hands free for use. Another device found helpful in some centres, for both standing and mobility is the swivel walker (Shrewsbury or the Orlau types).

In the discussions above of the different neurosegmental levels of spina bifida the recommended types of orthoses have been given (see Figs. 11.3 and 11.4). Some centres only use standing frames followed by orthoses.

Muscle activity.   Although the developmental training activates the muscles if innervation exists, additional physiotherapy techniques of facilitation and strengthening may still be required for specific muscles. Arms and trunk muscles often need extra strengthening and play activities or motivating exercises will be selected for each child. Reassessment of muscle actions is continuous during therapy sessions or at occasional check-ups by therapists so that information can be reported to surgeons and orthotists.

Deformities have been discussed above, with the hip and feet needing particular consideration for standing and walking. Adequate foot–floor contact must be obtained through correction of foot deformities. A minimum of two-thirds of the sole is thought to be necessary for weight-bearing when standing (Sharrard 1971). The spine also affects walking and the stance for gait.

Maintenance of joint range is helped by the development motor skills but passive full ranges still need to be carried out to avoid shortening of soft tissues and muscles. Care must be taken that no undue stress is placed upon joints and bones which do not have the muscular support around them. Increased risk of

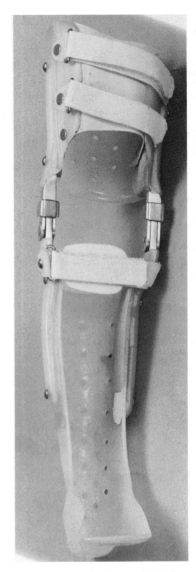

Fig. 11.3   Knee–ankle–foot orthosis.

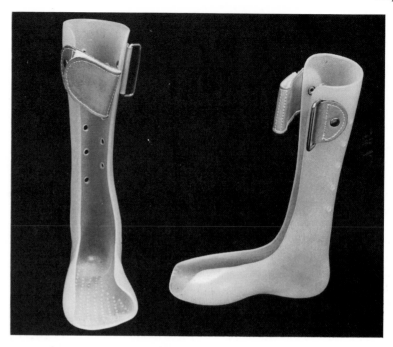

Fig. 11.4 Ankle–foot orthoses.

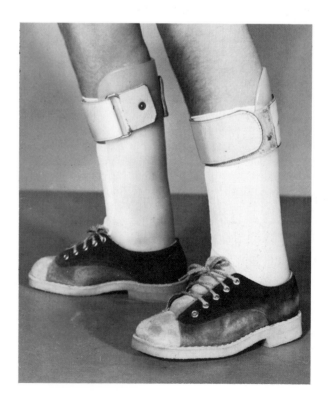

Fig. 11.5 Ankle-foot orthoses.

fracture is present. This risk is further increased during the first 3-4 weeks following removal of plasters and immobilization after surgery.

Mobility aids.   Before using as well as whilst moving in the orthoses, the child also needs other forms of mobility. In his prone development he reaches the stage when he can push himself along the floor on a prone trolley. This strengthens his arms, neck and back muscles and helps to extend his flexed hips.

Mobility in sitting can be facilitated by the caster cart or Chailey chariot. This allows the child to move around independently at floor level, which is appropriate for his early stage of development. He learns to manoeuvre himself and the cart, and also to get in and out of the cart with little or no assistance. Other mobility toys are being developed and designed for both indoors and outdoors. Special moulded seats can be incorporated in these aids for those children who need them.

Wheelchairs of correct measurements and types will be needed when the child is older. They may be used for longer journeys or used only outside or in special situations. The type of ambulation achieved and the motivation to use any independent walking will affect the choice and use of a wheelchair.

Walking aids will vary according to the child's level of development of postural control and neurological control of his limbs. The strength of his arms and his motivation influence how much aid is given. Fears and mental retardation will play their part in choice of walking aids.

Fig. 11.6 Caster cart.

The child's home, school and playground must be visited by therapists as part of their assessment of what constitutes the best mobility aid for each child (see Chapter 15). Other developmental aspects influencing motor control are discussed below.

Development of body image, exploration of the environment and counteraction of secondary mental and perceptual retardation; promotion of communication and social skills; development of fine finger actions and hand skills — in the development of the whole child all these aspects will need careful consideration and planning. The hospitalization, the anxious overprotection by many parents and the many problems facing the child tend to prevent his acquisition of many everyday experiences. Associated brain damage may add to these difficulties. All therapists must coordinate their work and, together with the child's teachers and playgroup workers, provide opportunities for the child's development.

Specific training or teaching will also be important. Self-care often needs specific occupational therapy sessions for the child. Physiotherapists and occupational therapists may use the training of dressing and undressing to teach not only the social skill, but also body image. The child should be taught to put on his orthoses as part of his everyday life. It provides an opportune time to reinforce learning concepts such as 'the strap goes over my feet' or 'the belt goes around my tummy', and so on. Hand skills are encouraged in performing these tasks. Extra hand coordination activities must be given, as many of these children have a developmental delay in fine motor skills whether their hands are neurologically affected or not. Should any visual problems be present additional training will be needed for these children (see Chapter 14). The loss of sensation in spina bifida requires that extra experiences be given to the child for body image, including body parts recognition, as well as for exploratory activities using his hands and body.

Muscle-strengthening exercises can be incorporated into all these activities. The child may learn to put on his standing brace while he sits on the floor. He then learns to roll over from supine to prone in his brace and take weight through his hands pushing up with straight elbows into standing. He will need to push or pull up using a stable piece of furniture or a ladder-back chair. Another benefit of using his arms to get up from and get down on to the floor is that he learns to deal with toppling over and overcomes his fears of falling.

All the motor training and the use of mobility aids, as well as suitable playthings and friends at school and home, help his all-round development.

PREVENTION OF SKIN AND TISSUE TRAUMA

At first, parents and therapists will take care of the child's insensitive skin, but gradually each child assumes this responsibility for himself. He must visually check feet and legs to make sure they are well away from hot radiators, not pressing against objects or that his feet are resting securely on the footrests of chairs or wheelchairs. Temperature of bath water will have to be tested and other such problems anticipated.

Orthoses must be put on with care and all pressure points checked and protected. The heels must be positioned well in, for example, a polypropylene ankle-foot-orthosis or the foot may become more deformed as well as tissue breakdown occuring. Felt, foam or lambswool can be used for lining.

Correction of any foot deformities is not only important for good weight-bearing and development of standing ability, but helps good fit of shoes. The child without sensation in his feet which are also deformed will take excessive weight through a reduced area of his soles. There will thus be increased pressure on these areas as well as against poorly fitting shoes. Tissue breakdown and skin ulcers are inevitable. The long period of non-weight-bearing required to heal tissues and the consequent disruption for the child is most undesirable.

Prolonged periods of sitting can cause pressure sores on the buttocks. A child should learn to relieve the pressure regularly by pushing up on the arms of the chair, lifting the buttocks off the seat. Special cushions designed to reduce the risk of excessive pressure should be an integral part of a wheelchair prescription. Skin of the feet, legs and buttocks should be checked daily for signs of pressure or breakdown. Undetected fractures should be looked for in any child who appears ill, has a swelling and is generally in discomfort. Exuberant callus formation may draw attention to the underlying fracture.

Fig. 11.7 Powered caster cart

SELECTION AND SUPERVISION OF EQUIPMENT. CHECKING FIT AND FUNCTION OF ORTHOSES.

These have already been discussed in relation to deformities and as part of the motor and other developmental needs of the child. There will be growth of the child with regular adjustments of equipment required as well as other changing needs throughout childhood. The therapists will have to contribute to the assessment, fit and correct use of all equipment and orthoses. The child's environment will also change as he grows up and he will often need patient instruction in the use of new aids and orthoses.

GENERAL ENCOURAGEMENT AND SUPPORT OF THE - CHILD AND HIS FAMILY.

The physiotherapist is often the liaison between teachers and hospital, between parents and other consultants and team members. This is because the focus on locomotion is inevitably the prime aim of the child's habilitation programme. However, as with other childhood disabilities, the needs of the whole child must be considered. Despite the many handicaps it is possible to emphasize the child's assets in each case. Many of these children do well in regular schools with therapists advising and supporting the school staff as well as giving therapy if and when it is indicated.

Appointments to see the many consultants should be coordinated so that the parents are not put under extra strain with repeated journeys. Surgery is often needed not only for the deformities but for the urinary problems and occasionally replacements of the shunt when it blocks.

Urinary problems.   Parents will have received appliances and instructions for training their child from consultants and nurses. Intermittent catheterization is taught to parents and later children learn to do this for themselves. The ileal loop operation where the ureters are diverted through the body wall into a special bag makes the child independent of nappies and he becomes more socially acceptable. Wet pads or nappies are an additional problem in the prevention of skin pressure ulcers. Some children may be trainable. Whatever approach is taken the therapist will reinforce the programme and help the parents to integrate this in the total treatment plans. They must be particularly aware of urinary tract infection, the common cause of hospital admissions of these children. Parents must know the signs and seek help.

Incontinence of faeces.   This is usually managed by establishing a routine that probably includes a high-fibre diet and regular toiletting. Children may be given medications, disempaction and enemas in some cases. The routine is taken over by the child when he can understand this. The ability to get to the toilet, transfer on to it and generally deal with sitting and other related aspects must be considered in the therapist's management. Lack of control of the bowel is not only socially embarassing but may lead to chronic constipation or perhaps pressure of hard stool on a catheter of the ventricular-peritoneal shunt. General malaise, often associated with constipation, will affect the child's motivation and other physical abilities. Fortunately, the great majority of these children manage to achieve some control, especially since new methods of urinary control of the urinary diversion operation has dealt with keeping the child dry.

Emotional and social problems have already been mentioned above; this is more fully discussed in Chapter 1. Parents' Associations are in existence in many countries and much strength and information is drawn from them for the family as well as for the child, adolescent and adult. Easy to read brochures and books are available from ASBAH, Tavistock House North, Tavistock Square, London WC1 and from the Ontario Crippled Children's Centre, Rumsey Road, Toronto M4G IR8, Canada (see also Lorber 1970, 1972; Nettles 1972).

Parents need one person they can always contact when they are anxious. They may be the first to notice subtle changes in the child's ability and health. The shunt may be blocking or there may be early neurological signs such as from a tethered cord. They need to report excess irritability, vomiting, shunt-drowsiness, tightness of the skin or a bulge over the myelomeningocele repair, increased head size and bulging of the fontanelle in a baby or headaches, neck or back pain in a child. Skin and fracture problems and many other concerns may occur. Parents' observations may not be any cause for concern and it is important that there is someone immediately available to reassure them, or arrange immediate assistance. Recreation, education, training, sex and marriage are today subjects which have been studied, with encouraging information for many people with spina bifida. Parents and child must have someone to talk to about all this and with whom they can work out their individual problems.

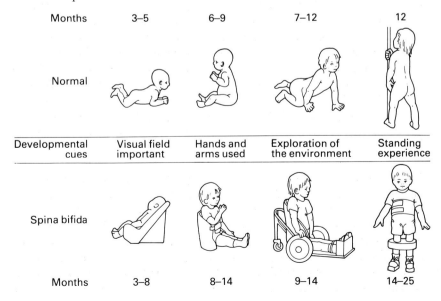

Months	3–5	6–9	7–12	12
Normal				
Developmental cues	Visual field important	Hands and arms used	Exploration of the environment	Standing experience
Spina bifida				
Months	3–8	8–14	9–14	14–25

Fig. 11.8 Developmental therapy for children with spina bifida.

ACKNOWLEDGEMENT

I would like to express much appreciation for helpful discussions and advice for this Chapter from Christine White, formerly of Ontario Crippled Children's Center, Toronto, and Christine Howell, Deputy Superintendent Physiotherapist, Queen Elizabeth Hospital for Children, London, and to Doctor Werner Schutt, paediatric neurologist, Bristol.

REFERENCES

ANDERSON E.M. & SPAIN B. (1977) *The Child with Spina Bifida.* Methuen, London.

BROCKLEHURST GORDON (ed.) (1976) *Spina Bifida for the Clinical.* Spastics Int. Med. Publ. Heinemann, London.

DURHAM SMITH E. (1965) *Spina Bifida and the Total Care of Myelomeningocele.* Charles C. Thomas, Springfield, Illinois.

LORBER J. (1970) *Your Child with Hydrocephalus.* ASBAH, London.

LORBER J. (1972) *Your Child with Spina Bifida.* ASBAH, London.

LEVITT S. (1982) *Treatment of Cerebral Palsy and Motor Delay.* 2e. Blackwell Scientific Publications, Oxford.

NETTLES O.R. (1972) *Growing Up with Spina Bifida.* Scottish Spina Bifida Association, Edinburgh.

ROSENBAUM P., BARNITT R. & BRAND H.L. (1975) A developmental intervention programme designed to overcome the effects of impaired movement in spina bifida infants. In *Movement and Child Development* (ed. K.S. Holt), pp. 145–56. Spastics International Medical Publications, London.

SHARRARD W.J.W. (1971) *Paediatric Orthopaedics and Fractures.* Blackwell Scientific Publications, Oxford.

STARK G. (1977) *Spina Bifida: Problems and Management.* Blackwell Scientific Publications, Oxford.

FURTHER READING

ELLISON-NASH D.F. (1969) Urinary problems of spina bifida. *Developmental Medicine and Child Neurology* **11**(1), 105.

FORSYTHE W.I. & KINLEY J.G. (1970) Bowel control of children with spina bifida. *Developmental Medicine and Child Neurology* **12**(1), 27.

HAMILTON E. (1972) Developments in techniques for ambulation for spina bifida children. J. Canadian Physio. Assoc. **24**, (1), 17–19

HASKELL S. & PAULL M. (1976) *The Nursery Years.* ASBAH, London.

LLOYD-ROBERTS G.C. (1971) *Orthopaedics in Infancy and Childhood.* Butterworth, London.

LORBER J. (1971) Results of treatment of myelomeningocele. *Developmental Medicine and Child Neurology* **13**,279.

MENELAUS M.B. (1980) *The Orthopaedic Management of Spina Bifida Cystica,* 2e. Churchill Livingstone, Edinburgh.

NETTLES O.R. (1982) Spina bifida and hydrocephalus. In *Cash's Textbook of Neurology for Physiotherapists* (ed. Downie P.A.) pp. 348–77. Faber and Faber, London.

SHARRARD W.J.W., ZACHARY R.B. & LORBER J. (1967) Survival and paralysis in open myelomeningocele with special reference to the time of repair of the spinal lesion. *Developmental Medicine and Child Neurology Supplement* **13**, 35.

SHEPHERD R.B. (1974) *Physiotherapy in Paediatrics.* Heinemann Medical, London.

STALLARD J., ROSE G.K. & FARMER I.R. (1978) The Orlau swivel walker. *Prosthetics & Orthotics International* **2**, 35–42.

CHAPTER 12
ASSESSMENT AND PRINCIPLES OF MANAGEMEMENT FOR MUSCLE DISORDERS IN CHILDHOOD

Sylvia A. Hyde

The physical management of children suffering from one of the 'dystrophies' presents the physiotherapist with a great challenge, requiring skill, expertise and vigilance if the optimum outcome for the child is to be achieved. Profound muscle weakness is the common feature shared by this group and it primarily affects the proximal muscle groups, causing considerable disability, particularly in tasks associated with standing and walking. Imbalance of muscle strength and the inability to move normally predispose to the development of severe contractures at the peripheral joints (hip, knee, ankle) and spine. Indeed, the presence of joint deformity is sometimes the pattern of the disease, as for example in congenital muscular dystrophy, but this is more rarely the case and deformity is essentially preventable. Inevitably normal skeletal growth has an adverse effect on the child's ability to attain an adequate level of physical performance given such marked muscle weakness. As the child experiences growth spurts the precariously balanced biomechanical system often falters and, therefore, great vigilance is required in monitoring the child's performance at these times if crises are to be averted. A further difficulty in infants and very young children is to determine how much of the apparent disability is simply due to delay in achieving normal motor milestones and how much is the result of the disease process.

The nomenclature and classification of muscle disease in childhood is often confusing and often complicated by the tendency for personal names to be attributed to specific diseases. Developments in the understanding of the genetic basis for many of the diseases and the development of histochemical processes permitting more definitive diagnosis have compounded the problem, because what was originally thought of as one disease is now often recognised as several different and separate disease entities. The most useful working classification is that advocated by Moosa (1974), who suggests an anatomical approach to the problem. Briefly the disease is then classified according to the antomical origin, anterior horn cell, nerve fibre, neuromuscular junction or muscle. Further subdivision of these groups of diseases is then possible based on genetic inheritance and characteristic clinical features so that the descriptive terms, muscular dystrophy, spinal muscular atrophies, congenital myopathies, metabolic myopathies, myotonic disorders and floppy infant are used.

In one chapter it is impossible to describe the pathology and detailed management of such a large group of diseases and the reader seeking such detail is referred to larger standard texts (Dubowitz 1978; Walton 1981). In the following paragraphs the general principles of physiotherapy for muscular dystrophy will be described and the particular problems of management and the methods of treatment used in some of the more frequently occurring forms of the disease will be discussed.

ASSESSMENT

The cornerstone of effective active management is a sequential comprehensive, quantitative assessment of the child's motor ability to provide a baseline from which to plan treatment programmes and to monitor the progression/regression of the disease and the effect of therapy.

There are various methods of assessment (Fowler & Gardiner 1967; Ziter *et al.* 1977) and they all endeavour to provide information on muscle strength, joint range of motion, the presence or absence of fixed deformity and some measure of physical performance. In this chapter the method developed and used at the Hammersmith Hospital is briefly described. The methodology has been thoroughly tested and its validity established (Scott *et al.* 1982).

METHOD OF ASSESSMENT

1   History — a complete history of the progress of the disease is essential.
2   General observations — of gait and posture both in sitting and standing.
3   Muscle strength — this is evaluated in two ways, namely by manual muscle testing and myometry.
(a) Manual muscle testing. The muscle group to be examined is placed in standard positions and its ability to work either with gravity eliminated, against gravity or against the additional resistance offered by the examiner, graded on a 0–5 scale (Table 12.1). The scale used is that of the MRC (1976).

Table 12.1   Voluntary muscle force. MRC grading of muscle strength (MRC 1976). Manual muscle test.

Score 0 – 5

0	No contraction
1	Flicker or trace of contraction
2	Active movement with gravity eliminated
3	Active movement against gravity
4	Active movement against gravity and resistance
5	Normal power

Overall total muscle strength is then expressed as a percentage where:

$$\frac{\text{Total score}}{\text{Total muscles tested} \times 5} \times 100 \text{ is used.}$$

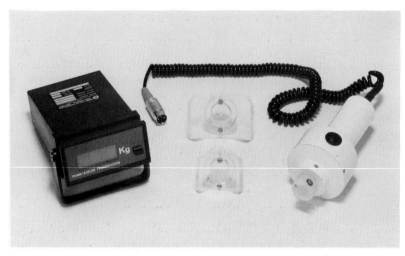

Fig. 12.1   The myometer.

This method, although useful in providing a global picture of muscle strength, is semi-objective relying heavily on the experience of the examiner.

(b) Myometry. This is an objective way of measuring the force output of muscle groups in kilograms force. The myometer used (Fig. 12.1) consists of a force transducer* mounted in the head of the apparatus and connected to a small recording box that provides a readout in kilograms force. The machine is small, completely portable and is powered by mains or battery and so is ideal for use in the clinic. Standardized positions for both placement of the myometer and the muscle to be tested are used. The child is encouraged to make a maximum voluntary contraction to break point and the best of three attempts is recorded. It is usual to examine eight key muscles, namely, hip abductors, hip extensors, hip flexors, knee extensors, foot dorsiflexors, shoulder abductors, wrist extensors and neck flexors. Normal values for these groups using a handheld dynamometer have been determined (Hosking *et al.* 1976).

MOTOR ABILITY	Score 2,1,0
Lifts head	
Supine to prone over right	
Supine to prone over left	
Prone to supine over right	
Prone to supine over left	
Gets to sitting	
Sitting	
Gets to standing	
Standing	
Standing on heels	
Standing on toes	
Stands on right leg	
Stands on left leg	
Hops on right leg	
Hops on left leg	
Gets off chair	
Climbing step – right leg	
Descending step – right leg	
Climbing step – left leg	
Descending step– left leg	
Total out of 40	

Fig. 12.2

4   Range of motion and joint deformity — these are measured using a goniometer and recorded according to the standards accepted by the Joint Meeting of Orthopaedic Associations, Vancouver, 1965 (AAOS 1965).

5   Motor ability — a progression of twenty movements based on a normal developmental sequence are performed and scored according to achievement; where he succeeds = 2, minimal reinforcement = 1, fails = 0. The child attempts each movement and a maximum score of 40 is thus possible (Fig. 12.2).

6   Physical performance — two standardized timed walking tests are used to measure the time in seconds taken to walk as quickly as possible over a standard distance of 28 feet (8.5 m) and 150 feet (46 m) respectively.

*Penny and Giles Transducers Ltd, Airfield, Christchurch, Dorset, BH23 3TH

Table 12.2 Functional classification (Vignos & Watkins 1966).

Class	Level of mobility
1	Walks, climbs stairs
2	Walks, climbs stairs, needs a railing
3	Walks and climbs stairs with great difficulty
4	Walks, rises from chair, cannot climb stairs
5	Walks, cannot rise from chair or climb stairs
6	Walks with assistance; walks independently with long leg braces
7	Walks in long leg braces, requires assistance for balance
8	Stands in long leg braces, unable to walk, even with assistance
9	Wheelchair bound

7 Functional classification — this provides an indication of the child's general functional level and the nine point scale of Vignos (Table 12.2) is used (Vignos *et al.* 1963).

8 Anthropometric measurements of height and weight should be recorded.

9 Supplementary information.

(a) Neurological. Where the child has a mixed problem or there is reason to suspect more central involvement, other methods of assessment described elsewhere in this book will be used to supplement the information obtained.

(b) Gestational age. In the newborn the neurological examination is greatly affected by gestational age and the reader is referred to the methods described by Dubowitz and Dubowitz (1981).

(c) Gait analysis. It is occasionally necessary to use more sophisticated and specific methods of gait analysis to provide detailed information on the many variables of gait cadence, stride length, etc. (Sutherland *et al.* 1981).

(d) Radiological Examination. Although the physiotherapist does not request this diagnostic test it is essential that she is aware of skeletal deformations as these will often influence the therapy programme designed for the child.

10 Patient records — The exact format of these will more frequently be determined by the institutional code of practice. However, it is absolutely essential that adequate and detailed records are maintained and that the information is easily retrievable and meaningful.

AIMS OF PHYSIOTHERAPY

These may be summarized as:
1. maintenance or improvement of muscle strength;
2. prevention of contractures and deformity;
3. maintenance or improvement of function;
4. promotion or prolongation of ambulation.

METHODS OF TREATMENT

Exercise

This is used to fulfil two purposes in the treatment of muscle disease of childhood, first to strengthen muscle and second to encourage motor learning. It is proven that muscle, and in particular the type II fibres, responds to working against a maximum load. Maximal-resisted exercise is, therefore, given to the affected groups; maximum resistance being defined as the greatest resistance that can be applied whilst yet still permitting a smooth, coordinated movement to occur through the range of motion. The ability of a muscle to develop tension and its force output varies through range, that is from the lengthened to the shortened position, manual resistance is, therefore, the best method of applying resistance.

The most useful and selective techniques are those of proprioceptive neuromuscular facilitation (Fig. 12.3 Knott & Voss 1968). Repeated contraction, in the shortened range pivoting on the appropriate joint, is often the technique of choice. Resisted mat work is particularly helpful and affords the opportunity of strengthening the trunk, neck flexors, extensors and gaining head control. Mat work is also beneficial because in this position the child feels quite secure in activities such as resisted rolling, bridging and kneeling, all of which work the trunk muscles effectively. Resisted walking and stabilization in standing, sitting and kneeling are also helpful in improving trunk stability and mobility.

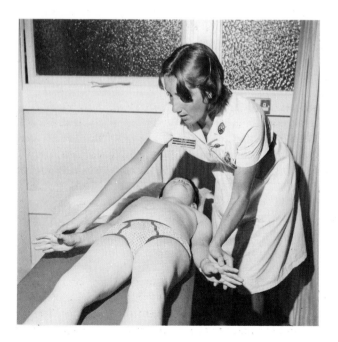

Fig. 12.3   Resisted exercise.

The use of weight and pulley systems to offer resistance to muscle activity has limited benefit in these children since these techniques are rarely sufficiently selective and often encourage bizarre movements.

Parents have been found to comply with manually resisted exercise and with skilled instruction develop considerable expertise. Free active exercise is also encouraged both as a treatment medium and as a recreational activity as developed in sporting activities.

For many years there was divergence of opinion about the use of resisted exercise in Duchenne muscular dystrophy largely based upon the concept that the disease was of neurogenic origin. It was felt that undue fatigue associated with activity might accelerate the destruction of muscle fibres and enhance the replacement of muscle tissue with fatty tissue. However, Vignos and Watkins (1966) reported no such findings when they evaluated the effect of a vigorous rehabilitation programme and, more recently, a controlled feasibility study using resisted exercise in boys with Duchenne muscular dystrophy reported no such finding (Scott *et al.* 1981b).

Passive stretching

The development of contractures leading to fixed deformity is the most disabling and often painful sequelae to poor management. Prevention of these is essential and passive stretching of the tight soft tissue and ligamentous structures around the affected joint should be performed on a regular daily basis. The most commonly affected structures are the tendo achilles, knee flexors, hip flexors and iliotibial band; in most of the muscle diseases these are synonymous with the pathomechanics of the disease, all tending to occur as weakness advances and the child, in an attempt to maintain equilibrium, adapts extreme postures. Inevitable as some degree of tightness of these structures may be, every effort to contain them must be made. Contracture at the knee, shoulder, elbow and wrist should never occur and where they are present, represent a failure of management.

A regular daily programme of passive stretching has been found to be effective in preventing deformity and there is evidence to suggest that this also enhance the child's mobility (Scott *et al.* 1981a). It is essential that parents and even older siblings are carefully instructed in the performance of passive stretching and their technique should be checked at each clinic attendance to ensure that this continues to be performed correctly. The development of contractures is insidious and, regrettably, still too many clinicians wait until there is measurable tightness before commencing treatment.

Night splints

The provision of lightweight plaster of Paris night splints is invaluable in controlling contractures, especially of the tendo achilles and of the wrist flexors. The splints should be made so that the tight structures are held on stretch but no attempt should be made to achieve an over-corrected position as this will be uncomfortable and lead to child and parent rejecting them; further correction can be achieved as subsequent splints are made. The splints must be carefully made and lined to avoid producing pressure areas. In recent years many new splinting materials have become available but plaster of Paris remains the material of choice for this application.

The splint for the tendo achilles is moulded to fit from the most distal part of the toes to an inch below the head of the fibula. When making the splint the physiotherapist must ensure that the calcaneum is held in neutral rotation, equinovarus corrected and that the tibia is not rotated. Attention to detail in finishing the splint will ensure that it is comfortable and does not produce pressure areas, such detail includes using a plaster cream to smoothe the inside of the splint and lining it proficiently with lint so that rough edges are covered. Reinforcement strips are added to the very light shell to make it stronger and robust.

When the completed splint is dry, it should be fitted on the child and carefully appraised. The parents are cautioned to observe the skin for any signs of pressure areas developing, and advised to contact the therapist if this should occur. Pressure areas do not disappear spontaneously and the splint must be modified.

In Duchenne muscular dystrophy it is rarely necessary to splint joints other than the ankle, except in the late stages of the disease, but in spinal muscular atrophy and congenital muscular dystrophy the varied pattern of joint involvement may necessitate splinting other joints. The necessity for splinting will become obvious through assessment and appropriate splints should be provided.

Serial splinting

Serial plasters are often indicated in the treatment of congenital muscular dystrophy, arthrogryposis and in those cases of dermatomyositis where prevention of deformity in the active phase of the disease has not been successful. Serial plasters are used for gaining range of motion at the ankle, knee and wrist. It is essential to ensure, by radiological examination, that the joint space and bone density are normal before attempting this technique. Serial plasters are made using gypsona and the bony prominences must be very carefully padded with felt to avoid pressure areas. The plaster cylinder is then applied with the joint and its attendant ligamentous structures held in the optimum position of stretch that the child can tolerate. After three days the plaster is carefully wedged to gain a few more degrees of correction. This procedure is repeated several times. Alternatively the plaster may be bivalved and the plaster of Paris splint removed several times a day for periods of strengthening exercises.

Regardless of the method chosen, it is essential that an intensive programme of strengthening exercises is given so that the child develops control over the additional range of movement obtained.

Positioning

Careful attention to sitting posture and adequate attention to the detailed requirements for chairs and wheelchairs will help to prevent peripheral joint deformity and scoliosis of the spine (see Chapter 15).

Prone lying

Encouraging the child to spend at least half an hour each day lying prone to passively stretch the hip and knee flexors, an activity easily accomplished whilst watching television, will do much to prevent contractures developing. It is important to ensure that the hips and knees are really stretched and that the feet are at 90°. It may, therefore, be necessary to place a small wedge just above the knee but not under the hip, with the feet positioned over the edge of the bed.

Breathing exercises and postural drainage

These are usually only needed in the late or terminal stages of Duchenne muscular dystrophy or in the rare case that experiences troublesome, recurrent chest infections with difficulty in expectoration. Children with the intermediate and severe forms of spinal muscular atrophy encounter more problems with respiratory embarrassment due to the involvement of the intercostal muscles; these children also often have a very narrow antero–posterior diameter at the apex of the chest. The detailed positions for postural drainage and exercises to improve lateral costal breathing are found in the standard texts (Gaskell & Webber 1980).

The use of adjuncts, such as intermittent positive-pressure breathing (IPPB) apparatus, to respiration in the terminal stages of muscle disease is a controversial subject. Fortunately, it is not the physiotherapist who must make the decision and this will be dictated by the ethos of the unit and the wishes of the parents. Where the child is in distress and IPPB is requested a face mask must be used because these children lack the ability to close their lips over the mouth piece.

Home Programme

In children with chronic or progressive disease it is essential that interruption of their schooling and leisure hours by attendance at hospital out-patient departments is kept to an absolute minimum, such attendances being restricted to follow-up clinic appointments and short periods of intensive treatment at critical points in management.

An individually structured, short, simple programme of exercise that can be done at home is , therefore, taught to parents and child. This programme should be revised, reviewed and amended as necessary following each assessment. Various voluntary organizations produce helpful literature on home treatment and recreational activities (Harpin 1981 a & b; Hyde 1983).

Patient and Parent Education

Every effort must be made to ensure that both the child and parents understand the objectives of physiotherapy and the methods by which these are going to be achieved. Time spent explaining in simple terms 'the why, when and how' is well rewarded in cooperation and trust. The physiotherapist must remember that listening is often more important than talking and to do so will often reveal problems or anxieties that the parents were too shy to mention in case they sounded too trivial or complaining.

MANAGEMENT OF NEUROMUSCULAR SCOLIOSIS

In order to maintain the spine in equilibrium over the pelvis, the gross architecture of the skeletal spine and rib cage must be intact and the muscles acting on and over the bony articulations must be in balance.

In neurogenic scoliosis the cause is obviously one of muscle imbalance and often gross muscular insufficiency; the precipitating cause, however, is often postural asymmetry of the pelvis arising from tightness of hip flexor tendons and/or the iliotibial band. Unlike idiopathic scoliosis, where the progression of the curve is more predictable and usually associated with growth, neuromuscular scoliosis is not predictable and tends to progress very rapidly, so much so that it is frequently described as the 'collapsing spine'.

In Duchenne muscular dystrophy, scoliosis usually develops as the boy begins to spend more time in a wheelchair since, whilst still ambulant, the extreme lordotic posture with facet locking militates against scoliosis. The best method of treatment is by prevention, so careful examination of the spine at the early stage, attention to sitting posture and the provision of a seat mould for the wheelchair-bound child will do much to retard the development of the inevitable scoliosis (Gibson *et al.* 1978). Unfortunately, although many different types of spinal brace have been tried none have proved to be really effective except for the mildest curves.

In the intermediate spinal muscular atrophy child and the hypotonic infant the scoliosis often begins as the child attempts to achieve sitting balance and, if allowed to develop, it deteriorates rapidly and prejudices the chance of a successful outcome. The application of formal spinal orthoses (Boston, Milwaukee) is not possible on small infants under two years of age, so the physiotherapist makes a jacket out of Plastazote reinforced with Vitrathene. The jacket usually extends from the occiput to the level of the hip and is firmly moulded over the iliac crests; anteriorly the jaw is supported with the head held in the neutral position. The jacket is side fastening with Velcro straps. Initially some clinicians and parents were concerned that immobilizing the trunk would inhibit the development of muscular control, however, our experience has been that, by controlling the trunk, useful movement in the legs and arms has been enhanced and the promotion of motor achievement encouraged. As muscle strength and control improve the jacket is modified.

Increasingly, surgical intervention is advocated to stabilize the spine. Formerly the most frequently used procedure was that of Harrington (1962) but now intervertebral wiring after Luque and Cardoso (1977) has gained favour in these very young children.

MANAGEMENT OF SPECIFIC DISEASES

DUCHENNE MUSCULAR DYSTROPHY

This is an x-linked recessive disease and the course of the disease is one of progressive loss of muscle strength, most marked in the knee extensors, hip extensors and hip abductors producing a marked impairment in the ability to walk.

The child with Duchenne muscular dystrophy typically presents with a slightly toe-stepping, wide-based, waddling gait, which becomes more marked and bizarre as he attempts to run. It is often this that is first noted by the parents, although sometimes it is not until the child has difficulty in rising from the floor and mounting steps that they realize their child is handicapped. This pattern reflects the symmetrical muscle weakness initially affecting the proximal muscles and in particular the hip extensors, hip abductors and knee extensors; as the disease progresses the weakness becomes more profound until all the muscles are involved. The severity of the disease varies but the rate of deterioration is said to be uniform in an individual boy (Ziter *et al.* 1977).

The pathomechanics of ambulation have been widely investigated and well discussed (Sutherland *et al.* 1981). Essentially the child adopts an increasingly severe lordotic posture and the feet are held in equinus, this is an attempt to maintain his centre of gravity within his base and is a direct response to the weakness affecting the hip abductors and extensors, knee extensors and trunk muscles (Fig. 12.4).

Physiotherapy is given to prevent flexion contractures at the ankle, knee and hip; in the later stages of the disease it is also necessary to avoid contractures at the elbow and wrist. The treatment of choice is the early use of night splints and passive stretching of the tight structures as previously described.

Resisted exercise should be undertaken to preserve muscle strength using the techniques described earlier.

Unfortunately, somewhere between the age of 8 and 10 years the muscle weakness becomes so profound that the boy ceases to walk independently. Careful and regular assessment, as outlined, will enable the physiotherapist to predict this critical event and, hopefully, to have prepared the boy and his parents for that moment. At this stage child and parents are faced with the choice of accepting total wheelchair dependency or attempting to prolong ambulation by the use of appropriate orthoses. Correct timing of surgical/orthotic intervention is crucial and should be just as the boy goes off his feet; delaying action until the child is already completely wheelchair bound

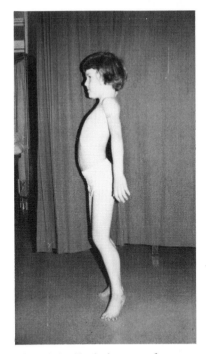

Fig. 12.4 Typical stance of Duchenne muscular dystrophy child, note the plantarflexed foot, slightly flexed knee and hip with increased lordosis of lumbar spine.

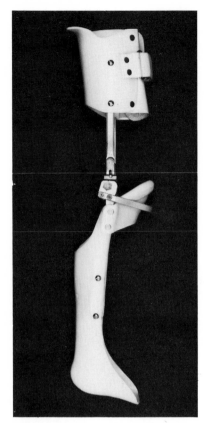

Fig. 12.5 Knee–ankle–foot
orthosis.

prejudices the chance of a successful outcome and once the boy has been wheelchair dependent for three months or more, it is very unlikely that he will walk again.

The desirability of attempting to prolong ambulation in Duchenne muscular dystrophy was for many years a subject for controversy amongst clinicians, some putting forward the view that it was unfair to subject the boy to possible discomfort and effort in the face of a progressive disease, whilst others felt that a measure of independence made it worthwhile. However, the development of improved orthoses and the use of modern lightweight manufacturing materials has largely resolved the problem.

An ankle-knee-foot orthosis, modified after Siegel (1975) is used (Fig. 12.5). It is made of polypropylene and consists of a quadrilateral thigh piece with a well-developed posteromedial lip connected to the lower leg section by lightweight steel side supports. The lower leg is moulded round the calf and extends over the ankle and foot to the base of the metatarsals. The knee hinge is made so that it can be locked in weight-bearing and is fitted with a ring release mechanism so that the child can unlock the knee joint himself. The orthoses are worn beneath trousers and the foot piece fits inside ordinary shoes, so that they are cosmetically very acceptable. It is usually necessary to perform subcutaneous tenotomies of the tendo achilles prior to fitting the orthoses. This is a simple procedure, the child is then put in plaster of Paris, long leg casts and walking re-education begun twenty-four hours later. The formal orthoses are then fitted approximately one week later.

The outcome and benefits of this method of attempting to prolong ambulation have been reported on favourably by several investigators (Siegel 1977; Ziter & Allsop 1979; Hyde *et al.* 1982).

Inevitably the disease progresses to the stage where the child is confined to a wheelchair. Regrettably, there is then a tendency for parents and professional staff to neglect measures to prevent deformity. However, this is when vigilance is really required and the therapist must be diligent in pursuing passive stretching and splintage. Deformity, once advanced, causes considerable discomfort to the child and makes transfers from bed to chair, and chair to toilet difficult. Scoliosis tends to develop rapidly, ultimately causing respiratory embarrassment. Various methods for controlling scoliosis at this stage have been described, these include seat mould inserts, prophylactic jackets and spinal bracing. Few of these methods claim noteworthy success.

SPINAL MUSCULAR ATROPHIES

This is a group of hereditary diseases presenting with proximal symmetrical muscular atrophy associated with degeneration of the anterior horn cells. Although clinically classified as occurring in three forms, mild, intermediate and severe (Table 12.3), in practice there is considerable overlap especially between the mild and intermediate forms of the disease. The child with the severe form

Table 12.3   Clinical Classification of Spinal Muscular Atrophy.

Classification	
Severe	Unable to sit
Intermediate	Able to sit but unable to stand
Mild	Able to stand and walk

(Werdnig Hoffman) only places a demand on the physiotherapist in terms of managing respiratory distress; this arises from the paralysis of the intercostal muscles. Intercurrent chest infections cause the infants early demise, usually within the first year of life. The extent to which active physiotherapy, consisting of postural drainage, vibrations and suction, is required will be much dictated by the physicians', and, hopefully, parents' philosphy. Certainly every effort should be made to ensure that the child (and parents) are not distressed. The physiotherapist, therefore, teaches the parents how to perform postural drainage and, if necessary, suction at home. Sometimes, it is also necessary to advise on positioning of joints unprotected by muscle tone and, therefore, subject to trauma.

The intermediate and mild forms of the disease require far more aggressive treatment and seldom is the need for thorough assessment more important. Active resisted exercise to develop potential muscle strength is essential, whilst splinting is used to prevent contractures, to stabilize unprotected joints and to encourage function.

Scoliosis develops very early in these children and every effort must be made to prevent and control this whilst the child's potential muscle strength is exploited. Until the child is old enough to fit formal orthoses, a Plastazote jacket extending from the pelvis to occiput is used (Galasko 1977).

Some of the children with the intermediate form of the disease will achieve ambulation with assistance; for example, a child may wear lightweight splints to control the knees and ankles in standing whilst being encouraged to use the arms, hands and trunk in activities such as drawing on a blackboard. This not only stimulates the child mentally but encourages the development of postural control. The approach to the provision of splints and formal orthoses must remain flexible and the effects of these carefully monitored; this may mean considering the biomechanical implications on joints far removed from those splinted; for example, in fitting a child with below-knee orthoses and elbow crutches, one may be giving greater freedom at the knee, without doubt an important feature in negotiating stairs, but by encouraging forward flexion of the spine predisposing to the development of scoliosis. The difficulties of managing the neurogenic spine and controlling scoliosis have been described earlier.

In the mild form, ambulation is certainly possible but the child will need frequent courses of intensive physiotherapy particularly during growth spurts.

CONGENITAL MUSCULAR DYSTROPHY

These children present at birth with weakness and usually associated hypotonia. Contractures of muscles are often a major feature of this disease causing more disability and impairment of function than the muscle weakness itself. In general, this is not a progressive disease and, therefore, a positive attitude to mobilization should be taken. General strengthening exercises are essential and an aggressive, but as far as possible conservative, approach to the reduction of contractures is needed.

The use of serial plasters to improve joint range of motion is definitely advocated and often provides the most rewarding results. The application of plasters must be done with extreme care to avoid pain and the possibility of creating pressure areas. It is essential that an intensive programme of resisted exercise is undertaken at the same time to strengthen the muscle in the range of motion that has been gained. Failure to do this will make the child more unstable.

INFLAMMATORY MYOPATHIES

This term covers a group of diseases where in some the cause is known but in others the exact aetiology remains unclear. Only one member of this group will be discussed.

Dermatomyositis

This disease although classified with polymyositis in the adult form is recognized as a quite seperate disease entity when presenting in childhood and is probably due to an underlying angiopathy (Banker & Victor 1966). Muscle weakness is one of three cardinal signs of the disease and is usually proximal and symmetrical in presentation, often starting in the pelvic girdle and progressing to the thighs and upper shoulder girdle.

The aims of physiotherapy as described in earlier paragraphs are to prevent deformity and improve muscle strength; there is, however, an additional and important contribution to be made in providing accurate measurement of muscle strength for the determination of drug therapy. The course of the disease is unpredictable and varied, with periods of remission punctuated by acute exacerbation.

In the chronic stage the child often presents with contractures at hips, knees, shoulders and ankles, these are primarily due to the replacement of muscle fibre with fibrous tissue during the healing process but in childhood dermatomyositis the deposition of calcium in the interstitial tissues of muscle itself or in the subcutaneous tissues is marked and may cause further disability.

Corticosteroids are usually effective in treating the disease but immunosuppressive drugs such as methotrexate are sometimes needed. The most efficient way of determining dosage is clinically to carefully monitor change in muscle strength. It is usual for the physiotherapist to choose three or four muscle groups and measure the strength of these weekly using the myometer.

Detailed instructions for the physiotherapy required for this group can be found elsewhere (Hyde 1980).

OTHER CONDITIONS

In the preceding paragraphs no attempt has been made to detail the physiotherapy treatment but rather the general principles have been outlined. There are many omissions, for example that wide group of diseases known as the congenital myopathies, the limb girdle dystrophies and fascioscrapulo-humeral dystrophies; the list is manifold. However, the principles of management are similar.

CONCLUSION

In summary, active physiotherapy has an important part in the management of the 'dystrophies' and muscle disease in children. The contribution made by techniques of exercise, splinting and passive movement and attempts to prolong ambulation have been the subject of research and have been found to be very beneficial in achieving the best outcome. There is no longer reason to accept the idea that because there is no cure available there is no treatment either. The basis of effective management is continuous, comprehensive, quantitative assessment of all the physical parameters so that treatment programmes can be clearly defined.

REFERENCES AND FURTHER READING

AAOS (AMERICAN ACADEMY OF ORTHOPAEDIC SURGEONS) (1965) *Joint Motion: Method of Measuring and Recording.* E. & S. Livingstone, Edinburgh and London.

BANKER B.Q. & VICTOR M. (1966) Dermatomyositis (systemic angiopathy) of childhood. *Medicine* **45**, 261.

DUBOWITZ L. & DUBOWITZ V. (1981) *The Neurological Assessment of the Preterm and Full-term Newborn Infant.* Clinics in Development Medicine 79. William Heinemann Medical Books Ltd, London.

DUBOWITZ V. (1978) *Muscle Disorders In Childhood.* W.B. Saunders Co. Ltd, Philadelphia.

FOWLER W. & GARDINER G. (1967) Quantitative strength measurements in muscular dystrophy. *Archives of Physical Medicine and Rehabilitation* **48**, 629–44.

GALASKO C.B.S. (1977) The 'difficult' spine. *Israel Journal of Medical Science* **13**, 197–202.

GASKELL D.V. & WEBBER B.A. (1980) *The Brompton Hospital Guide to Chest Physiotherapy,* 4e. revised by B.A. Webber, Blackwell Scientific Publications, Oxford.

GIBSON D.A., KORESKA J., ROBERTSON D., KAHN A. & ALBISSER M. (1978) The management of spinal deformity in Duchenne's muscular dystrophy. *Orthopaedic Clinics of North America* **9** (2), 437–50.

Harpin P. (1981) With a little help. *Mobility* VI. Muscular Dystrophy Group of Great Britain.

Harpin P. (1981) With a little help. *Leisure* VII. Muscular Dystrophy Group of Great Britain.

Harrington P.R. (1962) Treatment of scoliosis — correction and internal fixation by spinal instrumentation. *Journal of Bone and Joint Surgery* **44A**, 591.

Hosking G.P., Bhat U.S., Dubowitz V. & Edwards R.H.T. (1976) Measurements of muscle strength and performance in children with normal and diseased muscle. *Archives of Diseases of Childhood* **51**, 957–63.

Hyde S.A. (1983) *Parent's Guide to Physical Management.* Muscular Dystrophy Group of Great Britain.

Hyde S.A. (1980) *Physiotherapy in Rheumatology,* Chapter 11. Blackwell Scientific Publications, Oxford.

Hyde S.A., Goddard C.M., Scott O.M. & Dubowitz V. (1982) Prolongation of ambulation in Duchenne muscular dystrophy by appropriate orthoses. *Physiotherapy* **68**(4), 105–8.

Knott M. & Voss D.E. (1968) *Proprioceptive Neuromuscular Facilitation Techniques.* Harper and Row, London.

Luque E.R. & Cardosa A. (1977) Sequential correction of scoliosis with rigid internal fixation. *Orthop Trans* **1**, 136.

MRC (Medical Research Council) (1976) *Aids to the Investigation of Peripheral Nerve Injuries.* Her Majesty Stationery Office, London.

Moosa A. (1974) The investigation of neuromuscular diseases in early childhood. *British Journal of Hospital Medicine* **12**, 166–74.

Scott O.M., Hyde S.A., Goddard C.M. & Dubowitz V. (1982) Quantitation of muscle function in children: A prospective study in Duchenne muscular dystrophy. *Muscle and Nerve* **5**, 291–301.

Scott O.M., Hyde S.A., Goddard C.M. & Dubowitz V. (1981a) Prevention of deformity in Duchenne muscular dystrophy. *Physiotherapy* **67** (6), 177–80.

Scott O.M., Hyde S.A., Goddard C.M., Jones R. & Dubowitz V. (1981b) Effect of exercise in Duchenne muscular dystrophy. *Physiotherapy* **67** (6), 174–6.

Siegel I.M. (1975) Plastic-moulded knee-ankle-foot orthoses in the treatment of Duchenne muscular dystrophy. *Archives of Physical Medicine and Rehabilitation* **56**, 322.

Siegel I.M. (1977) Orthopaedic correction of muscular skeletal deformity in muscular dystrophy. *Advances in Neurology* **17**, 343–64.

Sutherland D.H., Olshen R., Cooper L., Wyatt M., Leach J., Murbarak S. & Schultz P. (1981) The pathomechanics of gait in Duchenne muscular dystrophy. *Developmental Medicine and Child Neurology* **23**, 3–22.

Vignos P.J., Spencer G. & Archibald K. (1963) Management of progressive muscular dystrophy of childhood. *Journal of the American Medical Association* **184**, 89–110.

Vignos P.J. & Watkins M.P. (1966) The effect of exercise in muscular dystrophy. *Journal of the American Medical Association* **197** (11), 843–8.

Walton J. (1981) *Disorders of Voluntary Muscle,* 4e. Churchill Livingstone, Edinburgh.

Ziter F. A. & Allsop K.G. (1979) The value of orthoses for patients with Duchenne muscular dystrophy. *Physical Therapy* **59** (11), 1361–5.

Ziter F.A., Allsop K.G. & Tyler F.H. (1977) Assessment of muscle strength in Duchenne Muscular Dystrophy. *Neurology (Minneap.)* **27**, 981–4

CHAPTER 13

CHILDREN WITH BRITTLE BONES

Alison Wisbeach

Osteogenesis imperfecta (OI) is a group of disorders characterized by abnormal fragility of the bones. Together they are the most common heritable abnormality of bone and have an incidence in western Europe of about 1 in 20 000. At a molecular level these disorders appear to result from defects in collagen, the fibrous framework of bone, skin and tendon. These collagen defects cause the additional features which may be observed in some, but not all, people with OI; they include blueness of the sclerae ('whites of the eyes'), deformities of the long bones and/or spine, excessive sweating, joint laxity, abnormal teeth (dentinogenesis imperfecta) and impairment of hearing. The disorder is often referred to as 'brittle bones'.

Although the birth of a baby with OI is traumatic for the parents, they soon become experts on the disorder, and may well acquire more knowledge than the professionals who are supporting them. Children with OI may sustain fractures when being examined or treated by doctors, nurses, radiographers and therapists who feel guilty despite their professional training and knowledge of the disorder. Parents without these advantages may feel very guilty about incidents for which they are blameless. Parents who have passed on the disorder to their child often feel guilty about it and must be handled sensitively. It is not usually helpful to ask how a fracture occurred in a case of OI since the information does not affect the treatment and the question increases the parent's feeling of inadequacy.

These children are extremely dependent on their parents during the first few years of life; this may make them very demanding, using a parent to meet the motor needs that their intellectual development demands. Some children take advantage of this even when able to do things for themselves, taunting when they misbehave 'You can't hit me!'. Support for the parents and behaviour modification for the child can both be helpful. Parents often have a dilemma of how much protection and how much freedom to give their child.

CLINICAL FEATURES

FRACTURES

Some babies are stillborn, or die within the first few weeks of life, usually because of respiratory difficulties due to rib fractures, or because of intracranial haemorrhage. Most babies with OI survive into adult life and have a good life expectancy. These children often have fewer fractures with increasing age so that after puberty fractures occur mostly as a result of appreciable trauma. Some parents are advised that their baby will 'grow out' of the condition; unfortunately this is not true and they remain susceptible to fracture throughout life.

Childhood may be punctuated by fractures; often parents detect a cyclical pattern with three or four fractures consecutively followed by a fracture-free period of several months or even years. These variations are not yet understood. Other patterns can be seen. Although many children have fractured all of their long bones at one time or another, there are some whose fractures are confined entirely to their lower limbs and others with a tendency to fracture just one limb, or bone. Awareness of this can be helpful when planning a management programme.

Fractures occur very readily, even turning over in bed or sneezing may cause a fracture. At other times children may unaccountably escape fracture despite trauma. Some children get a 'feeling' that a bone is likely to break, and sadly they are all too often right. There are times when it is not possible to identify the cause of a fracture or when it occurred, and others when the child or the parents heard the crack.

DEFORMITY

Bowing of the long bones is seen commonly in severely affected children (Fig. 13.1.). Often the femora and humeri are particularly shortened. Scoliosis is common and the chest frequently has a 'beehive' shape. Flattening of the vertebrae results in short stature and the appearance of 'not having a neck'. The skull shape is often triangular, being broad at the temples and flattened antero–posteriorly. As a result unrelated people with OI may have a marked resemblance to each other.

JOINT LAXITY

This may be limited to the extremities but in some patients can also be seen in the elbow, shoulder, knee and hip joints. Many children enjoy performing tricks, such as sitting with their feet behind their head. Joint laxity can also be put to practical use in compensating for the restriction of movement caused by bone angulation.

SCLERAE

A frequently described feature of OI is the blue or grey colour of the sclerae. The colour is the underlying choroid pigment seen through the unusually thin sclerae. Blue sclerae are not seen in all patients with OI; normal sclerae are seen in a small proportion of families with the milder varieties of OI and the majority of patients with severe OI. In many patients the colour of the sclerae

Fig. 13.1   A child with brittle bones.

varies and parents may report that their child's sclerae becomes a deeper blue just before a fracture occurs. Such changes are not understood but may serve as a warning for a child to be extra careful.

SKIN

The skin may be fragile and wounds heal slowly. Small blood vessels rupture easily causing bruising, which is a common feature of OI. These children also have a tendency to excessive sweating, often preferring to sit in the shade during the summer and rejecting warm clothing during winter.

TEETH

In some types of OI the teeth are discoloured and appear opalescent (dentinogenesis imperfecta). The enamel chips away from the soft dentine and the teeth rapidly wear down, sometimes to the gum margins. The deciduous teeth are more severely affected than the permanent teeth. Mandibular prognathism and maxillary retrusion may affect the child's ability to bite.

HEARING

In the second and third decades of life patients may develop a conductive type of deafness which often responds well to stapedectomy. It usually occurs in the milder types of OI.

FATIGUE

Children often tire easily, even those who are mildly affected, possibly because the generally low muscle tone requires them to exert more effort to fulfil normal motor activity. Short rests usually enable them to keep pace with their normal peers.

CLASSIFICATION OF OI

The most widely accepted classification of OI is that described by Sillence and his colleagues from Australia (Table 13.1).

Recognition of the variety of OI is important to provide the parents with an idea of the outlook for their child. It is also important for genetic counselling.

Table 13.1   Classification of OI (after Sillence)

OI type	Clinical features	Teeth	Inheritance
IA	Generally mild, a few patients may have several hundred fractures in a lifetime. Deep blue sclerae. Presenile hearing loss in about 45% of patients over 40	Normal	Autosomal dominant
IB	As IA but with dentinogenesis imperfecta	Opalescent	Autosomal dominant
II	Extreme bone fragility causing death in utero or early neonatal life	Not known	Autosomal recessive
III	Variable but often severe bone fragility in infancy: progressive skeletal deformity: usually normal sclerae	Opalescent	Autosomal recessive
IVA	As IA but with normal sclerae: very variable severity	Normal	Autosomal dominant
IVA	As IB but with normal sclerae: very variable severity	Opalescent	Autosomal dominant

DIFFERENTIAL DIAGNOSIS

It is not surprising that a disorder that can cause fractures and bruising with little or no injury can occasionally be confused with child abuse. The problem of diagnosis is particularly severe in children with no family history of the condition and expert medical help is needed. Idiopathic juvenile osteoporosis may also cause difficulties in diagnosis but the first fracture is usually in late childhood or early adolescence.

MEDICAL TREATMENT

Several forms of drug treatment have been tried in OI but with no clear evidence of value. The fact that some parents feel that the fracture rate has been reduced must be treated with caution since the fracture rate in people with brittle bones is so variable. Some children are given extra milk to 'build up their calcium' but this has no known value since the basic disorder is in the collagen and not in bone mineral. Advances in this field are most likely to come from better delineation of the various disorders included in OI and from increased knowledge of the chemical basis of the disorder.

ORTHOPAEDIC MANAGEMENT

Orthopaedic treatment aims to prevent or correct bony deformity as well as fracture care.

Fractures may be treated in a variety of ways. In very small babies simply binding the limb with a crepe bandage, possibly with a pad of soft cotton or lint, usually holds the limb sufficiently to reduce discomfort and promote healing. Alternatively, lower limb fractures may be treated by gallows traction, and to reduce hospitalization many families have their own traction frames at home. In some instances, following reduction of a fracture by gallows, the traction can be removed once union commences, and can be replaced with a simple plaster cast.

For older children plaster of Paris remains the most widely used method for splinting fractures but some of the newer, lightweight splinting materials such as Baycast or Scotchcast are increasingly used. Some orthopaedic surgeons use Thomas splints or traction with weights, but these methods must be applied carefully as children have been known to disappear down the bed!

Intramedullary rodding is used to straighten long bones and prevent fractures. The Sofield-Miller procedure is sometimes known as the 'shish kebab' method (Fig. 13.2). The deformed bone is exposed and osteotomies allow the bowed part of the bone to be removed. A rod is selected with the largest diameter that can be inserted into the medullary canal and long enough to extend from epiphysis to epiphysis. The removed length of bone is cut into segments appropriate for correction and are then threaded on to the rod which is then replaced. The limb is usually immobilized in plaster for six weeks.

One of the main disadvantages of the rod is that it may require frequent replacement because the bone grows and angulates beyond the part supported

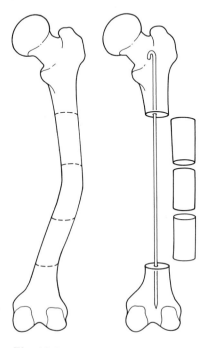

Fig. 13.2

(a)

(b)

Fig. 13.3   (a) Milestones of a child with OI. (b) Milestones of a normal child.

by the rod. This problem is avoided by the recently introduced Bailey-Dubow rod which is telescopic and elongates with growth. Experience of the value of this type of rod is still very limited.

Scoliosis is frequently seen in children with OI and, when combined with deformity of the long bones, can cause severe disability. Attempts to maintain and correct spinal deformity using bracing is seldom effective and can be harmful as the pressure may cause fractures and inhibit respiration. Spinal fusion has been valuable in progressive scoliosis. Cotrel traction, which the children can use regularly at home, also seems helpful in some cases.

THERAPY

The therapist is most regularly involved with severely affected children; patients with the milder varieties may only require help immediately after a fracture to encourage them to get back on their feet.

The therapist's aims are to prevent fracture and deformity and to promote as normal a life as possible. The programme must be planned for each individual for, whilst there are many common features of the disorder, the combination is unique for each child. However, there are some general points to keep in mind.

1 Ask the parents how to lift their baby or, if the child is old enough to speak, ask him how he prefers to be handled. Many babies and young children scream when approached by a stranger — very sensible when bones break easily with incorrect handling. If a child cannot move away from danger, screaming is the most effective warning he can give.

2 Remember that fractures are painful, even for children with OI. Unfortunately some parents are told that the child should be used to it. Knowing that fractures are painful causes anxiety which may increase the pain and induce a fear of hospitals.

3 Handle the children firmly, but gently, once you know how. Even small babies can sense that you are nervous; if you are confident they in turn will feel confident in you.

4 Believe the child if he says that he feels he is about to fracture, or that a limb aches. The chances are that he is right. On more than one occasion we have heard of children who have mentioned this to their doctor or therapist only to be told that it is 'imagination'; efforts to continue an activity caused fractures and sapped the child's confidence in the skills of the professional.

5 Bear in mind that these children have a biochemical not a neurological disorder. It is well recognized that milestones will be delayed. There is no virtue in testing for reflex reactions in development as one is more likely to injure the child than learn anything useful to help plan a programme.

6 Recognize that the 'floppiness' is another feature of the collagen defect. Trying to stimulate extension by placing severely affected babies prone is unlikely to be effective and may restrict breathing and cause unnecessary pressure on the arms.

7 Be cautious in making an assessment of the baby's abilities. Checking head and trunk control in transition from supine to sitting, by pulling on the arms, could cause upper limb dislocations or fractures, and could damage the cervical spine. Several children with OI have sustained bilateral femoral fractures as a result of being tested for hip dislocation.

8 Let the child do as much as possible for himself, handling him only when necessary; for example, if a child in nappies is able to roll to either side, he can practise this at nappy changing times rather than being lifted.

9 Keep therapy enjoyable. 'Exercises' are usually boring. Therapy can be done effectively through a carefully structured daily living and leisure programme. Motor activity may improve bone and muscle quality, and prevent the complication of osteoporosis.

10 Remember that these children are usually of at least average intelligence; either be careful of your comments in front of them, or include them in the discussion. One little girl overheard 'There's no flies on her'. That night as she was put to bed she refused to have her duvet over her, but settled with a blanket. As her mother was leaving the room she heard her whisper to her teddy, 'There's no flies on me'. It was only then that her mother remembered that the duvet cover was patterned with bumble bees and polka dots!

DEVELOPMENT

Babies who are mildly or moderately affected by OI usually follow a normal developmental pattern interrupted by fractures. More severely affected infants have delayed and deviant motor milestones (Fig. 13.3).

The ages at which the children attain these stages vary. Some children never learn to sit, and a larger group remain confined to a wheelchair. OI children are generally of normal intelligence; they are often thought to be very bright because their small stature leads to their being thought to be younger than they are.

Some children who have spent much of their early years supine, or being pushed in a pram, may have perceptual difficulties especially in relation to body awareness and spatial relationships. They respond well to developmental therapy.

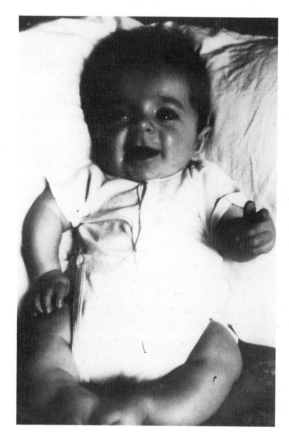

Fig. 13.4

PRACTICAL SUGGESTIONS

It is usually advisable to nurse the baby supine. The skull is often particularly soft in infants and has been described as feeling like a bag of jelly. The anterior fontanelle is wide and takes longer than usual to close. The arms and legs are held flexed and abducted; sometimes the thumbs are held tucked inside fisted hands. Skin creases are noticeable where the bones are bowed (Fig. 13.4).

Parents are often told to 'treat their baby like china' and should be supported in their everyday handling. Some babies have Plastazote or Orthoplast carrying cocoons made for them. Although these 'exoskeletons' allow the child to be handled easily, he may become reliant on them and fuss when handled without it. A useful compromise is the Bexi bath foam, designed to support infants in the bath. This offers some support when carrying and is especially useful if the baby has a fracture since it helps reduce handling. The best way to lift an OI baby is to support him with one hand behind head and shoulders, and the other hand between the legs supporting the buttocks and lower spine (Fig. 13.5). This minimizes the danger of rib fractures.

Fig. 13.5 Carrying position tilted backwards.

Although the baby cannot be hugged it can be cuddled, cradled in the foam support or held vertically against its parent's shoulder.

There are many other practical activities which should be introduced at this early stage.

1 Encourage the baby to fix visually and follow moving toys. This will help the child to begin rolling to either side and so perhaps reduce the extent to which the soft skull becomes moulded.

2 Lay the baby in the three-quarter supine position on either side each day to accustom him to the position. Care must be taken not to move him over too quickly as this might cause a fracture of the underneath arm and leg. One way of doing this is to initiate the movement by asking him to track a toy to the side to which he is to be turned. As he follows gently raise the opposite side of his play mat so that the pull of the fabric gradually moves him over on to his side. He can then be supported with a rolled blanket or pillow beneath the play mat. This position is also useful for the development of hand regard, hands together and hands to mouth (Fig. 13.6).

Fig. 13.6

3 Look out for small lightweight toys. Like everything else toys tend to come and go in fashions and so, sadly, there is no guarantee that any particular toy that proves useful will continue to be available. Currently some shops have a range of extremely soft and easy-to-squeak toys in a variety of shapes and sizes. They are far easier than the usual squeaky toys which tend to be rather heavy and require a lot of effort. Another useful range of soft toys includes an inflatable 'jungle gym', an inflatable mobile, an inflatable cot bumper and a padded activity centre. It is possible to find miniature jumping jacks and miniature kellys.

4 Some babies need encouragement to open their hands, especially to extend the thumb out of the palm. Each time the baby is handled, gently ease open his fingers and thumb. It is worthwhile to suggest that a cotton wool ball is placed in the hand to try to maintain the thumb position; a small home-made dumb-bell rattle can be used. Hartz jingle balls for cats (available from most pet shops), make good 'ends' for a rattle or useful toys in themselves.

5   When the baby is taken out in a pram, put a notice on the pram to say 'Please don't touch me, I have brittle bones'. It may be necessary for the parent to go into a shop to which a pram cannot be taken. On one occasion a mother came out of a shop to find a well-meaning lady removing her baby's cardigan, berating her for overdressing the sweating baby!

6   Use natural fibres in preference to manmade fibres to help reduce sweating. For the young baby complete back openings are advisable to reduce the lifting and struggling needed to get head and arms through openings. If the baby has a fracture, an open-backed garment can easily be laid across. Garments with raglan sleeves are often easier to put on than those with fitted sleeves. Collarless clothes look smart and prevent chafing when the baby has a short neck.

7   Make sure the baby is protected from his loving but boisterous siblings and their friends. A 'cat net' over a playpen allows the baby to be part of the group but protects him from toys 'dropped overboard' for him to play with, or from being accidentally trodden on. They can go on to the floor when their sibling is asleep or visiting friends, or when a parent is there to supervize.

8   Bedding should be light to minimize pressure on fractured limbs and to allow the baby to move. A single sheet or blanket is often adequate in warm weather but otherwise a duvet is useful.

9   Babies with OI often prefer several small feeds to a few large ones.

10   Gaining bowel control is difficult for some OI children. Toilet training is often interrupted by fractures or delayed by poor sitting. Constipation adds further difficulties and may cause a sudden loss of control. A regular toiletting programme is essential together with medical advice on diet and laxatives. Increased motor activity can be helpful.

11   Most OI babies love water. They can be bathed on a Bexi bath foam support which allows the parent to have both hands free. Nappy changing is a good time to encourage extension, internal rotation and adduction of the legs. The legs can be gently mobilized at these times, releasing immediately there is any resistance. Some babies practise by propelling themselves around the floor in supine. Once the family is confident in handling the baby new activities can be built into the day.

12   It is most important, but admittedly difficult, that the family should encourage relatives and friends to hold and feed their special baby. If this is achieved it will allow the parents to go out together for an evening; it will also build up the baby's confidence in being handled by others.

SITTING POSITIONS

A variety of sitting positions can be introduced bearing in mind three factors. First, the child should not be brought fully upright too suddenly as femoral fractures can occur when weight-bearing while sitting. Second, the child should always sit symmetrically. Third, children with OI are susceptible to backache; at first, sitting should be interspersed with frequent rests in the supine position. If sat too long initially, the discomfort which may follow could deter a child from trying again.

SEMI-SITTING

One simple way for a baby to begin sitting is to use a bouncing cradle. Generally those are rather soft and tend to sag but the recently available Chicco bouncing cradle has the advantage of being firm at the back and having sides padded so that waving arms and legs are protected from damage. Handles allow the baby to be carried in the seat; this is helpful when doing housework.

A foam wedge makes a useful semi-reclined support. If necessary a portion can be scooped out to prevent the baby slipping off. A groin strap sewn to the cover could serve the same purpose.

The Biemme Dastynove pushchair is a chair with a firm base and a choice of three back positions. The most reclined position is useful for beginning sitting training. The side wings and armrests help give protection from swinging shopping bags! The footrest elevates to an almost horizontal position; although the baby's legs do not usually reach it until it is much older, it does act as a bumper. It is often helpful to make a retaining apron to keep the baby's bottom to the back of the seat as standard restraints are too large. This pushchair is ideal for making a cardboard box tray, so that there is a suitable play surface (Fig. 13.7).

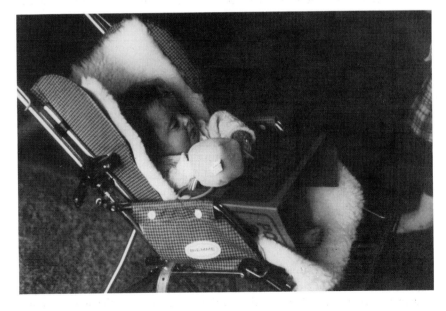

Fig. 13.7

Fig. 13.8

The Cindico super seat, Baby Relax 7 in 1 or Mothercare Super Sitter are also suitable in their reclined position. OI babies may have short femora which do not allow them to sit in these chairs with their knees at right angles. They tend to sit on a broad base with their legs abducted and externally rotated. If the lower legs or feet extend beyond the seat, they should be supported by an extended seat of Plastazote or Evazote to prevent fracture or deformity. Washable sheepskin or synthetic sheepskin can be used as a chair lining for comfort and protection.

To prepare for upright sitting, encourage the baby to roll actively to either side. If the baby rolls into a prone position, this may cause distress. In severe cases this position should be avoided altogether.

During the day, trunk extension can be encouraged by the parent holding the baby up against a shoulder and gradually reducing the amount of support given. It is important that the baby has something interesting to look at, perhaps in the mirror or out of the window (Fig. 13.8).

Other ways of developing sitting are supported on mother's lap (Fig. 13.9a) or on the floor between her legs (Fig. 13.9b). Both positions provide an opportunity to assess how much weight can be brought forward safely, and how much the baby can do to control his head and trunk.

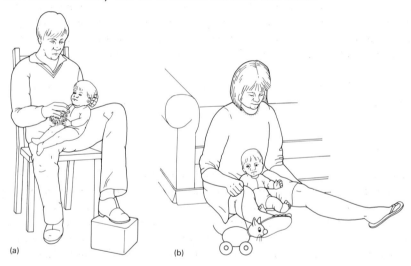

Fig. 13.9   Sitting positions for play.   (a)   (b)

UPRIGHT SITTING

Once the child has head and trunk control the big step towards mobility is independent floor sitting. Like all small children he has to be placed in this position and it is not until some time later, if at all, that he is able to move from the supine position to sitting by himself. Independent floor sitting can be encouraged either sitting between a parent's legs, surrounded by soft plump cushions, or in an inflatable boat or bath. It is essential that he is well protected; if he has to use his arms to save himself from falling, a fracture is likely. Some children with severe upper limb deformity do not have arms long enough to sit and rest their hands on the floor. This makes independent sitting hazardous since there is a danger of hitting their heads should they lose balance. The Jonsport trolley can be invaluable in helping to train balance and reduce dependence on parents and siblings.

The natural progression from floor sitting is to bottom shuffling, usually backwards at first! Deep pile carpets, although soft, often make the going more difficult. Squeezing through chair legs can be difficult when going backwards and they soon learn to shuffle forwards. It is important that no one gives a 'helpful' push from behind since the forward shunting of their weight through their femora can cause fractures. Bottom shuffling becomes a rapid and effective method of mobility which many continue to use in adult life. It also forms a basis for independent transfers. Once able to bottom shuffle the children usually learn to move from supine to sitting through elbow propping, which they work out for themselves.

STANDING

Many children will never stand and bear weight unaided, usually because of instability at the hips, knees and ankle joints, and bowing of the long bones. Baby walkers can be useful in providing an enjoyable alternative to sitting. Being suspended in the hammock allows the legs to extend and many children are able to scoot effectively and safely around the room. If there is a tray, toys can be carried.

From a baby walker some children learn to hold on to the sides and stand. They might then graduate to using a toddle truck or rollator.

EQUIPMENT

Generally OI children have great determination and devise their own ways of achieving independence. Many items available in the commercial nursery market can be used or modified effectively for these children. In other instances special items of equipment are needed, which may have to be made to order. It is important to evaluate carefully the child and family as well as the environmental restraints. At one house visited much of the house furniture had been cut to suit the family member with OI, as a result everybody else had to stoop and developed backache. The provision of an elevating chair for the OI child would have solved the problem.

Stairs are a frequent difficulty which may be overcome with a shaft or stair lift. However, many young children enjoy the exercise of going up and down stairs on their bottom, although this is not very dignified in adult life.

Basic safety around the home is important, such as avoidance of slippery floor surfaces.

Since some children have a tendency to become 'chesty' the rooms should preferably be kept free from damp.

CALIPERS

Long-leg or below-knee calipers are appropriate for some children and can be an effective support. They allow a good range of movement at the hip and are less constricting than a space suit. The main disadvantages are their weight and the possible occurrence of stress fractures at the level of the support bands.

'SPACE SUITS'

These are currently undergoing clinical trials with some encouraging results. The suit is an inflatable orthosis designed to support and protect the child's legs (Fig. 13.10). Selection of the patients is vital. It has been used successfully with children as young as 18 months old who have not been attempting to bear weight, and with teenagers who have been off their feet for several years because of a series of fractures. It is hoped that if introduced at an early age, deformity and the need for rodding might be prevented. For children who already have intramedullary rods the need for renewal might be delayed. The suit cannot be fitted if a bone has appreciable bowing.

One of the disadvantages of the suit is that it is restrictive, since the child is held stiffly from waist to ankles. However, many children are able to achieve

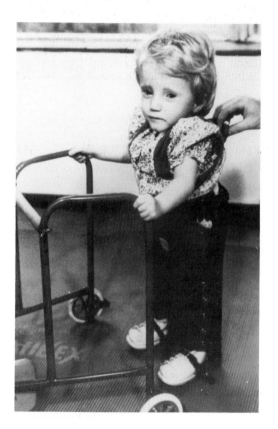

Fig. 13.10a 'Space Suit'

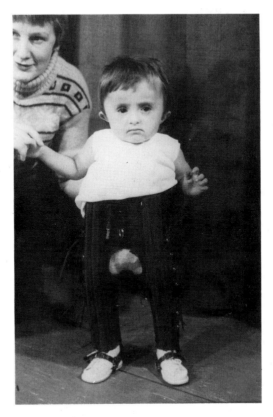

Fig. 13.10b 'Space Suit'

an effective gait using trunk rotation, supported by a rollator or crutches.

The waist zip can be undone to allow the child to sit forward for school work, although he still has to sit with straight legs. The aim is to discard the suit when confidence in walking has increased, and the fracture rate stabilized.

SPLINTS

To ease handling, for additional support or for management of minor fractures, lightweight leg splints are often helpful. They can be made directly on the child or on a positive cast for a more intimate fit. These are usually made from Plastazote or Orthoplast although plaster of Paris can also be used. Usually a backslab is adequate but sometimes a bivalved splint is preferable.

SPORT

Although some mildly affected children are good at sports, most vigorous sports are generally contraindicated. With thought some games such as indoor hockey, badminton, ball games and indoor cricket can be played.

Swimming is enjoyed by most children with OI, many of whom prefer to swim on their backs because of their short necks and tendency to be 'top heavy'. It is excellent for muscle strengthening and provides an opportunity for competition.

EDUCATION

Educational provision for OI children varies from place to place. A few receive home tuition; while this is often satisfactory educationally, children may lack experience of the outside world and the opportunity to make friends.

Most children attend special or mainstream schools; the choice is not necessarily related to the degree of handicap. Some severely disabled children attend ordinary schools and some mildly affected children attend special schools.

Many problems are similar whatever type of school a child attends:

1   loss of school time through fractures;
2   danger of fracture by accident;
3   physical limitations of speed and quality of writing which may call for special equipment;
4   inability to cope independently with toileting, the need to lie down at some time in the day and other special assistance;
5   safe transport to and from school.

Additionally, mainstream schools may have architectural barriers, such as stepped entrances, internal stairs and narrow doorways.

OI children make popular and lively classmates with good academic ability. Many adults are able to complete further education courses at college or university, obtain employment, drive their own cars, marry and raise families. Their requirements change accordingly and we must be flexible in our approach to meeting their needs.

Further details from: The Brittle Bone Society, 112 City Road, Dundee DD2 2PW (Tel: 0382 67603)

REFERENCES AND FURTHER READING

ALSTON J. (1982) Children with brittle bones. *Special Education: Forward Trends (British Journal of Special Education)* **9**, 29–32.

MAETANI T., TAMAMOTO M., MIYOSHI R., KAWAZOE Y. & HAMADA T. (1981) Prosthetic treatment of a patient with osteogenesis imperfecta. *Hiroshima Journal of Medical Sciences* **30**, 15–19.

MARAFIOTI R. & WESTIN W. (1977) Elongating intramedullary rods in the treatment of osteogenesis imperfecta. *Journal of Bone and Joint Surgery* **59**A, 467–72.

PATERSON C.R. (1978a) Osteogenesis imperfecta and fractures in childhood. *Health Visitor* **51**, 174–6.

PATERSON C.R. (1978b) Unexplained fractures in childhood. *Social Work Today* **9**, 14.

PATERSON C.R. (1978c) Medical management of osteogenesis imperfecta. In *Bone Disease and Calcitonin* (ed. Kanis J.A.) pp. 163–9. Armour, Eastbourne.

RENSHAW T.S., COOK R. & ALBRIGHT J.A. (1979) Scoliosis in osteogenesis imperfecta. *Clinical Orthopaedics and Related Research* **145**, 163–7.

SILLENCE D.O. (1981) *A Handbook for Medical Practitioners and Health Care Professionals.* Osteogenesis Imperfecta Society of New South Wales, Australia.

SOURCES FOR EQUIPMENT

Bathing

Bexi bath foam	Starters, 38 Tydraw Street, Port Talbot, W. Glam.

Chairs

Tripp Trapp Chair	Joncare, Radley Road, Industrial Estate, Abingdon, Oxon (Tel: 0235-28120)
Britax-Handicapped Child Seat	Britax, Chertsey Road, Byfleet, Surrey KT14 7AW (Tel: 093-23-41121)
The Craddock Chair	R.C. Hayes (Leics) Ltd., 12a Wood Street, Earl Shilton, Leics LE9 7ND (Tel: 0455-46027)
Mothercare Super Sitter	Mothercare, PO Box 145, Watford, Herts. (Tel: 0923-40366)
Luxury Padded Bouncer Chair (Chicco)	Kiddy Mail Ltd., (UK Dist. of Chicco), 9–10 Rich Industrial Estate, Crimscott Street, London SE1 5TE (Tel: 01-403-5514)
Jubilee Luxury Chair	Baby Relax Ltd., Rainham, Essex (Tel: 04027-53344)

Karts & trikes

Jonsport Trolley Jonsport Electro	Joncare, Radley Road, Industrial Estate, Abingdon, Oxon (Tel: 0235-28120)
Comet Mini Kart Rally Special Go-kart	Malden Care, 579 Kingston Road, Raynes Park, London SW20 8SD (Tel: 01-543-0077)
Big 'T' Trike	R.C. Hayes Ltd., 12a Wood Street, Earl Shilton, Leics LE9 7ND (Tel: 0455-46027)

Pushchairs & baby walkers, etc.

Chicco de luxe Baby Walker	Kiddy Mail Ltd., 9–10 Rich Industrial Estate, Crimscott Street, London SE1 5TE (Tel: 01-403-5514)

Sealand Inflatable Orthosis	Sealand Medical Products Ltd., Tower Road, Four Bridges, Birkenhead, Merseyside (Tel: 051-647-4764)
Biemme - Dastynove pushchair	Thistle Products, 24 Beswick Street, Ancoats, Manchester M4 7HS (Tel: 061-273-5756)
Mini Max pushchair	Alvema Range of Chairs, Carters (J. & A.) Ltd., Alfred Street, Westbury, Wilts. BA13 3DZ (Tel: 0373-822203)
Cindico Recliner pushchair	Cindico, Skeme Road, Driffield, N. Humberside (Tel: 0377-46841)
Wheelchairs	See D.H.S.S. range

Toys

Shelcore
  Crib-soft Gym
  Crib-soft
    Playground
  Crib-soft Activity
    Bumpers
	Kiddy Mail Ltd., 9–10 Rich Industrial Estate, Crimscott Street, London SE1 5TE (Tel: 01-403-5514)

Soft Squeaky Toys (Lanco Inter.)	Dantoll Ltd., (GB Distr.) 15–16 Leather Market, London SE1 3EZ (Tel: 01-403-1636)

Others

Myers - County Cot Bed	Myers Contract Div., Vauxhall Walk, London SE11 5EN
Mothercare Bed Guard	Mothercare, PO Box 145, Watford, Herts. (Tel: 0923-40366)
Small Keyboard Typewriter	Possum Controls Ltd., Middlegreen Trading Estate, Middlegreen Road, Langley, Nr. Slough, Berks. (Tel: 0753-79234)

SEVERE VISUAL HANDICAP

Sophie Levitt

Vision is a significant part of every aspect of a child's development. He starts life by looking at his caring adult promoting affection and concern. The rich interplay of a mother's and her infant's eyes is fundamental to their love affair. Eye contact and facial expression encourage development in communication. The child's social and emotional development grow out of this mother–baby closeness. Later, after having left the safety of his mother's lap, the child will look back towards mother's face for reassurance or warning when he explores new experiences. The discovery of the child's new experience begins with 'catching sight' of its potential fascination. Visual lures promote reaching out and moving, so developing motor abilities. Exploration by the child also encourages speech and language development.

Vision is rich in information, for it simultaneously combines colour, shape and the function of things. Touch only gives a few aspects of an object. Only immediate and local events and things can be reached to touch, to hear and to smell. Localization of sound and smell may not be as easily or as accurately made as with vision. Vision is continuous whilst other sensory stimuli are fleeting, unpredictable and thus take more time to comprehend if received on their own. Vision acts as a tutor for the other senses. What made a sound, where it is, what pleasure or danger the sound conveys are explained by seeing these meanings. The sensations of touch, proprioception (pressure, stretch, muscular contractions, joint traction and compression) and vestibular input may be received by the blind child but having no meaning may make him fearful or overwhelmed. If so, he may prefer to be safe and remain immobile. Vision helps enormously to obtain a predictable, reassuringly reliable and more comprehensive world. Through vision the child has more control so that stimuli do not suddenly impinge on him without warning. He can anticipate and protect himself as far as he is able. A child also learns more from what he can control.

The severely handicapped child with additional visual handicap and the otherwise 'normal' child with severe visual impairment are understandably unsure, often fearful and suspicious of the unfamiliar. They hesitate more about the unknown stage of development and cling more to what they know. Delay in development is obviously inevitable. One could say it is 'normal' to be delayed if there is severe visual handicap. However, with early intervention, developmental delay has been considerably reduced. Norris

(1956) showed how 66 congenitally blind children with no major physical handicap reached the same levels as their sighted peers at school age, if given early intervention. Others such as Fraiberg (1977) have demonstrated similar results.

ASSESSMENT

Medical consultants, psychologists, social workers, teachers, physiotherapists, occupational therapists and speech therapists can all contribute to the assessment of visually handicapped children. However, it is wise if the baby and young child is not handled by too many strangers. Parents can be used to handle and instruct their child under the supervision of the professionals. Simultaneous observation by other professionals in a one-way viewing room is helpful to avoid having too many people in the same room. The parents will be more relaxed and the child will not be distracted by the sounds of other observers present. By observing through the one-way mirror, with each professional's specific interest, many examinations may not have to be repeated by every professional; for example, the physiotherapist may observe motor patterns of arm and hand whilst the psychologist studies the understanding behind the use of the hands and the paediatrician obtains information about the vision during hand function.

Therapists will need information on the following areas.

Vision. Is the defect in the eye itself, visual pathway or cortex? What vision is available? What size of object and at what distance can it be seen? The therapists will also need to know if any field defects exist. Is visual acuity the same in each eye? The use of particular visual ability remaining in any child will be developed with training. Therefore the stage of visual development or functional use of residual vision should be assessed. When using residual sight the child's sphere of visual interest and any head posture he needs to adopt to get his maximum visual competence must be known.

Assessment must be made for any visually directed reach and for which sizes and near distances he uses it.

Hearing. Can the child hear normally? Does he prefer one side — which may often be the side on which he has more vision — or is it more central? When a sound is heard, many babies still, open their eyes wider or change the rhythm of breathing. The blind baby may sometimes look down as if disinterested, though he may be concentrating strongly on the sound and what it could mean. Later the child turns to sound to localize it. This is automatic around 4 months of age but is lost when he gets no visual feedback or reward. Active turning towards a sound is achieved by intelligent 10-month-old babies and soon becomes linked with reach for sound (Fraiberg 1968). Reach for sound in front and centre of the baby precedes turn to sound and reach. Turn to sound is first in the horizontal, then horizontal and above or below, and finally behind him, via the horizontal of the child's eye level. These two-stage searches for sound will be progressed to a one-stage or direct localization of sound. Reach for sound will follow this same manner of development (Sonksen 1979).

The therapist who has more accurate information on the child's use of sound will appropriately apply it to stimulate movement; for example, reach and roll, reach and crawl, and reach and step are aspects of motor development, when reach for sound may be used.

The child must also have the intellectual capacity to understand that objects make sounds and later that, though the sound comes and goes, the object may still be there. Such conceptual information is given to the therapist by the psychologist (see also Chapter 5, p. 54).

Selection of appropriate sounds which appeal to the child rather than startle him should be made. Parents often know what rattles and toys are best for their child's pleasure.

Touch, proprioception, vestibular sensation.   These stimuli will be used more for the blind child. However, assessment must be made as to whether these sensations are present. In spina bifida, and other conditions where sensory pathways are absent, the therapist will not be able to use tactile and proprioceptive input according to the particular part of the body involved. In others, sensations are there but lack of experience and lack of comprehension may demand a gradual introduction of such stimuli. Developmental levels for localization of touch and reactions to proprioceptive and vestibular stimuli are present in both sighted and visually impaired babies. The development of the postural reactions depends on proprioceptive stimuli and they only appear as any child develops (see Chapter 2).

Assessment of sensory appreciation, sensory integration and perceptual activity or interpretation are part of psychological, neurological and developmental paediatricians' reports. Some physiotherapists and occupational therapists have their own assessments of these areas and work together with the medical and psychological consultants.

Other handicaps.   Various studies have shown that about 50 –70% of blind children have additional handicaps (Robinson 1977); Fine 1979; Griffiths 1979). There may also be convulsions, cerebral palsies, hydrocephalus and spina bifida, different degrees of mental handicap, deafness, speech defects and behaviour problems. These handicaps augment the visual disabilities, and vice versa.

Therapists must assess these handicaps with the team. The effect of vision on normal development must be appreciated so that the complex interaction of other handicaps is understood. Specialized knowledge of other handicaps must, therefore, be combined with the effect of blindness on child development.

Social problems.   It is, unfortunately, very common to find social and emotional problems in the families of visually handicapped children. A social worker's assessment as well as assessments by psychological staff are important to therapists. The selection of therapy techniques and treatment plans must recognize what is acceptable for the family. The 'key worker' may be the mother or father or someone visiting and supporting the family. Therapists will work closely with whoever is the best person to handle and train the child. As discussed in Chapter 1, the relationship with parents needs to be particularly good.

DEVELOPMENTAL ASSESSMENT

This consists of gross motor development, development of hand function, residual visual and hearing development, other sensory development, self-care, social and emotional development and development of speech and language. The Reynell-Zinkin Scales used at the Wolfson Centre (Reynell & Zinkin 1975) assess babies and young children with visual handicap and additional disabilities. The assessment given to me of the child's levels of learning in the following areas is especially helpful in planning appropriate therapy. These are the areas of sensorimotor understanding, social adaptation (which includes self-care), exploration of the environment, communication, response to sound and verbal comprehension, language structure and the meaningful use of language. Therapists in other Centres receive other test results or psychological assessments.

The motor developmental levels are taken from normal schedules but are adapted for the visually impaired child; for example, sequences to walking may omit crawling using bottom shuffling instead. Use of the index finger may be omitted whilst fingers rake small objects into a stationary thumb (Zinkin 1979). Various patterns of motor abilities are used by the blind child such as toe-walking or crawling backwards or using the forehead to 'feel along' the ground in crawling forward. These and other unusual patterns should not be labelled abnormal. Hand-function assessment must include more assessment on searching actions of the hands, orientation of the hand to grasp, finger moulding and fingertip feeling. These motor developmental assessments are still being studied by many workers.

Psychological assessments are also particularly concerned about the development of the permanence of objects which is so difficult for the blind child. The physiotherapist must be advised when the child appreciates the permanence or continuity of the floor, the recognition that whether a sound comes or goes, the sound-making object is still present and other aspects which affect her therapy plans. The correct timing of motor developmental training and of training feeding, dressing, toileting and other aspects of self-care depend on the child's levels of concept, social and emotional development. It is possible in some blind children to focus too much on, say, gross motor development which makes them 'motorized' without purpose. They may move about too much, too dangerously and lose essential learning experiences with their hands, residual vision or hearing.

Body image development is obviously delayed in children who cannot see where their body parts are, what their potential for movement could be and what they and others look like when they move. Assessment of body image as such is difficult as it includes assessments of tactile, proprioceptive, vestibular and motor development as well as concepts of self in relation to others and in relation to objects. Body image is also an emotional experience, feeling positive body awareness and what one can achieve and experience. However, in child development any assessment of the child's appreciation of body parts, where they are, what they do and how they are used in dressing and self-care and play are helpful in the therapy programme. Language development in each child overlaps into whatever speech is used in such assessments so that 'lack of body image' may mean 'lack of speech and language development'. Teamwork is, once again, essential for comprehensive assessment of each child.

THERAPY PROCEDURES

Speech therapy is discussed in Chapters 4 and 5.

Physiotherapy and occupational therapy are closely allied to the contributions of special teachers of the visually handicapped. When neurological handicaps also exist the therapy techniques must be modified to take account of the vision problems and their associated hearing, sensation, emotional and home problems. The teaching methods for the visual problems will also have to be modified according to any physical handicap or, when physical handicap is absent, in relation to any developmental motor disabilities (Sonksen *et al.* 1981; Sykanda & Levitt 1982).

The therapy programmes overlap into the educational programme because the child develops as a whole. The main areas for training are:

1   development of any residual vision;
2   development of the use of hearing; speech and language;
3   development of tactile, proprioceptive and vestibular functions and of body image;
4   development of posture, locomotion and hand function;
5   emotional and social development;
6   development of self-care.

Emotional development must be given special consideration in selection of all developmental techniques, as there is so much shock and stress surrounding a blind baby or child. Mother-child bonding must be fostered and the programme must create confidence in the parents in handling their child. Methods suggested should also come from parents and the family, and those used should be enjoyable for child and family.

Although the above developmental aspects are structured, separated for therapy and more precise training, they cannot be completely isolated from one another. All developmental channels of the blind child will interact and should be trained to do this. The child should not, however, be struggling to learn two different and *difficult* aspects simultaneously. The established ability in one area should be the base for learning and also interacting with another area of function; for example, once sitting balance is present, training vision or hearing is done in sitting. Once hearing provokes good reach laterally, this could be used to train unstable sitting balance ('counterpoising', see p. 22). Interaction is more successfully achieved this way.

VISUAL DEVELOPMENT

There is rarely a totally blind child except in those obvious cases without eyes or anatomical structures, or progressively deteriorating vision. Using the visual assessments from the medical consultants, the therapist provides interesting visual stimuli in the central or peripheral field, or in the one side or area where vision exists. Distance and size of object become more important after the child's interest is aroused at close range. Visual stimuli are then moved out and back into his adequate visual areas.

The object used is first in movement, being shaken to catch light or sparkling as it whirls. Use shiny Christmas decorations, torch with a toy face on it, unbreakable mirrors, silver, white, bright yellows in toys and soft flashing lights, 'glass' beads made of plastic and similar glittering objects. Usually these objects are used whilst attempting face-to-face contact with mother. Some babies first respond to shiny objects which their mothers can wear as necklaces, hats or brooches to help them respond more. Mother's face may have bright make-up, 'eye glitter', spectacles or she may wear earrings to obtain the child's interest, eye fixation and to follow or scan her face. The stages of training visual efficiency are generally as follows.

1 Achieve awareness and attention.
2 Establish eye-to-eye contact.
3 Look at moving object and then at stationary object.
4 Track the human face or an object, increasing range of track.
5 Track horizontally, then up and down and in circles.
6 Track the object moving further away from the child such as mother moving about the room, ball rolling to and from the child, shiny paper strips floating in the air, wind-up flashing toy 'walking' across the table/floor. Change the speeds of bright moving toys by pulling on attached string, rolling marbles slower and faster and blowing silver balloons about. Help eye convergence on to a light playfully brought to the child's nose when this can be trained in some visually impaired children. Accomodation of the eyes is also developed during tracking games as well as the child's focusing and refocusing on objects at different distances from himself. An immobile child should, therefore, not have visual interest playthings placed at the same spots near him out of consideration for his 'blindness'. At all times increase the variety in distance, size, colour and situation of whatever catches his visual attention. Take the child close up to such interests or create the interest for him so he keeps wanting to look and see from his babyhood through childhood.
7 Visual use develops perceptual abilities first as interpreting light/dark. If, in the future, increased vision is achieved with training, better perceptual

interpretations can be learnt. More advanced perceptual learning with vision, trained by teachers and psychologists includes perception of form, discrimination, part-whole appreciation, figure-background discrimination and visual memory. Such important visual abilities depend on mental ability and experience. Therapists have also helped prepare the way with early training of visual efficiency. Linking any vision with smell, touch and movement builds up some of the fundamentals for perception.

The blind child still is blind in that he may not use vision for academic learning. However, he uses light and any poor visual impressions to understand his environment and to enhance all the other avenues of development, and to decrease the severity of multiple handicaps. Mentally handicapped children will need any scrap of vision to learn. However, the stages of visual development, like other developmental areas, will progress much more slowly in the developmental sequences. Physically handicapped children, relatively immobile, need visual abilities more to learn as well as to initiate, guide and check their poor motor actions. Clumsiness in children is closely connected with poor development of existing sight, various perceptual problems or conflicting information of vision and motor control of their bodies. This is discussed elsewhere (see Chapter 10, Parts 1 and 2). Developmental levels of normal visual development may be followed with residual vision but are not applicable to all children as visual diagnostic problems are so variable. Ages should be adjusted, especially if the child has had no intervention and is treated as totally blind, or his other areas of function such as hearing and motor development have been emphasized and vision left as hopeless (see chart, Table 1.1, p. 8).

8 Visual scanning also occurs when visual learning is more advanced. Teachers have special methods to develop this important ability. Therapists may be asked to assist when offering toys or play material to the child, during motor training and training of hand function. Looking to find things in the room, on the table and in the playground involves practise in scanning. Gentle encouragement to 'set his eyes' on what he wants and not only grope with his hands should be given when there is the potential of doing so in the child.

Note Although visual training has been presented separately to clarify the aspects needing concentration, it must be combined with touch-what-is-seen, hear-what-is-seen and move-what-is-seen. The sound is regularly used to alert the child to the visual stimulus before having him look and see it with sound removed. Rolling or other locomotor activity is initiated or rewarded by the sight of a sparkling, clinking plaything or, especially, mother's voice.

Hand–eye coordination. This is intimately interwoven with visual development and begins with searching and reaching for the seen object. Use of hands to search, reach and manipulate will depend more on other sensations in the blind child but any reach to residual vision should be developed.

Eye-foot and eye-body as well as eye-hand actions should be encouraged whenever possible. Although acuity may not be totally absent, the children fall over objects and often bump into things and need conscious training 'to look'. 'Looking' behaviour later becomes as automatic as with any of the sighted driving a motor car or skating. Increased motor incoordination and mental handicap may also be responsible for these problems.

Development of the use of vision in apparently totally blind children is often rewarding but could create false hopes that sight is being restored! Until the baby is 2 to 3 years old results of visual stimulation are increasing. Therapists should not be misled for the future and should discuss the visual diagnoses and the child's intellectual capacities with the team to understand what is possible. On the other hand, today there should not be a pessimistic ignoring of the vision when one is told the child is blind.

DEVELOPMENT OF USE OF HEARING

When assessment is given of the child's hearing development the therapist can reinforce the training to help the child use sound. Speech therapists and teachers concentrate on this whilst other therapists use sound to motivate or to reward the child's efforts. Development of hand function must involve the child creating sound himself as well as responding to the sounds that appeal to him. Development of posture and postural reactions are possible with the use of sound; for example, the child should lie, roll over, sit, crawl, step and fall on paper that rustles, vinyl or leather couches that squeek and smell, and exercise mats that make a sound *and* have textures of different kinds. Sounds of the child's footsteps on floorboards and other surfaces, splashing water and the sounds associated with training feeding, dressing, bathing and toiletting should be clearly emphasized to the child. This means working and playing with the child in a quiet room and switching off the television set or radio.

Observation of children at play reveals how the unexpected sound of an object catches their interest and then they will repeat the movement or postural adjustment which will once again reward them with that sound. Training movement depends on placing the desirable soundmaking objects near the child, on the side that action is needed and leaving the child to treat himself ! Once touched, he may feel with hand and with mouth, taste, and even put the object to his nose to smell it. Observation of ability to use weaker parts of the body is needed by the therapist, so that frustration does not occur. Once purposeful turn and reach for sound is learnt, as outlined under 'Assessment', this is used in motor development and play therapy.

Help the child to practise rising reactions and locomotion, by going to investigate what made the sound. Teaching the concept of related object permanence depends again on his readiness and what his teacher has decided in his programme. The therapist should train the inefficient, unreliable and unsteady motor patterns using searching games when the child is ready and can experience success. Learning difficult, new, intellectual tasks is only attempted once motor abilities are well established or else the child is unable to learn easily.

Words, speech and explanations should accompany motor experiences in therapy. The therapist observes and knows what the child is capable of understanding either mentally or visually; he cannot conceive of 'visual language' that we use such as colours, 'the sky', 'the bus', 'the roof' and the abstract feelings. However, we must talk naturally and use 'sighted' language, giving the child time to adjust to the sighted world in which he lives, and to obtain his own perception of what is being said.

Speech and language development overlaps into development of hearing, as does intellectual development.

DEVELOPMENT OF TACTILE, PROPRIOCEPTIVE AND VESTIBULAR EXPERIENCES AND BODY IMAGE DEVELOPMENT

Some blind children dislike being touched, others are wary of strangers and others have abnormal neurological reactions or abnormal reflexes which are elicited by touch. Encourage the child to accept touch from his own hands and those of his mother first. The absence of mother–child bonding, especially in babies who were isolated in intensive care 'prem' units or from any 'special' adult, greatly contributes to withdrawal from touch and physical contact.

During therapy, gently 'desensitize' the child by mother's handling and by placing attractive textures and tinkling, light-catching, glittering objects on the mother for the child to lean against, accidentally place his feet and hands on them and so he will indirectly accept their touch. Later, he may search and reach out for these objects, not only on mother but elsewhere.

Whilst training gross motor development, stroking of the child's naked back, trunk and buttocks with powder, oil or pleasant-smelling soaps is easily introduced. Back extension activity is traditionally accompanied by stroking down the patient's back in paediatric physiotherapy! Speech or words or songs naming body parts can be easily and naturally used by the child's parent.

Place crinkly paper, vibrating toys, warm and cold objects, water, sand and other intriguing stimuli on the child's body, especially after stroking, kissing, blowing, making funny noises and other human contact, encourages children's acceptance of being touched. Let the child remove bracelets and coloured sticky paper from his limbs and let him pull off bells hung on his wrists and ankles to make him aware of his body parts.

All the hand function and gross motor activities are involved with tactile and proprioceptive experiences. Every time we move, the receptors in our muscles, joints and vestibular apparatus are activated, therefore, the fearful, inexperienced, blind child who refuses to move or has no inclination to move will cut down these afferent stimuli which he needs so much. Never push the child to move or force objects into his hands if he is withdrawn. Let his mother carry him around in a sling on her body, swing him and bounce him on her lap. Encourage the child's father to have rough-and-tumble play with his child *but* avoid throwing and shaking certain children with retinal problems.

The physiotherapist's assessment of available and emerging postural reactions helps to grade and select activities for parents. Motor-play activities can easily be enjoyed by parents and children, and aid self-confidence and bonding. The postural reactions of tilt in head and trunk can be specifically achieved with the child on his parent's lap or sitting on father's shoulders. Progress can be made to postural reactions stimulated on therapy balls and rolls. This is done because blind children often have fears on balls and rolls.

The child should have particular attention paid to his awareness of his hands as part of body image development. Absence of 'hand regard' allows him to continue to keep his hands out at the sides of his shoulders. With enjoyable sensory stimulation, songs and even messing with his food, the child will become aware of his hands, bring them together in midline to touch each other and so develop hand use.

As the blind child does not see how his hands or body move, he will be taught through kinaesthetic methods how to carry out motor actions. In Chapter 2 these methods are outlined. In addition, neurological physiotherapy methods can be selected to give proprioceptive input; for example, joint compression, manual resistance for postural holding or for movement patterns, push-and-pull exercises and all the methods provoking body sway/weight shift and tilt reactions.

DEVELOPMENT OF POSTURE, LOCOMOTION AND HAND FUNCTION

The development of reach, search, touch, grasp and release take priority, although all motor development is important. Techniques have been discussed in Chapter 2. The modifications for the visually handicapped child consist of the following.

1   Consideration of developmental levels of the 'non-motor' aspects.
2   More practice in orientation of the hand to grasp, finger-tip feeling and moulding, and bilateral hand function.
3   Training motor abilities which can be directly used to explore the environment, to play and to carry out self-care.
4   Specific movement techniques, splintage, calipers and special equipment should only be used when absolutely necessary for the physical handicap.
5   The postural reactions will be more delayed than in sighted children (Levitt 1982). This is associated with decreased tone or floppyness, often seen in blind babies. The development of the postural reactions is, therefore, an important part of the gross motor programme.

Poor posture in sitting, in standing and in walking will require extra training even in blind children who have no motor handicap.

Postural stability is achieved more easily than moving into or out of these postures (Fraiberg 1968). Techniques to elicit the rising reactions which create postural change will, therfore, need extra practice. Abnormal postures, such as unusual head tilts or hunching in order to see, create muscle aches which require therapy. Furniture should be corrected as well.

Selection of developmental sequences such as in the prone position is discussed in Chapter 2.

MOBILITY TRAINING

This is trained in older children by specialized instructors and teachers working for organizations such as the Royal National Institute for the Blind or at schools for the blind. The therapist will have contributed the hearing development and orientation to sound, to light and the basic development of body image and motor development which will be developed further by mobility experts.

THE OLDER CHILD

The physiotherapist may work with physical education and other teachers to increase experience in motor activities, music and movement, dance, gymnastics and various sports and field games.

Balance, coordination and poor posture and weakness often need further physiotherapy sessions. Tight hamstrings, knock knees, round shoulders and lordosis, as well as flat feet, are common. Blind children who have had early motor developmental training do not seem to have many postural abnormalities.

Physical fitness may need building up and is increased by swimming, horse-riding, skiing, and track and field activities.

GENERAL POINTS ON TRAINING VISUALLY HANDICAPPED CHILDREN

Besides the assessment and developmental ideas presented above, the therapist must remember the following points.

1 *Always warn* the child with touch and voice before you pick him up, carry out a procedure or place him in equipment.

2 *Positioning for function* must be shown to all who train the child. Cerebral palsies, weaknesses, and paralyses should be considered so that posture and movement cn be facilitated (see Chapters 2,8,9,15).

3 *Furniture and equipment* should be planned for each child to maintain positions for function rather than positions for perfect postures. The furniture should always be very stable as the child leans on it and uses it for exploration.

4 *Specialized neuromuscular techniques* in various treatment systems should be critically selected to take account of the vision problem. Make sure that the neurophysiological, touch, pressure and other sensory stimuli to move do not confuse the child. If they act as cues to move, they must tune in with the cues given by teachers, since they use the same sensory clues to train the children. Sensory clues must not be contradictory to the development levels.

5 *Clear information* given to the child is of paramount importance. He does not move only for the sake of moving. He moves to find out, to learn. He is

particularly disadvantaged in learning and this is the priority in intervention.

6 *Handling and treatment near and on the parent's bodies.* All babies and young children should be treated on parents' laps. Close physical contact should be made acceptable to the child. Avoid handling by too many different therapists until the child has matured enough to accept this.

7 *Work from in front* of the child so that he does not lean back to your voice or body for support. This is also needed to develop face-to-face contact.

8 *Mannerisms* such as rocking, hand flapping over light sources, eye poking and others may occur in intelligent blind children as well as in mentally handicapped ones. Advice from psychologists should be obtained in order to decrease these mannerisms, usually by distraction to other activities. Occasionally use of gloves or elbow splints may help in cases where eye destruction is likely. Other behaviour modification methods are also helpful (see Chapter 8).

9 *Hospitalization.* Blind children especially the multiply handicapped can be severely disturbed by the experience in hospital. They may still be very dependent on their mother, which is normal for much longer than in the sighted child. Separation from her and strange noises, smells and other

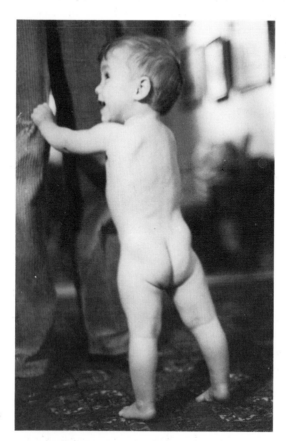

Fig. 14.1 Walking holding father's trousers.

experiences threaten the child into withdrawal. Marked delay in development has been known to occur. As these children often have to go into hospital, mother should accompany them and nursing staff should be helped to understand the effect of blindness.

10 *Self-care training methods* should be obtained from the Royal National Institute for The Blind and peripatetic teachers of The visually handicapped (see Appendix on Addresses).

CONCLUSION

The field of visual handicap is a new one for therapists, particularly physiotherapists. It is impossible to remain isolated in one's own specific therapy discipline as vision affects all functions in man. Contributions from various disciplines concerned with the blind have been studied and summarized in this chapter. Working with others and drawing on their expertise concerning visually handicapped children enriches the physiotherapist, occupational therapist and speech therapist. The therapist's own expertise is extended and given a new perspective.

REFERENCES

FINE S.R. (1979) Incidence of visual handicap in childhood. In *Visual Handicap* (eds Smith V. & Keen J.). Spastics International Medical Publications, London.

FRAIBERG S. (1968) Parallel and divergent patterns in blind and sighted infants. *The Psychoanalytic Study of the Child* **23**, 264–300.

FRAIBERG S. (1977) *Insights from the Blind.* Souvenir Press, London.

GRIFFITHS M.I. (1979) Associated disorders in children with severe visual handicap. In *Visual Handicap* (eds Smith V. & Keen J.). Spastics International Medical Publications, London.

LEVITT S. (1982) *Treatment of Cerebral Palsy and Motor Delay,* 2e, p. 69. Blackwell Scientific Publications, Oxford.

NORRIS M. (1956) What affects blind children's development? *New Outlook for the Blind* **50**, 258–67.

REYNELL J.R. & ZINKIN P. (1975) New procedures for the developmental assessment of young children with severe visual handicaps. *Child: Care, Health and Development* **1**, 61–9.

ROBINSON G.C. (1977) Causes, ocular disorders, associated handicaps, and incidence and prevalence of blindness in childhood. In *Visual Impairment in Children and Adolescents,* eds J.E. Jan, R.D. Freeman & E.P. Scott. Grune & Stratton, New York.

Royal National Institute for the Blind. Parents' pamphlets.

SONKSEN P. (1979) Sound and the visually handicapped baby. *Child: Care, Health and Development* **5**, 413.

SONKSEN P., LEVITT S. & KITZINGER M. (1981) *Motor development in the visually disabled child: identification of constraints and principles of remediation.* Proceedings of International Symposium on Visually Handicapped Infants and Young Children, Tel Aviv, June 1981 (in press).

SYKANDA A.M. & LEVITT S. (1982) The physiotherapist in the developmental management of the visually impaired child. *Child: Care, Health and Development* **8**, 261–70.

ZINKIN P.M. (1979) The effect of visual handicap on early development. In *Visual Handicap* (eds Smith V. & Keen J.). Spastics International Medical Publications, London.

FURTHER READING

CRATTY B.J. (1971) *Movement and Spatial Awareness in Blind Children and Youth.* Charles
   C. Thomas, Springfield, Illinois.
JAN J.E., FREEMAN R.D. & SCOTT E.P. (1977) *Visual Impairment in Children and
   Adolescents.* Grune & Stratton, New York.
TURNER M. & SIEGAL I.M. (1969) Physical therapy for the blind child. *Physical Therapy*
   49, 1357–63.
WARREN D.H. (1977) *Blindness and Early Childhood Development.* American Foundation
   for the Blind, New York.

CHAPTER 15

AIDS TO DAILY LIVING

Patricia Kennedy

A ramp leads up to the door, inside the hall we have to squeeze past the large and heavy outdoor wheelchair with its footplate at a disconcerting angle to trip the unwary. A game of chess played with the family's bikes enables us to reach the living room. (On later visits the route changes, and we are shown through the kitchen.)

The living room is dominated by the large television, the child's window on the world, and various other pieces of equipment, including a foam wedge, a standing frame and chair. The table loaned for standing play is now in the garden, as there is no room for it except at night.

Upstairs, the small bathroom is occupied by a hydraulic bath seat, and the mother has to exercise superb spatial skill to fit herself and the handicapped child into the space available.

This is not a picture of one child's home, but it could easily be. Families often accept the items offered without wishing to seem ungrateful, even though they may not want them. Other parents may seek equipment because someone else has had it for their child, and they feel it may help their own child, even though the needs are quite different.

Disability does not occur in isolation; it occurs in communities, and more specifically in families. Disabled living affects not only the handicapped person, but those who share his life, and those on whom he depends for many of the services that enable him to function at all in the wider community. Parents bear the greater part of the care at home, but brothers and sisters often take a great deal of responsibility for the handicapped child. The family's lifestyle is very important when considering what aids should be provided in the home, just as the requirements of education will affect planning for the handicapped child in school.

ASSESSMENT

Assessment of need and provision of equipment may be shared by a number of professionals. This in itself may create difficulties for the family if cooperation between professionals is fragmented. Those involved in provision of aids are most likely to be occupational therapists or physiotherapists, but speech therapists have an important role with the child who has communication difficulties. Teachers will also be concerned with equipment that enables the child to function better in school.

The family may have contact with more than one source of advice: therapists in hospitals and clinics; therapists and teachers at school; local authority advisers to the disabled, and possibly a voluntary body such as the Spastics Society or Royal National Institute for the Blind, Royal National Institute for the Deaf, and others.

Whenever possible, one therapist should seek to maintain liaison between these different parties. This role is most readily assumed by a community-based therapist, who knows the family and is familiar with the school and services that are available locally. If there is no community therapy service, a therapist at the child's treatment centre may be the best person to do the job.

When providing aids for handicapped children, both the nature of the specific handicap and the natural process of development, and of growth, from dependent infancy to independent adulthood, must be assessed and especially re-assessed as he changes (see also Assessment, under Wheelchairs, p. 237).

Development may be uneven, with more rapid progress in one aspect and little in another. Aids should assist the child to function as adequately as possible in the tasks that a child of his age and intellectual ability might reasonably tackle with competence. For many children this achievement will come only after periods of careful training and help. For some more severely handicapped children, skills may be severely limited. For profoundly handicapped people, aids should assist the parents and those who take care of such disabled people to keep them as active and comfortable as possible, while minimizing the risks of strain and injury to the carers.

The needs of children are governed by three broad aspects of their development: the total pattern of handicap, including physical, intellectual, sensory and perceptual deficits; the maturation of the child and his family's attitude towards realistic independence.

Practical factors affecting the child's progress will be the home and local environment, including the schools available; the health and needs of other family members; and the services available to the child and his family.

There are now many sources of information on aids and equipment for the disabled, and much of the work has been done by voluntary organizations. The Disabled Living Foundation has a permanent display of aids that are available, but not for sale, in London, and produces a regularly updated catalogue of equipment divided into various sections. There are also travelling exhibitions, and specialist units have their own exhibitions (see 'Useful Addresses', Appendix 1).

THE YEARS OF CHILDHOOD

The needs of the child change as he grows and develops. Many solutions to daily living problems, established in these early years, remain useful skills throughout childhood and adolescence.

The parents are most frequently concerned for their child to achieve the developmental 'milestones' that are slow in coming, particularly sitting up and standing, which they recognize as being essential stages on the way towards independent mobility and personal care. They are also anxious for the child to speak, but may accept the child's failure to play and develop manual skills as being the unavoidable result of the child's physical limitations.

PLAY

Playthings stimulate activity, providing the child with reward for his efforts. There are many suitable toys available in nursery and childcare shops, and from specialist mail order firms such as Galts and Arnold's 'Offspring' However, for the severely handicapped child there may be few toys which he can control and manipulate, especially as he gets older when nursery toys with large pieces are too babyish. A number of specialist toys have been made for the disabled, including the profoundly handicapped child. Simple switching systems that allow the most severely restricted child to activate a mechanical or illuminated toy like the 'Atari' games have been designed. Mechanical games with appeal for older children, but having large pieces and strong base trays can be found. 'Perfection', 'Connect 4', 'Track 4' are examples produced by Merit and by Denys Fisher. Microelectronic games such as 'Simon', TV games controlled by paddle switches, and joy-sticks, now make recreational activity accessible to handicapped children. Personal computers can provide much leisure activity.

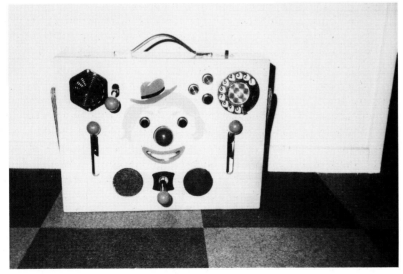

Fig. 15.1 Multi-activity box

By using magnetic strip and metal boards, games can be adapted for the older child. Large parquetry tiles (from Task-Master Catalogue) can be arranged on a vertical or horizontal board. Thick card dominoes, pair-matching games drawn on large squares can be used in a similar way.

For the parent or technician who is able to make wooden toys, a series of working drawings are available from 'Active'. Most of these designs have come from parents or professionals who have made toys for children with severe handicaps.

Toy libraries have been established in many areas, and their use can increase the child's play experience. Some toy libraries have a particular interest in toys for handicapped children and may stock some of the special toys for the severely handicapped.

Toys can be fixed in a number of ways to avoid the frustration of involuntary displacement. Suction pads or small clamps can be used on firm surfaces, and a variety of toys are designed to be suspended from cots or playpens. A small wooden frame can be used to fix toys in front of the child, becoming a new toy whenever the objects are changed. Aprons or table tops can be made from textured fabrics, and a variety of items pinned or tied on. The apron is particularly useful for the mobile, mentally handicapped child or the visually handicapped child.

Positions for play are discussed elsewhere (see Chapters 2,8,9,13,14).

FURNITURE

Many items of furniture or domestic equipment can be used for the handicapped child at home. Normally available things should be explored before recommending specialist equipment for the child. The schoolchild may

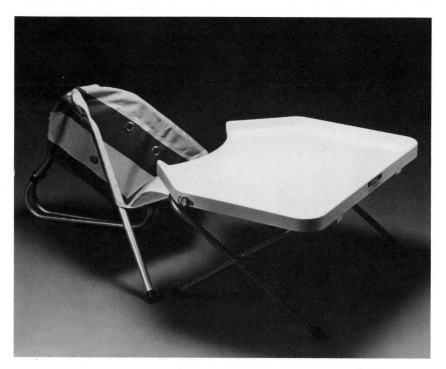

Fig. 15.2

wish to appear more grown-up using things in the adult world but may still require some adaptations. The general rules for equipment apply equally well to those things used by all children. Furniture should be sturdily made, safe for its purpose, easily cleaned, compact and useful over a reasonable period of time. This last point is particularly important when recommending something to be bought by the family.

Cot-beds, cot-bumpers, wooden high chair/table combinations, playpens and safety gates are just some of the items that can be bought at local shops. The child's therapist should be able to advise on the most suitable furniture, both for the child's needs and the family's home.

Seating is a very important aspect of the child's care, and a good sitting position can lead to many opportunities for play and the development of independence skills. The Baby Corner seat and folding table, from Nottingham Handcraft Ltd., suit many young handicapped children, and are welcomed in the home for their pleasant appearance and ease of storage when not in use. At school, tables and chairs should be of the correct measurements. Special chairs may be made by school technicians or other workshops.

TOILET TRAINING

For the child to co-operate with toilet training, he must feel comfortable and secure when using a potty or toilet seat. There is a wide selection of potties and seats in local stores. The styles that give a secure base, and some support to the child, are most suitable for young handicapped children. The Baby Relax toilet seat has a firm, supportive seat, and a safety strap.

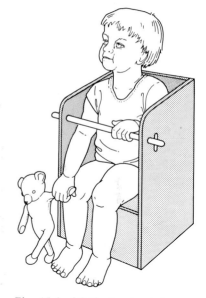

Fig. 15.3 Watford potty-chair

For the child who needs more support, a number of designs based on the Watford potty chair are usually available through Social Services Departments. Toilet aids can be replaced with larger models, or a seat fitted over the toilet or a commode to suit the child's needs. An unsteady child needs a sturdy platform as a foot stool to avoid his holding on to the toilet seat with both hands. Grab rails fixed to the floor or wall near the toilet may be sufficient for independence for some children.

Bathing may present problems of safety for the child, and as he grows, for the parents or carers who lift him in and out of the bath, and support him during bathing and dressing. Parents' backs need to remain healthy for a long time.

A bath aid such as the SAFA bath seat (Fig. 15.4) may help a child with reasonable sitting balance, whose stability in the water, however, is affected by the bouyancy of flaccid limbs. A suction-attached bath mat is often sufficient to provide a non-slip standing area and comfortable sitting place for the more physically able child, like the hemiplegic child who can stand and walk. A stable wooden stool with a larger surface area is preferable to the small plastic stool for helping the child reach the basin.

For the more severely handicapped child and his parents, the Sunflower bath-aid reduces the amount of lifting and bending for the parent, and provides a secure and comfortable reclining position for the child. It drains quickly and efficiently when bathing is over, and can be used as a drying table.

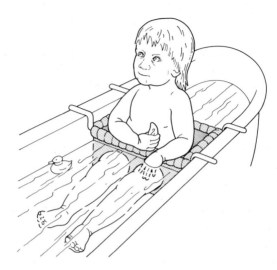

Fig. 15.4   Safa bath seat

The older child needs grab-rails on the edge of the bath and a safe non-slip floor surface. Lever taps, and flexible shower attachments increase the child's independence.

A nailbrush with suction pads, sponges or brushes on long handles, soap on a rope, sponges enclosing soap, towel-mittens, bubble bath all help the child bath alone.

For the older child who needs to be lifted in and out of the bath, more comprehensive adjustments to the bathroom may have to be made. Aids should be kept as simple as possible. Bath-boards, free-standing bath seats and fitted rails may enable the child with stronger arms to transfer himself into the bath from a chair or wheelchair.

If there is severe limitation of the child's arm function, a more complex system such as the Auto-lift may be needed. Baths or shower units specifically designed for the disabled may need to be installed for the most severely disabled children, particularly if the parents have medical problems themselves which make lifting a considerable risk to their own health.

Social Services Departments will be responsible for the assessment, provision and installation of any major aids or equipment for the bathroom. Cooperation between professionals before and after installation, should be maintained to ensure that the adaptation is adequate, and, where necessary, to train the family to use the equipment efficiently. Ineffective or redundant equipment should be removed from the child's home as soon as possible, as space is at a premium in the average home.

DENTAL CARE

This is particularly important for the handicapped child. Many children with speech impairment cannot perform the simple tongue and mouth movements that assist the natural cleaning of teeth during and after eating. They cannot push their tongue over their teeth and gums to remove particles of food, nor can they suck at their teeth with their tongue to remove irritating bits from between the teeth.

For the child who can hold a toothbrush, but who cannot achieve the fine movements needed for cleaning the teeth, or for the child who needs his teeth cleaned by someone else, a battery operated toothbrush can be a great asset.

CLOTHING

Suitable clothing can greatly assist the family where a child is still very dependent on others for his personal care, but it can also help a child who is struggling for independence or who is attending school. This need not mean abandoning current fashions, but can, by selecting certain basic features of size and design, make dressing and undressing very much easier.

Cotton or wool mixtures for sweaters and T-shirts have much greater elasticity than most artificial fibres. They do not tend to cling to other garments or to the skin as much. Clothes should fit loosely but not be too large. Wider sleeves such as raglan or cap sleeves, open necklines and front-fastening clothes assist dressing. Nylon roll-necks, nylon socks, shiny fabrics and tightly elasticated waists should be avoided. Stretch towelling socks and shoes with elastic gussets are easier for independence.

In the early stages of independence, the child has quite a task learning to manage himself and his clothes, particularly if he has perceptual problems. It is generally not advisable at this stage to use separate aids, as their introduction may add new problems. However, a number of aids can be part of the clothing: loops to help pull up pants or trousers; rings or loops on zips; and Velcro fastenings.

Parents should be encouraged to take a child in his wheelchair when buying a coat, so that the ease of getting it on and off, and the comfort of the child wearing it while sitting, can be judged before buying. Footwear may present problems, particularly in the winter, as many children have poor circulation to the feet, and parents may not know how important warm wool or cotton mixture socks can be. Thermal insoles, socks or tights may help to avoid problems resulting from long draughty journeys to and from school in the winter.

EATING AND DRINKING

There is a wide variety of nursery tableware available at local chemists and nursery stores, including trainer cups, shaped bowls and non-metal cutlery. If the child is to master self-feeding, a good sitting position and firm table top are necessary. For some children a standing frame may provide a better posture than a chair.

Non-slip mats or bowls with a suction base help to control the plate in the early stages of self-feeding, and a 'Keep-Warm' plate can help the very slow child to remain interested in the food. Spoons may be adapted by lengthening or thickening handles, or by altering the angle of the spoon handle according to the child's particular needs. Many young children respond badly to the hard texture of a metal spoon: an unwanted reflex action of the mouth, and the head and shoulders, may be caused by the contact of the metal with lips and teeth. Plastic spoons should be of the safer polythene type, to avoid the risk of the child biting through the spoon where reflex biting occurs during eating.

Some children are reluctant to maintain a grip on the spoon and may need a loop fitted over the hand. Swivel-spoons may help the child with limb deformities or joint-restricting conditions such as arthrogryphosis, but generally are not satisfactory for the cerebral-palsied child.

Specially adapted equipment is available from several suppliers and can often be lent by the child's therapist before being ordered for the child. Some children may only need the aid for a few weeks or months before learning to use ordinary cutlery or plates.

When the child is reluctant to feed himself it is important to establish a pattern that has a good chance of success before being too insistent on self-feeding at home. Many children enjoy the opportunity to fight the parents over feeding, and for the handicapped child, experiencing boredom and fatigue in attempting to feed himself, failure will only increase such chances. The aim should be to make mealtimes pleasant and relaxed giving the child the chance to enjoy his newly acquired skill.

MOBILITY

Mobility in some form is essential for the child and his family. The form that mobility takes will be the result of differing objectives for the child and those caring for him. Standing and walking aids will be used as part of the child's physiotherapy programme and will be supplied to the child. They may include standing frames, rollators, quadrupods and may be changed as the child progresses.

For the child who is pulling to standing and cruising round the furniture, the furniture itself can become an aid by placing toys on the settee or coffee table so that the child stands for longer, and is encouraged to move round to reach what he needs.

Push-round toys are excellent for these children. The toys should be sturdy, have a low centre of gravity, and allow room for the child to step forward without being obstructed by the frame of the toy. A low centre of gravity can be created by weighting the axles or the lower part of the frame. A sandbag weight rather than loose metal pieces should be used, as this is safer, and the weight distribution can be more easily adjusted.

Various forms of low trolley can provide early mobility. The prone trolley is used by the child lying on his tummy and propelling himself by pushing with his hands. The SHASBAH trolley and the Yorkhill wheelchair (available from DHSS) are suitable for the young child with reasonable balance and adequate arm function.

Parents may have bought a pushchair for their child, but if it is unsuitable or needs replacing as the child grows, the McLaren Baby Buggy and Cindico Traveller are available from DHSS. Lie-back or twin models can be supplied if the child is severely handicapped, or the parents have to transport another toddler or baby with the handicapped child. These models are usually supplied on request if a form is signed by the child's doctor. If a special inset seat is needed, a DHSS technical officer may need to see the child. The child's therapist should try to be present at the assessment or should send written details of needs.

Buggies can be of great benefit to the families of ambulant disabled children where the child becomes tired easily, as they enable the child to go with the rest of the family to local shops and parks, and on longer trips away from home.

For the child with trunk balance, reach and grip in the arms and hands, and with functional leg movements when sitting, many ordinary mobility toys provide play activity and can act as mobility aids, particularly out of doors. The bike, push truck or pedal car can also be adapted to the needs of the individual child by making sitting a little more secure, or by ensuring that the child can maintain a firm, comfortable grip on the handles or on the steering wheels.

There are several playcarts and chairs designed for handicapped children, particularly those with lower-limb paralysis, but they do tend to be expensive and limited in their use. Foot-pedal and hand-pedal trikes and bikes can be supplied by DHSS.

CAR SEATS AND WHEELCHAIRS

The family car is an important factor in mobility. Safety of the handicapped child in the car is essential, and all the safety rules that apply to children should be emphasized for the handicapped. A child with limited movement and poor sitting balance is at great risk sitting in a car without some form of restraint. The restless, distractable child can cause accidents if he is left to move around in the car, or if the parent relies on holding him.

There are several commercial car seats and harnesses that will give the child security, but for the severely disabled, and the larger child, a special seat or harness may be needed once the standard baby and toddler sizes are no longer adequate. (See References: car safety equipment in *The Disabled Child* in the Equipment for Disabled series.) Some parents find the Orthokinetic chair useful as a car seat. Therapists should draw the attention of parents to legislation as it affects children in cars. The Transport Act of 1981 prohibits any child under the age of 14 from travelling in the front seat of a vehicle unless restrained. Children under one year old are allowed to travel in the front seat only if they are protected by an approved form of restraint that is specifically designed for them.

Wheelchairs for the growing child will depend on the degree of handicap and on the intended use of the chair which might be:

Fig. 15.5 Hansa Booster Seat for the car (distributed by Joncare, UK, see p. 211).

1 Self-propelling
(a) as an independent mobility aid in conjunction with other aids used for walking (calipers, sticks, crutches, etc.);
(b) as the child's major means of mobility and seating during the day.
2 Controlled by an attendant
(a) as supportive and remedial seating where mobility is controlled by an attendant.

The type of chair will be further defined by the child's physical and mental ability to control it; his build and weight; and by special requirements for avoiding postural deformity; or preventing pressure sores and similar problems.

SELF-PROPELLING WHEELCHAIRS

The propelling wheels are usually mounted at the rear of the chair, with forward castors and adjustable footrests. The DHSS model 8C has a well-balanced frame and is adequate for most children in this group. A variety of similar models are available privately, including sports models which will suit the active child who is interested in greater speed and manoeuvrability.

Powered chairs are suitable for children with limited hand function and those with medical conditions requiring a less fatiguing means of mobility. Such chairs are operated by batteries controlled by a four-way switch which is usually a joystick mounted on the arm rest. A variety of alternative switching systems, to be operated by the head, chin, foot, or by hand pressure pads, can be used. BEC supply a range of powered indoor chairs available through the DHSS, starting with the wooden-framed 'Bambino' for nursery and infant age group; the 'Fireball' for children from about six; and models 12 and 14 for older and larger children. All except the 'Bambino' can be folded down for transporting. There is a wide range of powered chairs and go-karts available commercially, and features such as kerb-climbing, easy folding and reassembly, neat battery packs, and various aspects of appearance may all affect choice. However, the major concern should always be the best possible form of mobility and seating for the child.

For the profoundly handicapped child a wheelchair which assists desirable posture and reduces the risk of fixed deformities is needed. The 'Avon' tilting pushchair with upholstered seat, headrest, sides, and leg support is the only model supplied by the DHSS. Orthokinetics have produced a chair with a great number of finely adjustable features which enable it to be adjusted to suit very particular needs. Its easy translation from wheelchair to car seat without the need to move the child is appreciated by parents.

A standard wheelchair can be adapted to special needs through various forms of cushioning; pommels to prevent forward sliding; and harnesses to assist the maintenance of posture. A built-up upholstered seat, link-adjusted or vacuum-moulded seats can all be accommodated in a standard wheelchair by being anchored to the chair's frame. Where such a seat is used, its effect on the balance of the chair for the child and the attendant should be assessed.

ASSESSMENT

Assessments for wheelchairs should be carried out, whenever possible, by the child having the opportunity to try out the model(s) himself, before the final acceptance of the chair. Physiotherapists and occupational therapists should work together with the child and the parents to choose the most suitable chair.

The following important points should be observed while taking measurements for a chair.

1   The child should be sitting in the required posture, and also be observed during a period of time to note detrimental changes of posture (e.g. sliding forward and downwards in the seat).

2   Measure height of chair back, from base of the spine, when in the correct position, to the shoulders. Make a separate but linked measurement if a headrest or extended back is required. Allow for any extra height if a seat cushion is to be used.

3   Seat length should be measured from the back of the chair (with the child in the correct position) to just behind the knee joint, allowing for 3–5 cm clearance between the edge of the seat and the joint to prevent pressure. (Add to the measurement if a back cushion is to be used).

4   Width should be measured with the child in the correct position and wearing any form of prosthesis or aid (calipers, splints, etc.). Allow extra width for supportive cushions and for wearing outdoor clothes.

If a self-propelling chair is ordered, the hands should rest on the propelling wheels comfortably, and the shoulders should not be abducted more than 30° as this reduces mechanical efficiency and increases fatigue.

5   The length from the seat to the footrest should enable the feet to rest at right angles on the footplates (unless this is impossible) and they should not slide off. If the footrests are at full extension when the chair is tried, then a larger model, or use of a seat cushion, is indicated.

6   Observation of the child's posture and use of the chair may indicate the need for additional adjustments which should be listed in full detail when ordering a chair, e.g. removeable pommel for toiletting; hard- or soft-backed cushions; position and handedness for joystick controls.

All wheelchairs should be fitted with a safety strap at waist level; other safety or practical adjustments may include extensions and enlarged handle-grips for joysticks, brakes and switches. Chairs may be fitted with attendant-operated brakes for safety when using tail-lift coaches. Parents may request folding backrests to enable the chair to fit into the family car. If the chair's use is altered by the child's being in plaster splints, or requiring a leg extension board, then it should be checked for balance and safety, particularly the level of armrests, safety belt and supporting cushions or harness.

SCHOOLDAYS

If the child attends a special school he is likely to be in an environment which is adapted to his needs. He not only will find toilets, and handbasins appropriate to his size but may have rails, special seats, lever taps and non-slip floor surfaces to assist him in his personal care and safety. The school is likely to be on the same level throughout, or will be ramped where levels vary. Corridors will be wider, doors designed for wheelchair users and, classrooms and cloakrooms will have sufficient space to manoeuvre a wheelchair or trolley.

For the child who attends a mainstream school, these built-in aids are unlikely to exist. When the child's future schooling is being discussed, the paediatric therapist may be asked to give an assessment of the school being considered. Using her knowledge of the child, the therapist can observe the school's layout, and the way in which its activities are organized, assessing how to exercise the child's personal independence, and recommending the adaptations, aids and assistance that the child may need if he is to participate in the school activities, and establish satisfactory relationships with his peers. At the present time in Britain, schools tend to accept a handicapped child provided that the child can cope with the school as it is, or with fairly minor adjustments. Where structural alterations might be required such as ramps, or enlarging toilet cubicles for chair-bound children, or to accommodate a child using a rollator or other walking aid, the school may feel unable to cope, particularly if there is a local special school to suit the child's needs.

Schools may respond to the request to take a handicapped child by asking for support, by requesting additional services both within the school (nursery-nurse or welfare staff), and access to the professional services provided by the local authority, local health services and hospital units. The school may also demand quite a high commitment from the parents in supporting both the child and the school, but much depends on the school staff as well.

The child should be trained to manage without aids or use neat and unobtrusive ones which are conveniently carried to the right place at the right time.

EDUCATIONAL AIDS

At school the child must have reasonable access to all areas of the building, adequate space to use toilets, washing facilities and cloakrooms and room to move freely around the classroom. The child should be responsible for his own books and equipment, unless too severely disabled to do so. Storage cupboards and drawers should be at the correct height for the child, and appropriate seating and work surfaces are essential if the child is to function adequately in the classroom.

Position in relation to boards and display materials is of great importance to all handicapped children. Informal groups of desks or tables in the classroom may present particular difficulty to children with physical or sensory handicaps, particularly where there are visual defects or visuoperceptual problems. Ideally all children should face blackboards and wall displays and not need to turn themselves in order to see something at an oblique angle. This is particularly important for copying from the board. For some children, even the angle from the board to his own desk top can cause difficulties and alternative layouts of work should be used.

Physically handicapped children who use wheelchairs may prefer to use their chair at all times. For many children some form of alternative seating during lessons is desirable and should be encouraged. If the child does remain in a wheelchair, work surfaces should be adjusted to allow the wheelchair to fit adequately beneath the desk or table. Sloping work surfaces assist children with a variety of physical and visual limitations, particularly where there are problems of head control.

Functional deficits of the upper limbs will require careful assessment of the most suitable working surfaces for different activities. Trunk-balance problems may lead to severe postural difficulties when writing, and assessment in the classroom is essential for establishing the most satisfactory working position for the child. Prone boards linked to the work surface may provide a satisfactory position for some more severely handicapped children.

WRITING AND DRAWING

Large-size pencils, pens and crayons are often used by young children, but their use may continue well beyond the infant stages if they assist the child to draw and write more effectively. Felt pens are particularly useful as they are available in several thicknesses, both for line and grip. The bright colours give clear contrast between line and paper and will give visible results even from the most tentative of movements.

Grip on the pen or pencil can be improved by thickening the shaft with foam or strapping. Task-master supply small triangular rubber grips that fit standard size pencils. Some children may be able to guide a pen if it is pushed through a gamester ball (normal or golf ball size to suit the child). The child can then use a full palmar grip on the ball, and the pen remains firmly in position.

Paper can be fixed to table tops with 'blue tack' or clipboards. Alternative surfaces such as white-boards may facilitate writing skills as the surface offers less resistance to the pen than paper. For many children with visual or visuoperceptual problems, a vertical work surface such as an easel or small black-white board appears to help the child in early shape and letter formation more than a horizontal surface. Positioning of all work materials, particularly for copying, should be considered very carefully for vision and postural security. All work surfaces should be well illuminated, using an angle-poise lamp if necessary.

TYPING AND ELECTRONIC AIDS

Typing may be used for children:
1   who are unable to write;
2   who are excessively clumsy or uncoordinated;
3   who have perceptual and/or spatial deficits or visuomotor handicaps.

Some children will be able to use an ordinary portable machine, particularly if they are in mainstream schools, but for many physically handicapped children its use requires too much energy, and an electric machine is better. Bulletin, or Jumbo-type machines should be used with young children but are also indicated for older children. If the typewriter is a teaching-machine as well as a writing aid, the keys should be covered with lower-case letter stickers. Visibility of the script can be improved by using a magnifying glass on an adjustable stand. Work being copied should be placed on an adjustable rest, as close to the typescript as possible.

The child should be seated so that he can see down on to the keys and script that he is producing. The machine may need to be tilted at an angle by using a secure wooden frame on the desk top, the frame may include a forearm rest which supports the wrist and restricts unwanted movements. Key-guards can be fitted to most makes of typewriters, but the Brother Bulletine-print typewriter has an excellent perspex guard that is pleasant to touch for the child, and can easily be removed if the keyboard is to be used by a teacher to produce class materials.

For the severely disabled child who cannot use a normal electric typewriter, there are several electronic alternatives available. Possum produce three such machines: the Type IA/5A which works through a switching system and illuminated letter grid. This is very slow and it is difficult to place the child so that he can use the switches and see the script. The expanded keyboard models normally use a golfball typewriter which presents very serious problems of visibility of the script, even with a magnifying glass. The mini keyboard is only suitable for the child with severely weakened arm function but accurate finger location.

The DHSS may issue a Possum typewriter if the child has a severe communication problem, but will not supply them to children with severe physical handicaps who have comprehensible speech.

The Electraid typewriter control 5600 is similar to the Possum IA/5A machine, but is more versatile as it can be adjusted to take more than one pattern of switch inputs. This makes it available to more than one pupil, or to the same child advancing from two to four or eight switches. (It is not available through the DHSS.)

Microprocessors and personal computers are affecting the world of the disabled very rapidly. Many new communication aids are being developed. They nearly all use some form of keyboard and television display. MAC (Microprocessor Assisted Communicator) developed by Patrick Poon at Kings College, London, consists of a briefcase containing the electronic parts with a keyboard or switching system. Plugged into any television set, which becomes the display area for the text, work can be corrected and edited while displayed on the screen and then transferred through an electronic printer on to paper. MAC has the facility for setting out column maths and for word lists. It can also be used to replace the keyboard input to a computer.

As with much microtechnology, MAC is already being superseded. A MAC floppy disc has now been produced for use with Apple-computer, and includes an Etcha-Sketch drawing programme. A geometric drawing programme is also being developed. The MAC–APPLE computer system for severely disabled users is being developed and marketed through the Electraid Company. Another personal computer being developed for handicapped users is the Commodore Pet, but many of the computers now on the market could be used by anyone able to type using a normal keyboard.

An Apple microcomputer specifically adapted for the handicapped may cost £1500 (1983). However, many normal schools have opted for the cheaper BBC microcomputer which has also had programmes designed for the handicapped child. Cash is still needed to provide the severely handicapped child with an adapted keyboard or switching system.

Parents may ask about insurance cover for privately owned electronic aids and other equipment. The Sun Alliance Company is one of the companies with special policies for such equipment.

ADAPTATION OF THE HOME ENVIRONMENT

The bathroom and kitchen may need adjustments for safety and for the child who is poorly coordinated or in a wheelchair. Most children in wheelchairs will not be able to see above the level of the kitchen units or the top of the cooker, spina-bifida children may not be aware of the risk to their legs from a hot oven or radiators.

Few parents encourage their child to cook or even use an electric kettle, but they should let the child do what he can manage. The parents of a

Thalidomide-damaged child bought Melamine tableware so that their son could take his turn setting the table, clearing away, and washing up with his brothers, without losing his confidence through breakages.

Simple kitchen aids can be introduced appropriately as the child seeks to become more independent. Parents may need advice and encouragement to let the child use skills in the home that he uses in the school's domestic science room (Handscombe *et al.* 1981).

The home environment itself may place severe limitations on the disabled child, this is particularly so where the house is old and built on different levels with split staircases, half-landings and steps leading to bathroom and kitchen areas. Access to the home may be limited by steps to the front door, several flights of stairs and lifts that break down. Besides access problems there may also be narrow corridors and doorways. Very small rooms may make it very difficult for a wheelchair user to turn, move close enough for safe transfers, be able to close bathroom or bedroom door, or be unable to open it once inside. Adaptations, particularly involving structural alterations, may be impossible in system-built houses or flats and may lead to recommendations for re-housing. Parents need medical, social work and educational help when they approach housing authorities for re-housing.

For ramps, widening of doorways and installation of lifts, bathroom fittings and kitchen alterations may be recommended by the Social Services advisers. Structural additions and adaptations can be planned to accommodate the handicapped person in the home, particularly where provision of toilet and washing facilities will result in greater personal independence.

The cost and possibility of installing equipment, adaptations and extensions will depend on the ownership of the property. Therapists involved in an advisory role with the family about to embark on such a scheme should try to ensure that the family fully understand what the alterations hope to achieve in terms of personal independence for the child, or easier care by the parent. Parents should also be helped to prepare for the disruption and inconvenience that will arise while the work is being done. The therapist can help alleviate anxiety by directing the family to the appropriate agency should they experience problems in relation to improvement grants, permission from landlords for work to be carried out, and clarification of plans for alterations. Therapists other than those employed by the local authorities as advisers to the disabled, do not generally have direct access to the relevant departments and should always work on the family's behalf through the appropriate social work agency.

The stage at which housing problems are dealt with will vary according to the severity of the child's handicap, his size and weight, and health or other factors affecting the parents themselves. Some parents welcome any adaptations or alterations to their home that increase the child's independence or those which help the parent to care more easily for the severely handicapped child. Other families may resist making consessions to their child's special needs and may not want their home life to be disrupted. Their feelings must be respected. Professionals caring for the child may experience personal frustration, but should continue to support the family in such a way that the parents feel free to return and ask for help, previously declined, when they accept the need for changes within their family and home.

ADOLESCENCE — TOWARDS ADULTHOOD

As the child grows into adolescence, parents may begin to raise fears and anxieties previously unspoken. For some families this is the point at which they seek and accept help previously declined. For the child, all the preoccupations of adolescence arise, but there may be a marked preoccupation with his own self-image, anxiety about what it means to be a handicapped adult, and concern with what lies beyond school.

Reassessment of the child's personal independence is vital at this stage, particularly for the child with incontinence and for those with such severe handicaps that full independence in self-care is not possible.

For many adolescents, a partial degree of self-care is more desirable than total dependence, but it not always easy to establish with the carers (parents or care-staff).

A severely quadriplegic boy wanted to become independent in toiletting as he no longer wished to be dependent on welfare assistance at school, where even slight delay might lead to accidental wetting. He was able to use a urine bottle when wearing adapted trousers, provided he could reach the bottle and replace it. A pedestal table at wheelchair height was placed in the school's toilet, with the bottle on it. After use it was replaced on the table to be sluiced later by care staff. A closomat toilet with elbow control for washing and flushing gave the same boy a measure of privacy after help with his clothing and transfer from wheelchair to toilet by care-staff.

Physical changes during puberty may increase the problems of the incontinent child. Previously learned patterns may be disrupted, and greater external pressures for social conformity may interrupt carefully established routines. For these children, and those whose earlier training has been less successful, adolescence frequently brings strong motivation to master more socially acceptable patterns of hygiene. Timed routines can be assisted by a digital watch with an alarm, reducing the need for reminders from adults.

For the adolescent girl, the onset of menstruation brings new problems of personal hygiene, and emotional reactions to this very clear evidence of approaching adulthood. Suitable protection during periods is essential to the comfort of all handicapped girls. Those with sensory loss and incontinence need to take particular care at this time. Girls who have been trained in the care of their skin will not have any great difficulties in learning to be particularly vigilant during menstruation.

Girls should be encouraged to select their sanitary protection carefully. Tampons are unsuitable in several handicaps either because of the continuing risk of infection in the incontinent child, or because insertion is difficult. Tampons may be preferable for girls wearing artificial limbs or calipers (worn for conditions other than those involving incontinence). Chailey Heritage have designed a tampon aid for severely limb deficient girls which could also be used in other limb restricting handicaps. Towels should be soft and have a cotton covering rather than fibre-paper, they should also be of sufficient length for comfort when worn by a girl using a wheelchair. Most girls prefer the self-adhesive towel as it is easy to manage and generally more comfortable. Nikini briefs with clip-in towels are very comfortable for the ambulant girl.

MOBILITY

Greater mobility is a high priority for many adolescents and finding a suitable wheelchair during this period of rapid growth can be quite difficult. Those with powered chairs are particularly limited as the DHSS do not supply models for outdoor use. Some parents will use the child's mobility allowance to purchase a chair. Buying a wheelchair is also a popular project for fund raisers in pubs and clubs. In either case it is important that the family are advised by the child's therapist on the most suitable model for the child's disability, the home and local environment, and the ease with which it can be transported in the family's car. Whenever possible a demonstration by the sales agency should be arranged, with opportunity for the child to try out the chair, control positions and manoeuvrability in the local environment.

The DHSS will occasionally issue an alternative self-propelling chair (Everest & Jennings, Zimmer or Carter's model) if an adequate case is put to the assessing medical officer, demonstrating the advantages for a particular child over the standard 8L chair.

If a private chair is being bought or donated, the parents must accept all responsibility for maintenance, repairs and spare parts.

The DHSS will supply three-wheeler bikes ('Picador') to those able to pedal and maintain an adequate control over the bike. An assessment with the bike at the DHSS centre is essential before it is issued, but no formal training is given. Therapists are often responsible for teaching the child to use the bike, and for safety training if it is to be used on the roads. Many local police authorities will advise on cycling proficiency schemes and may be willing to organize such a scheme in special schools.

Many teenagers express a wish to drive, and details of the adaptations and aids for driving are listed in *Equipment for the Disabled, Outdoor Transport;* and in the Government booklet *Door to Door.* However, fitness to drive and ability to learn the coordinated patterns required for the safe control of a car can prove a considerable obstacle to many disabled youngsters, particularly those with neurological handicaps.

There is no central coordinating body for disabled driving information and assessment, but Banstead Place have set up a Mobility Centre. They have particular expertise in the assessment and training of disabled teenagers in all aspects of independence. The teenagers and their families should also be encouraged to explore alternative methods of transport especially for the ambulant child.

SOCIAL ACTIVITY

Teenagers are often keen to have closer contacts with able-bodied youngsters. Many local clubs and uniformed organizations will welcome the children, but the success of the venture often depends on the child's own personality. Where the child needs a less demanding introduction to his peers, local PHAB (Physically Handicapped and Able Bodied) groups may help, as the able-bodied youngsters have a particular interest in relating to the handicapped.

CONCLUSION

It is not possible to discuss all the aids available for disabled young people and new items are constantly being designed and added to catalogues. However, a general approach by a paediatric occupational therapist to helping the disabled child and adolescent in his daily living requirements has been given.

REFERENCES AND FURTHER READING

ASBAH (1979) *Sex and the Spina Bifida Child,* Association for Spina Bifida and Hydrocephalus, London.

CHAILEY HERITAGE (1977a) *Sitting Comfortably.* Chailey Heritage, Lewes.

CHAILEY HERITAGE (1977b) *Arthrogryphosis.* Chailey Heritage, Lewes.

DEPARTMENT OF TRANSPORT (1981) *Door to Door.* Department of Transport, London. (Available from DoT, Freepost, Ruislip. Middlesex HA4 0BR)

DISABLED LIVING FOUNDATION (1971) *Clothing for the Handicapped Child.* Disabled Living Foundation, London.

DISABLED LIVING FOUNDATION (1978) *The Garden and the Handicapped Child.* Disabled Living Foundation, London.

EQUIPMENT FOR THE DISABLED (1980) *The Disabled Child.* Equipment for the Disabled, 2 Foredown Drive, Portslade, Sussex BN4 2BB.

EQUIPMENT FOR THE DISABLED (1978) *Personal Care.* Equipment for the Disabled, Portslade.

EQUIPMENT FOR THE DISABLED (1977) *Outdoor Transport.* Equipment for the Disabled, Portslade.

GOLDENBURG E.P. (1979) *Special Technology for Special Children.* University Park Press, Baltimore.

GREENGROSS W. (1980) *Sex and the Handicapped Child.* SPOD, London.

HANDSCOMBE S., FOOT S. & LANE M. (1976) *The Disabled School Child and Kitchen Sense.* Heinemann Health Books, London.

HARPIN P. (1981) *With a Little Help.* Muscular Dystrophy Group of Great Britain, London.

See also 'Useful Addresses', Appendix 1.

CHAPTER 16

INTEGRATION OF DISCIPLINES IN THE TREATMENT AND EDUCATION OF CHILDREN WITH CEREBRAL PALSY

Ester Cotton

This chapter is concerned with the problem of how the work of many teaching and treating professionals can be best integrated for the benefit of the cerebral-palsied child.

With the development of atomic physics, the mechanistic view of Descartes and Newton is changing and a new view emerging that no longer sees the world as a machine consisting of separate objects, but rather as an organic whole, a network of relationships and an interdependence of objects. Most of us are still adhering to an out-of-date world view. When we meet problems we try to solve them by dividing them into parts and putting the parts right, but we do not concentrate on the connection between the parts.

The organization of management in cerebral palsy is an excellent example of this fragmented outlook. We deal efficiently with the physical, linguistic and functional disabilities of the child but fail to provide continuity and opportunities for reinforcement and transfer of skills.

ORGANIZATION OF TREATMENT AND EDUCATION

Since the Second World War, interest in both treatment and education of the cerebral palsied child has grown considerably. This advance was prompted by the high survival rate due to antibiotics and the conquest of other major ailments such as TB and polio.

Doctors, neurologists, therapists and educationists have used their knowledge, observations and experience to devise methods, systems of treatment and programmes of education according to their professional bias.

A few examples are:

Perlstein, Phelps	Orthopaedic procedures
Bobath, Kabat, Rood, Temple-Fay, Vojta	Neurophysiological theories
Bobath, Rood, Vojta	Ontogenetic development
Temple-Fay, Vojta	Phylogenetic development
Ayres	Sensory integration
Paget Gorman, Bliss	Communication skills
Cruikshank, Strauss, Tansley, Frostig	Educational theories

All these systems and methods vary both in theoretical background and in their use of aids and techniques, but certain features are common to them all.

1 Treatment is divided from education.

2 Treatment is divided into physiotherapy, speech therapy, occupational therapy, music therapy.

3 Treatment and education are divided from care.

4 Treatment sessions are episodic and outside the child's daily routine.

Figure 16.1 shows that in all these methods treatment and education are *linear,* i.e. each therapist, teacher, psychologist, or nursery nurse deals with the symptom that comes under her jurisdiction. The child moves from one to the other at prescribed times. Movement, function and language are taught as separate items and according to the method preferred by each operator. This fragmentation and the different handling of the child lead to confusion, and instead of concentrating on the here and now, the child will be anxiously worrying when he has to move on to the next operator again.

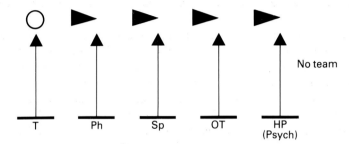

No team

T　　Ph　　Sp　　OT　　HP
(Psych)

○ = Child

● = Child

▬ = Teacher/Therapist/etc.

G = Goals

C = Conductor

Fig. 16.1

There are two exceptions from the linear approach. One is the concept of the cerebral palsy therapist created by Eirene Collis. The other is conductive education (Peto) as practiced at The Institute for The Motor Disabled in Budapest. We shall discuss this at the end of this Chapter.

SOME ASPECTS OF NORMAL DEVELOPMENT

For a long time now 'normal child development' has been the keystone in all treatment of cerebral palsy, but it seems to be ignored that this development is global, not linear or consecutive and that the normal child is not expected to cope with more than one teacher in nursery or school.

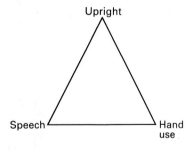

Fig. 16.2

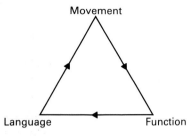

Fig. 16.3

Integrated development

Figure 16.2 shows the milestones reached at the age of two when a baby has matured into a person. He will have acquired the three main human characteristics, upright posture, use of hands for manipulation, and ability to speak and use language to regulate his behaviour. This learning/maturation process takes place in a totally integrated global fashion (Fig. 16.3).

Movement, language and function influence one another and develop together. Maturation leads to active movements, exploration and play; exploration and language lead to body awareness, and movement and language lead to spatial comprehension. This development is a continuous round based on the relationship between mother and child, as the following examples show.

(a)   At six months the baby has developed sufficiently to lie firmly in supine (maturation). Stability enables him to lift his legs and hold on to his toes (active movement based on stability). If noticed by the mother, this provides an opportunity for play around toes, socks, cold feet, etc., or to a game, 'Little piggy went to market', (language and body awareness).

(b)   The baby has learnt to sit (maturation). Sitting in his high chair he makes a mess, patting his food and smearing it over his face (sensory exploration and stimulation). Mother interferes, turns his hand over to wash it and to humour him she plays and sings 'Round and round the garden like a teddy bear' (language and play). She may follow this by giving him a flannel to teach him to wash his face (function, body awareness and movements).

Normal development is always global. If we insist on following a linear approach we must, at least, recognize that we are out of step with normal development.

Steps towards independence

A child's security starts with understanding himself, his body image and spatial awareness. A baby of twenty months may beat his chest and say 'Me, me, me'.

Spatial awareness grows with the ability to move and explore. The child's security in relation to his mother will increase as he is able to move away from her and find her again. To hide under tables and behind doors is not only fun, but teaches 'gone' and 'not gone'. This does not mean, however, that he will know where his mother is when she leaves the room or understand sophisticated expressions like 'Mummy back soon', which involves a time factor as well as a spatial factor. Neither can he grasp why his mother does not know where he is if he runs out of sight. 'But *I* know all the time where I am', answered the little boy when his mother said, 'You mustn't run so far away, I don't know where you are'.

From 2 to 5 years old the child moves from total dependence towards semi-independence. For this to be successful the relationship between mother and child must be one of trust. As we have seen, the baby gets to know himself and his surroundings, and his mother will guide him towards the outside world, the extended family, play groups, friends and nurseries. With some children this is an easy task, with others it needs most careful handling. All mothers have experienced the ever tightening grip round her finger when approaching the house where the child knows he will be 'abandoned', and all mothers long for the day when he will run away happily and confidently.

Even after such careful weaning, most children worry about their first day at school. It is, therefore, common practice to select a particularly suitable teacher for the reception class, someone who relates easily to the children. It cannot be overstressed how important this is. I remember asking a little girl if she was looking forward to going to school. 'Of course not' she said, '*I* don't know the teacher.' A teacher, who in an emergency had been removed from the reception class, told me that when she said 'Hello' to one of the boys in the playground, he did not answer. When she asked him why he would not speak to her, he ran away shouting, 'You left me, you left me!'

Nursery and primary schools are fully aware that an insecure child will not learn well. They recognize this by providing *one teacher* who will deal with all his needs, from teaching the three Rs to blowing his nose and doing up his shoe-laces.

THE CEREBRAL PALSIED CHILD

If the normal child needs security, the child with cerebral palsy needs it even more. Due to his many symptoms, he will not have acquired the typical human characteristics during his first 2 years of life (see Fig. 16.2). And at 5 years old, instead of reaching a stage of semi-independence, he may still be totally dependent on his mother. This dependence, coupled with the mother's anxiety for his progress and welfare, often results in a fearful, demanding and insecure child.

Figure 16.4 shows our provision for the cerebral palsied child, the mother's route from doctor, to assessment centre, and to therapists. When the child is able to attend nursery or school he will not, like the normal child, stay with his teacher, but will be taken out of the classroom by therapists and psychologists for individual and expert treatment or assessment. His sense of security will be undermined by constant interruption of his daily routine. In some schools the therapist works in the classroom to avoid taking the children out.

WORKING IN A TEAM

The linear approach provides neither the security needed for learning nor the possibility for intimate communication between members of staff. Holt (1975) says this about communication, assuming that 8 members of staff would have

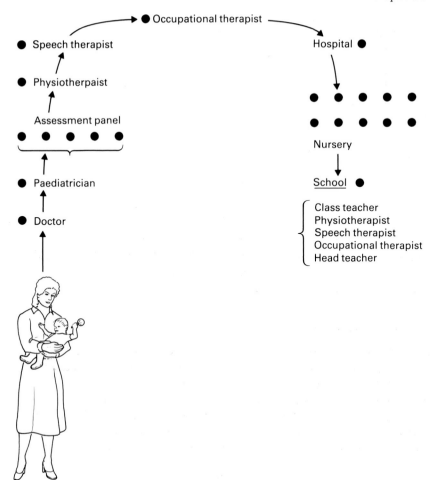

Fig. 16.4

to communicate with one another about the children, 'If all these 8 communicated with each other, assuming that each person communicates with each other once, there would have to be 28 initial communications. If any one wanted to recommunicate because of new information coming from another person, then the communication would have to begin again, and the number would assume astronomical proportions.'

On the following pages we shall examine various types of teams which have developed to deal with these problems.

The multi-disciplinary team (MDT)

The MDT is based on friendly cooperation amongst various professionals. The MDT does not recognize, in practice, the global development of the child and perpetuates the linear, fragmented approach to treatment and learning, and the division between therapies.

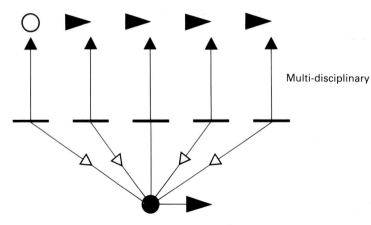

Multi-disciplinary

Fig. 16.5

Team meetings are, on the whole, similar to case conferences where each member reports on her specific treatment of the child; it is a backward-looking team. The quality of discussion very much depends on the leader of the team and what he/she is expecting from each member.

The inter-disciplinary team (IDT)

The IDT is a forward-looking team, closely knit and *goal directed*. Team meetings will include discussions about the goals to be reached by a child or a group of children within a certain period of time. Each member will consider in what way he/she can use his expertise to assist the child to reach these goals.

To plan a structured programme and set realistic goals is extremely difficult, but the advantage of such meetings lies in the necessity for much more accurate evaluations and the need for closer understanding amongst professionals.

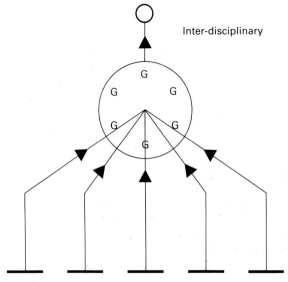

Inter-disciplinary

Fig. 16.6

The team will also have to learn to assess where the learning process has broken down, if goals are not reached.

The trans-disciplinary team (TDT)

The TDT, like the IDT, is goal directed and also based on integrating expertise, but the TDT aims at a further step in integration, one where any member of the team will be able to do another person's job so that the most suitable worker can be chosen to deal with a specific child. This involves regular training of the team over a long period of time and calls for a renunciation of all professional jealousies.

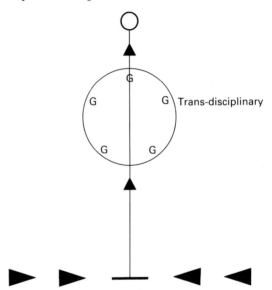

Fig. 16.7

The TDT is a most desirable model for community work, because instead of a stream of people visiting mother and child, one person (such as the health visitor to the normal child) can become the key person in this relationship. The TDT avoids conflicting advice being offered to mothers. It is also economical in time and expense.

It might be useful to illustrate with a simple example how each of the teams might deal with a specific problem. Let us imagine that the team is working in a boarding school for spastic children. The long-term goal is independence in dressing, and the short-term goal is putting on a pullover.

Multi-disciplinary team (MDT)

Dressing in the MDT comes under the heading 'function' which is the domain of the occupational therapist. If the school has no occupational therapist, the job will go to the physiotherapist, but morning and night the children will be dressed and undressed by the houseparents or supervised by them.

Therapists are only very rarely seen in dormitories as they work 9am – 5pm or a part-time shift. Houseparents may be taught during the day how to teach dressing skills, but it is extremely difficult to arrange for therapists and houseparents to meet for any length of time, as houseparents work mainly morning and night shifts.

In some schools the therapists run courses for the houseparents. In others the time before swimming lessons is used to teach dressing skills, but as time is limited, voluntary workers will be welcomed to help and these will, on the whole, do everything for the children. Very occasionally therapists will change their working shifts to enable them to work *with* the houseparents, sharing their difficulties.

The actual task of putting on a pullover involves many aspects of learning. There is a physical side, the actual ability to hold the pullover, separate front from back, put the head through the largest hole before putting one hand then the other through the holes on the sides, and later, the head through the middle hole (or the other way round). The task involves grasp and release, stretching elbows, some sitting balance, head control and hip movements.

Conceptually, the child must know, up and down, top and bottom, two sides, left and right, front and back, inside and outside, upside-down, apart and together as well as the topological properties of the garment. The normal child will have assimilated these concepts in his first year of maturation, but they will be taught to the cerebral palsied child by the teacher or the speech therapist as part of the acquisition of language. However, these two members of the team are not involved in dressing, although the teacher may help the children when going on outings, etc. A division remains between the conceptual understanding and the difficult practical task of learning how to put on the pullover.

It can be seen that the child is in a very confusing situation. He will be taught parts of the skill in unconnected situations and will have very little opportunity to *practise the task,* which is essential for learning.

Inter-disciplinary team (IDT)

For the IDT, putting on a pullover will be regarded as a goal. To reach this goal a programme will be discussed, and it will be decided how each member of the team can best help the child.

In one school, I observed how an IDT fitted this goal, putting on a pullover, into a project called 'winter clothes'. The teacher taught the children why we need warm clothes in the winter and what materials are used to keep us warm. She spoke about sheep, sheep shearing, spinning and knitting. The children discussed whether their own pullovers were made of wool and whether they were hand- or machine-knitted, and, if hand-knitted, who in the family had knitted them. The houseparent, who was working with the children morning and night, was also helping in the classroom. She was asked to show the children how she took off her pullover and to put it on again. Afterwards she was asked to repeat it while the children told her what to do, 'arms above the head, behind the neck, pull, grasp the cuff, pull off the sleeve', so that by using language they would understand the task better.

In this same programme, the teacher also taught the concepts involved. There were lessons on holes and the children learnt about different sizes of holes, how one could get through them and the difference between open and closed spaces. They also learnt many other concepts relating to the task such as top and bottom, up and down, left and right, back and front, apart and together.

The physiotherapist gave hand classes in the classroom and taught the necessary physical skills: how to stretch the arms, lean forward, lift the arms above the head. She showed them how a fist moves more easily through a hole than an open hand. The children pulled quoits over their arms and learnt how to push their hands through the sleeves.

Finally, the children learnt to place the pullover correctly on the table and to use such difficult concepts as right side up, and to transfer the front of the pullover from the vertical to the horizontal position.

In this team every member was aware how the children were taught the task. There was no confusion and everyone involved with the children would be able to replace each other and assist them, using the same approach and the same language.

Transdisciplinary team (TDT)

Here a key person in the team will be chosen and taught how to approach the problem from every point of view. She, the mother, teacher or therapist, will be able to tackle all aspects of the skill and for the small child will also use suitable books, illustrations and rhymes.

Difficulties when organizing a team

Although everyone admits that closer cooperation and better communication is necessary, it is surprising how many difficulties arise when putting theory into practice.

What are these difficulties?

1 *Professional jealousies.*   I know what to do with this child and want no interference.

2 *Professional insecurities.*   I am a professional, I know my own profession (although I know nothing about cerebral palsy) and I do not want to be exposed.

3 *Working hours.*   Teachers and therapists work shifts and do not want to change their hours to fit in with nursing or care staff.

4 *Class divisions.*   Teachers and therapists are paid more than nursery nurses or care staff; they have a higher professional status.

5 *Fear.*   One might discover that someone else, if trained, might do one's job equally well, even better. Perhaps one is not as important or necessary as one believed!

These and many other points lead to resistance against team work, especially the close integration of IDT or TDT, and only few centres have progressed further than the loosest form of MDT.

Working in a team demands a positive attitude, a positive personality and a desire to find solutions to problems. Much patience is necessary from the leader of the team and an ability to turn grumbles and criticism into positive realistic proposals. It needs a deeply democratic approach, rarely found in any establishments.

Conductive education, and the conductor principle

Although this Chapter in no way attempts to describe the different methods and systems which have evolved in the treatment of cerebral palsy, it is not possible to discuss integration of disciplines without considering the conductor principle, and this cannot be understood without some knowledge of conductive education.

The Institute For The Motor Disabled and Conductor's College was opened in Budapest, Hungary, in the early fifties. Professor Peto's system, conductive education, recognizes the *global* development of the child. Peto suggested that what the children with cerebral palsy fail to acquire in their first years must be taught to them like a skill, and they must not only be taught, but given the opportunity to practise their skills in many different ways. In conductive education everything comes under the umbrella of *learning*. The cerebral palsied child, like the normal child, will need *one educator* (the conductor) who will teach him everything 'from sitting on the pot to the ABC', and provide him with the *security* needed for learning. Peto regarded the cerebral palsied child as insecure, unsocialized and adult oriented, needing a special environment to learn new skills. The Institute in Budapest is, therefore, geared towards one major goal, to give children with cerebral palsy an intensive training to prepare them for normal school.

The conductor

In conductive education the conductor is the educator dealing with groups of children who are well matched in age and ability. People are accepted for training as conductors in the Institute when they have finished their A levels. They study for four years, doing at least six hours practical work a day, and they attend lectures and seminars. This gives them both the practical and theoretical background for their work.

The syllabus for the course consists of child care, nursery and infant teaching, educational theories, play theories, anatomy, physiology, pathology, movement theories and splint making. This horizontal training creates a new profession and a new professional outlook able to deal with all problems of a neurologically impaired child. (The conductors also learn to deal with adult neurological conditions such as: hemiplegia, parkinson's disease, multiple sclerosis, dystrophies and paraplegia.)

Conductors are paid during their training and the course ends with an examination for state registration. The Institute and the examination both come under the auspices of the Ministry of Education.

How does the conductor principle compare with teamwork?

Most importantly, the conductor principle eliminates the need for the team as the conductor embodies the team within her person. All conductors alternate their shifts (7 am to 2 pm, 1 pm to 7 pm) and are, therefore, able to see the children in all situations during the day, and as Peto said, 'turn any part of the day into a learning situation'. There is, of course, still a need for communication amongst the conductors. The overlap between morning and afternoon gives them the daily possibility of sharing information about the children.

Conductor
Principle

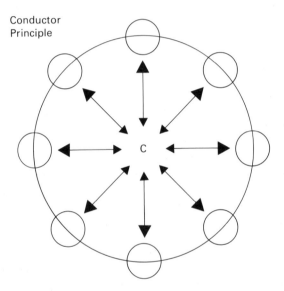

Fig. 16.8

The conductor principle leads to *continuity*. Walking, for instance, one of the most important achievements in cerebral palsy, can only be established if the child walks properly in all sorts of situations during the day, to lunch, in the classroom, to the toilet, etc. I remember saying to a little boy in a British school, 'Let us walk to dinner'. He answered, 'Why, you are not a physiotherapist', which clearly indicated that to him walking was not a means of getting from A to B but something one did with the physiotherapist. This is one of the reasons why so very few children, with more than a slight handicap, are able to walk. It is also more convenient, quicker yet quite wrong for the staff to bundle the children into wheelchairs.

Continuity means it is possible for the children to practise a skill in many different places, not only in a specific learning situation but in the many interconnecting, in-between situations of which life consists.

I remember observing the children in the Institute in Budapest learning different skills, such as dressing, walking, playing or writing. When I told Professor Peto what I had seen, he said, 'And what happened in between?' I then realized that as soon as one session had finished I went in search of another work session. The in-between periods, where the children were left to themselves to play or find their way to the toilet or to another room, had escaped my attention and I had failed to observe what use the children made of what they had learnt.

Continuity is necessary to reinforce a new skill. An opportunity to use the same skill for many different tasks is also essential. *Transfer of skill* is promoted by the conductor principle. If, for instance, a conductor sees a child pushing down his trousers using his previously useless thumb, she will make a mental note and see that he uses his thumb when holding a crayon. If the child has learnt to sit freely on the pot (the easiest position), she can use this ability to teach him sitting on the floor and on a chair. Such continuity and the organization necessary for transfer of skills are totally lacking in most schools and centres.

THE PRESENT AND THE FUTURE

This Chapter started by discussing the linear approach to treatment and education in cerebral palsy, and showed how teamwork developed from a desire to unite what different professions had divided. It also showed how the conductor principle arose from the concept of the whole, the child's indivisibility and his global development.

Although educational and treatment techniques have progressed, few steps forward have been taken in the field of integration. Poor teamwork is generally put down to personality clashes (MacKeith 1971), but it should be clear from the preceding analysis that personality problems are only the ripples on the surface, the real fault lies in our thinking or lack of thinking.

We think of professionals and their working hours rather than the children and their daily routine. We think of lessons and treatment sessions but make no use of the long periods before, after and between which present the children with many opportunities to fulfil their potential. Children who can walk a little do not walk to dinner or toilet. Children who can sit on a chair unaided are strapped in their chairs, children who can transfer from chair to chair will be lifted on to the toilet, and children who can remove a pullover or coat will have it done for them; all because it is quicker and easier for the staff.

There are several possibilities for the future. Efforts can be made to tighten up the MDTs into IDTs, i.e. change the emphasis from teams centred on personalities to teams centred on goals set for the children and the expertise necessary to reach them.

One might also seriously consider a new profession of a nurse/teacher/therapist based on the conductor principle (Holt 1975). I suggest that we have a new training course with very good aspirants being nursery nurses and pre-school teachers. They should start their training with the concept of the whole child rather than of individual symptoms. Centres staffed with such professionals would develop a totally new outlook on teamwork.

Although degree courses for paediatric therapists or developmental therapists are desirable, they will still leave us with a gap between therapy and care, and therapy and education.

Our dilemma is well summed up by the physicist Fritjof Capra (1982), 'Medical science today is no longer able to understand or treat many of the current serious diseases of our time, because it sees the human body as something like a machine made of separate parts. There are different specialists dealing with different parts who very often do not take into account how these parts interrelate, how body and mind are interdependent and how this whole organism is embedded in a social system and in a natural environment.'

REFERENCES AND FURTHER READING

CAPRA F. (1982) The turning point. *The Listener,* March 18th, 1982. (Wildewood House) London.

COTTON E. (1970) Integration of treatment and education in cerebral palsy. *Physiotherapy* **56.4**, 143.

HARI M. (1975) *Scientific Studies on Conductive Pedagogy.* Conductor's College, Budapest.

HOLT K.S. (1975) A single nurse-teacher-therapist *Child: Care, Health and Development* **1**, 45–50.

MacKEITH R.C. (1971) Who guides the therapist? *Dev. Med. and Child Neurology* **13**, 125.

VARTY E. (1975) What about the integrated child? *Special education* **62**.

For anyone wishing to know more about Professor Andras Peto's system of teaching called Conductive Education, the address is: The Institute of the Motor Disabled, Villânyi Ut 67, Budapest XI, Hungary.

APPENDIX
USEFUL ADDRESSES

Action Research for the Crippled Child, Vincent House, Springfield Road, Horsham, West Sussex RH12 2PN

Association for all Speech-Impaired Children (AFASIC), Room 14, Toynbee Hall, 28 Commercial Street, London E1 6LS

British Association of Occupational Therapists, 20 Rede Place, London W2 4TU

Chailey Heritage (School and Hospital), North Chailey, Lewes, East Sussex BN8 4EF

Chartered Society of Physiotherapy, 14 Bedford Row, London WC1R 4ED

College of Speech Therapists, Harold Poster House, 6 Lechmere Road, London NW2 5BU

Department of Health and Social Security (DHSS), Alexander Fleming House, Elephant and Castle, London SE 6TE

Disabled Living Foundation, 346 Kensington High Street, London W14 8NS

Down's Children's Association, Quinborne Community Centre, Ridgacre Road, Birmingham B32 2TW

Invalid Children's Aid Association, 126 Buckingham Palace Road, London SW1W 9SB

Lady Hoare Thalidomide Trust, 78 Hamilton Terrace, London NW8 9UN

Mobility

> Banstead Place Mobility Centre, Banstead Place, Park Road, Banstead, Surrey SM7 3EE
>
> Mobility Information Service, Copthorne Community Hall, Shelton Road, Copthorne, Shrewsbury SY3 8TD
>
> Airline Users Committee, 129 Kingsway, London WC2B 6TE (pamphlet: Care in the Air, Advice for Handicapped Passengers)
>
> Airline Users Committee, 129 Kingsway, London WC2B 6TE (pamphlet: Care in the Air, Advice for Handicapped Passengers)

Muscular Dystrophy Group of Great Britain, Nattrass House, 35 Macaulay Road, London SW4 0QP

National Association for Deaf/Blind and Rubella Handicapped, 164 Cromwell Lane, Coventry CV4 8AP

National Association of Swimming Clubs for the Handicapped, 93 The Downs, Harlow, Essex CM20 3RG

National Deaf Children's Society, 56 Hereford Road, London W2 5AH

National Society for Autistic Children, 1a Golders Green Road, London NW11 8EA

National Society for Brain Damaged Children, 35 Larchmere Drive, Hall Green, Birmingham B28 8JB

Paediatric Interest People, Secretary, Lorraine Clark, The Wolfson Centre, Mecklenburgh Square, London WC1N 2AP

PHAB (Physically Handicapped and Able-Bodied), 44 Devonshire Street, London W1N 1LN *or* Balfour House, 17 Bonnington Grove, Edinburgh EH6 4BL

Pre-School Playgroups Association, Alford House, Aveline Street, London SE11 5DJ

Queen Mary College (Design and Inventions Laboratories), Mile End Road, London E1 4NS

Riding for the Disabled Association, Avenue R, National Agriculture Centre, Kenilworth, Warwickshire CV8 2LY

Royal College of Nursing of the United Kingdom, Henrietta Place, Cavendish Square, London W1M 0AB

Royal National Institute for the Blind, 224–228 Great Portland Street, London W1N 5AA

Royal National Institute for the Deaf, 105 Gower Street, London WC1 6AH

Royal Society for Mentally Handicapped Children and Adults (MENCAP), 117–123 Golden Lane, London EC1 0RT

Spastics Society — Information Service, 16 Fitzroy Square, London W1P 5HQ

Association for Spina Bifida and Hydrocephalus (ASBAH), Tavistock House North, Tavistock Square, London WC1H 9HJ

Scottish Spina Bifida Association, 190 Queensferry Road, Edinburgh EH4 2BN

SPOD (Sexual and Personal Relationships of the Disabled), The Diorama, 14 Peto Place, London NW1 4DT

Toy Libraries Association and 'Active', Seabrook House, Willyots Manor, Darkes Lane, Potters Bar, Herts EN6 2HL

Voluntary Council for Handicapped Children, 8 Wakley Street, London EC1V 7LT

Woolwich College for Further Education (Engineering Centre for Special Schools), Villas Road, London SE18 7PN

INDEX